THE MURDER FILE
AN IRISH DETECTIVE'S CASEBOOK

To Jon,
Great meeting you
at last!
Come back soon,
Paul.

To (Alex sorry)
Jonathan
Best wishes

Best Wishes.
John.

Nice to see you
Ruth

D0043043

'If you don't get the murderer in the first twelve hours, or find him among the first twelve people you interview, or have to look twelve miles beyond where the body was found — you're in for a long drawn out investigation.'
Detective Chief Supt Dan Murphy

'How tragic . . .'
Detective Supt George Lawlor

THE MURDER FILE

An Irish Detective's Casebook

Tom Reddy

GILL AND MACMILLAN

Published in Ireland by
Gill and Macmillan Ltd
Goldenbridge
Dublin 8
with associated companies in
Auckland, Delhi, Gaborone, Hamburg, Harare,
Hong Kong, Johannesburg, Kuala Lumpur, Lagos, London, Manzini,
Melbourne, Mexico City, Nairobi,
New York, Singapore, Tokyo
© Tom Reddy 1991
0 7171 1905 X
Print origination by Seton Music Graphics Ltd, Bantry
Printed by
Colour Books Ltd, Dublin

Also for Maria

Contents

Acknowledgments

This book would not have been possible without the help of a number of people and institutions, all of whom I thank sincerely. In particular I wish to thank George Lawlor's sons, George, Peter and John and his daughters Nell and Mary for their patience, assistance and belief in this book.

I would also like to thank the Garda Commissioner Patrick Culligan, and Supt Denis Mullins of the Garda Press Office. Also the Editors of the *Garda Review* and *Garda News*, Stephen Rae and Austin Kenny respectively.

My thanks also to the staff of the Dublin Corporation libraries in the ILAC Centre Dublin and Pearse Street for their invaluable help — in particular Mr Jimmy McLoughlin for his continued assistance. The staff at the National Archives office in the Four Courts were also extremely helpful as was Mr Michael Daly, the librarian at Independent Newspapers.

I would like to thank former Commissioners Mr Patrick McLoughlin and Joseph Ainsworth and former Deputy Commissioner John Paul McMahon for their advice, along with Mr Anthony McMahon former chief of the Technical Bureau, Mr Eamon O'Fiachain and a number of other people who preferred not to be named.

Finally my thanks to Maria for her continued support.

Introduction

'In their reminiscences police officers recall how a leaning towards their profession in their youth attracted them towards that goal, but it was not so in my case. I had no love for police life and while I considered it dull and uninteresting and best suited to those destined for a lazy monotonous existence I had other and more potent reasons for disliking a "Bobby's" job,' wrote George Lawlor over thirty years ago. A young republican, arrested, beaten and interned after the Rising of 1916, he was a remarkable man of keen intellect, and an idealist who demanded rigorously high standards of enthusiasm and dedication from both himself and others. He was to join the fledgling Irish police force, champion the use of science as a weapon to fight crime, and rise to the rank of Detective Superintendent as head of the Technical Bureau. Prior to his death in January 1961 George Lawlor was to write about his pleasure and pride in being a member of the Garda Síochána and state that 'if we sincerely believe in truth and justice for all men then the only common basis for a real and true democracy is an active international police force to enforce international laws. I feel that it is the only way in which to prevent a recurrence of devastating wars and even perhaps stay the greatest disaster of all — the destruction of the human race.'

Throughout his career he wrote copiously about the Garda Síochána, including cases he had been involved in and the use of science to solve crime. He had intended to write a book about his career — I hope this is the book both he and his wife Bridget wanted to write.

1.

The Unlikely Detective

THE young George Lawlor was a most unlikely policeman. Yet he was to become the head of the Technical Bureau, a Detective Superintendent much admired and respected for his diligence, expertise and hard work, and a keen advocate of using science as an aid for crime detection. Yet in 1916 he was a teenage rebel.

'I had reached the age of 18 years when the rebellion of Easter week had awakened in me an urge to free my country from a foreign power,' he wrote in his diary. 'In 1917 I joined the Sinn Féin movement and became secretary of the local cumann in my home town of Monasterevin, County Kildare. The following year I was an officer in the Irish Republican Army and soon learned to hold in contempt the Royal Irish Constabulary — the police force then operating in Ireland. The years which followed found me an active member of both movements which aimed at the overthrow of British rule in Ireland and eventually the establishment of an Irish government. Thus I became engaged in many and varied activities.'

The young Lawlor put all his energies into political agitation, canvassing against the British conscription drive for troops for the trenches in Flanders. He moved on from this nationwide campaign by subsequently acting as election agent for Sinn Féin in the 1918 election, which saw a latterday Judge Arthur O'Connor and a latter-day Minister for Justice Kevin O'Higgins elected for the Kildare region. Lawlor also organised SF cumanns in the south of the county, collected subscriptions for the Irish Republican loan, and became a member of the Comhairle Ceannthair.

As an active member of the IRA, his home was raided regularly by the RIC. However no evidence was ever found on these many raids as he kept his revolver wrapped in an oilskin and hidden behind a loose stone in the chimney which he reached by climbing through a skylight and walking along the valley of the roof under cover of darkness.

He was part of a small and active group operating in the area, whose main activities included collecting arms and ammunition from people in the neighbourhood. 'This work had to be undertaken at night and while some weapons were handed over freely, others were secured only at the point of a gun,' he remarked drily in his diary.

The British military based in the Curragh camp were also active in the area, and there was a significant amount of support for them among the local population. Goods from Belfast, which were designated 'boycotted', were burnt by Lawlor's IRA group as they lay in a railway siding in the village on one raid. On another occasion Lawlor laid fog signals on the railway line and then held up the mail train as it went from Dublin to Cork. The seized mails were then examined by Lawlor as he hid in the attic of the station toilets while the alerted RIC and Black and Tans searched the station below him.

On 29 October 1920 a letter bearing the official crest of the RIC and signed 'By Order' was delivered to George Lawlor. It warned that should any subversive action take place in the surrounding locality he would be held responsible and suffer the consequences. Similar letters had been received by other members of the IRA in other counties, and the letters had been followed up with raids on their homes during which the IRA men had, as Lawlor put it, 'often been shot trying to escape'. On the advice of other members of the battalion he decided to sleep rough at night, but attended his parents' shop where he worked during the day.

On Monday 22 November 1920, a squad of British soldiers with bayonets fixed burst into the Lawlor home. George was searched, handcuffed and put into a caged lorry. With armoured cars at the front and rear of the convoy of trucks, they then drove off. The previous day, unknown to George Lawlor, in co-ordinated attacks around Dublin, a total of nineteen members of the British secret service were shot dead at eight different locations by the IRA. They had orders to locate and kill Michael Collins, but were thwarted by the Corkman's counter intelligence. That afternoon — forever known as Bloody Sunday — when Tipperary and Dublin met on the grounds of Croke Park, the Black and Tans surrounded the stadium and while the match was in progress, fired on the crowd with rifles and machine guns, killing fourteen and injuring hundreds.

Lawlor was driven to another IRA man's house, James Behan, in nearby Lughill. But Behan had made his escape, and Lawlor was ordered out of the truck and questioned about his movements on

3

the Saturday. He refused to answer questions and, still handcuffed, was beaten up and threatened with being shot. Somebody saw the beating, and assuming the worst was to come, told his family and friends that he had been shot. It wasn't until the following day that they learned he was alive and being held in Stewart barracks in the Curragh camp. He was held there for two weeks in solitary confinement, before being shipped to Belfast Lough aboard the gunboat *The Valorous* and then transferred handcuffed by train to Ballykinlar, Co. Down, where an internment camp capable of housing 1,000 prisoners had been established near the sea, overlooked by the mountains of Mourne.

George Lawlor was to spend the next thirteen months there acting as IRA banker and clerk in the canteen which was used for IRA meetings attended by camp leader Joe McGrath, Dr Tom McGrath, Sean Lemass, and others prominent in the movement.

'I had been released after the signing of the Treaty on 6 December 1921, as it were into a new world' he wrote in his diary.

'I could see no reason why at this stage, after agreeing to a pact at the Sinn Féin Ard Fheis, which I had attended as a delegate, that we could not agree to differ until the issue was settled by the free vote of the people. These and many other thoughts ran through my mind as I attended Comhairle Ceannthair meetings, the Sinn Féin Ard Fheis and an Irish Republican convention. Comrades who had stood shoulder to shoulder against the common foe were daily becoming disunited, dissention was rampant and appeals to settle our differences appeared only to annoy. We were so blinded by self-interest, trivial grievances, jealousy and pride that we appeared to forget our real enemy. As my appeals to agree to differ fell on deaf ears I decided to go my own way and remain 'neutral' as they afterwards styled it. Thank God I have never regretted my action. Like many of my comrades who had taken the same attitude of 'neutrality' I was being forced to take the only course open — emigration — but the serious illness and subsequent death of one of my six brothers kept me from doing so.

'The participants in the civil war became more active, brother fought against brother, and the jealousy and bitterness engendered remains alive to this day with us. About this period Kevin O'Higgins, then Minister for Home Affairs, announced his intention to organise an unarmed police force — An Garda Síochána — and as the force took shape I felt it was the only and proper way of dealing with the disorganised state of our country, and, coupled with the fact that I was sadly in need of employment, I decided to join the Gardaí,' wrote the young George Lawlor. In fact he was half an inch under the height requirement, but made it by standing on his tip toes!

Training was similar to that of the Royal Irish Constabulary because officers from that force had been appointed to the Gardaí and many of their ideas and advice were also transferred to the new force. George Lawlor, in common with many of his colleagues, felt the tensions inside the new police force and there were times when relations were strained between former members of the RIC and those from a Republican background.

He subsequently wrote — 'My dislike for the police force still remained with me, and my training as a recruit in the Depot under ex-officers and men of the RIC did not soften my feelings towards the profession I had reluctantly adopted. The position of things did not make for the best form of police training and most of the time was taken up with drill, physical exercises and lectures on simple Acts of Parliament from the British Law Code. Thus the knowledge obtained by men in law and procedure and general police duties was poor. It can well be said that in the investigation of crime the members of the force were dependent on their own resources and as the Irish law reports of that period record, there was a total disregard for the Judges' Rules. After a few weeks of this training I was sent to Galway as a guardian of law and order. Weeks of pounding the beat renewed my longing for America and were it not for the timely intervention of the Superintendent who took me into his office on the clerical staff, I would surely have emigrated.'

By 1924 political unrest had subsided, and there was better organisation of the force. That organisation brought the first examination which set a standard for promotion to rank in the Gardaí. Lawlor sat the written examinations, was successful and was promoted to sergeant, and continued working in Galway's Eglinton Street station as a clerk. Outdoor experience was necessary for anyone wanting to progress further up the career ladder, and Lawlor applied for a transfer, but the Chief Superintendent instead recommended his appointment to the newly-formed detective branch.

'Indeed I was very dubious of my ability to fill the post of Detective Sergeant after spending five years at office work. I had not sought the appointment and my main reason for giving up office work was to gain practical experience to fit me for Inspector rank. However, I soon came to like the work and to take a keen interest in the investigation of crime. My first case, which came within days of my promotion to Detective Sergeant in July 1928, whetted my appetite for this type of work,' he recalled.

On duty at the two-day Galway race meeting he was joined by three detectives whose job was to watch out for 'petty larcenies and kindred offences and to keep a sharp lookout for the usual type of criminal who frequents such places'. In the evening after the last race he acted as armed escort as the day's takings were brought to the bank in Galway city. When he returned to the Garda station he met a man called William Ryan who was reporting the theft of his gold watch and chain which bore the initials 'W.R.' on the inside of the case. He was in the city for the racing festival and in keeping with the practice at the time, when accommodation was at a premium, he shared a room with three other men who were strangers to him. After his room mates had left that morning he missed his watch and chain. His description of the three men was very vague, but they had spoken with pronounced Dublin accents.

The following day Ryan, accompanied by a detective, walked around the Ballybrit racecourse, but failed to spot his former roommates in the milling crowds. The last race had ended and as people either collected their winnings from the bookies or made their way to the exits, George Lawlor noticed a crowd of about thirty people shouting and in hot pursuit of a man. They caught up with him and, clamouring loudly, demanded payment of their bets.

'With two uniformed members of the Force who had come to my assistance I rescued the man and pacified the crowd, but only temporarily. He began to explain that he was only the clerk and that his employer the bookmaker had fled, or in racing slang had 'welshed', but the punters were not prepared to accept his explanation and to save him from further injury I had him conveyed in a police car to the station and I told the angry crowd I'd meet them there when my duties at the racecourse had been completed,' said George Lawlor.

The man was questioned, said he had no money and claimed to be the bookie's clerk. It transpired the man was known as 'the Masher' and when searched by George Lawlor only had some silver and loose change in his pockets as well as a gold watch and chain. He had been presented with it a few years earlier, the Masher said, but as Lawlor handled it the lid flew open to reveal the letters 'W.R.' inside. The Masher was made to undress for a more thorough search and as he did so, a roll of bank notes which had been hidden in his pants, fell to the floor. There was over £100 in five and one pound notes. With the evidence staring him in the face the Masher confessed. He had been trying to defraud the punters. William Ryan identified the watch as his that evening, and celebrated its return in a local public house telling everyone loudly about the work of the new detective sergeant. The following day the Masher received six months imprisonment. The District Justice directed that the punters should receive their money back and delegated· Detective Sgt Lawlor to act as bookie's clerk, paying out cash to those who had retained their tickets.

'I became more interested in my work. I eagerly read the accounts of cases, including murder trials, and I hungered for more insights into detective work. I came to realise and appreciate that in the investigation of crime many old methods were becoming outdated and that the time had arrived when science should be applied to assist in crime investigation. About this period I came in touch with developments in the USA and found that I could take a correspondence course in the science of fingerprinting and photography so I enrolled with the Institute of Applied Science, Chicago. My continued keenness in this line brought me in touch with Professor Tom Walsh, University College Galway, and I spent many happy hours in his company. The professor, besides his many qualifications as a doctor and pathologist, was a keen criminologist who visited police headquarters while on holidays on the continent and on his return kept me informed of developments in the police bureaux. During my visits to his laboratory I learned to appreciate the practical application of science in crime investigation. He demonstrated the various blood tests, the use of the microscope and photography, and as he had a good knowledge of the science of fingerprints we often discussed it. I had now acquired a good practical knowledge of the latter from my correspondence course and I was inclined to propound its usefulness in crime work, but many of my comrades in the force treated it as a new-fangled idea and were very skeptical as to its use in police work. Others however thought there might be something in it,' he wrote.

George Lawlor maintained his annual subscription to the Institute's *Fingerprint and Identification* magazine as part of his ongoing interest in scientific developments, and contributed to it on occasion. One of his favourite stories about the use of fingerprints dated back to the early introduction of a system of fingerprint identification in the Irish judicial system.

The chief warder of Galway prison was a friend of George's and met him sitting on the Salmon Weir Bridge after he had given fingerprint evidence in a trial. They sat chatting in the bright sunshine discussing the leaping salmon and the warder confided that the court action had reminded him of an incident in 1907 when the new infallible method of identification was still in its infancy. To operate the system, two warders from each prison were selected and sent to Dublin to learn how to take fingerprints. They returned and took impressions of inked fingertips of existing and new admissions to the prisons which were then sent to Dublin where a small group of civil servants would carry out classification and identification. About one year after two of the warders had received their training, the civil servants were surprised to find a large number of prints were being filed under the same classification. A closer examination of the sets astonished the examiners because several sets proved to be identical in every detail.

Two senior civil servants were despatched to Galway to check out an apparent problem in the supposedly infallible system that was already in use in large areas of Europe and both North and South America. The investigation established that the infallibility rule still held and the explanation was a simple one. One of the warders considered the premise that no two fingerprints were alike a huge joke and did not bother to take the fingerprint impressions of all the prisoners. Instead, to save time during the induction process, he inked his own digits and put them on the prisoner's form, and then forwarded it to Dublin. The new science had proved itself. However, despite the humour of the situation, the prison warder lost his job.

George Lawlor had drawn up notes to write a new detection manual, and had written a number of 'rules of thumb' to help identify corpses by examining their fingers as an aid to discovering their trade. Shoemakers, for example, suffer from frequent cuts on the index finger, whereas clerks have slight callouses on index and middle fingers, and washerwomen or domestic helps would have swollen hands and soft fingers of a bright colour, he wrote.

At this time Detective Sgt Lalwor's skills were becoming well-known throughout the force. From Dublin a leading lawyer of the time, Tom Finlay, K.C. had been in touch with the Garda authorities to suggest the establishment of a special investigation unit, aimed at providing vital experience and backup for Garda divisions where major crimes had taken place.

The suggestion was given added impetus after the embarrassing 'Missing Postman' case which ended with a series of civil actions for wrongful arrest taken against members of the Gardaí. The well-liked postman Larry Griffin went missing in Stradbally Co. Waterford at Christmas time 1930 while on his daily delivery round. He had no suicidal tendencies and no body was ever recovered despite the involvement of senior officers up to and including the rank of Garda Commissioner in the investigation.

The King's Counsel suggestion was that a Superintendent should be promoted to Chief Superintendent to lead a newly-established investigation unit. The named Superintendent asked George Lawlor if he would be interested in transferring to Dublin and becoming a Detective Inspector as part of this new team. However the imaginative measure never materialised as the idea died with the early demise of Tom Finlay.

It was in 1932 that a break-in at a bungalow at Roundstone, Co. Galway gave George Lawlor the first chance to use his fingerprinting skills. The burglar had absconded with a lot of valuable items including a pair of binoculars but during the burglary found time to help himself to a glass of port from a crystal decanter. The local Garda Superintendent had a number of suspects in mind for the crime and had heard of Lawlor's fingerprinting skills, so he asked him to join the investigation. Lawlor found a set of fingerprints on the decanter and he checked them against sets taken from a number of local suspects — one pair matched but the burglar denied it until he got to the Circuit Criminal Court where he pleaded guilty, and was sentenced.

It was shortly after this success that George Lawlor was to employ a new scientific technique to set the first of a number of precedents in the law courts as his career in crime detection progressed.

A wealthy farmer had sold a small herd of cattle at Galway Fair and returned to his home £200 richer. He was about to go to bed when he heard a knock on the front door and when he opened it was confronted by two masked men, one of whom carried a shotgun. As they shoved their way into the house, the farmer seized the barrel of the shotgun, and in the struggle a shot was discharged into the kitchen ceiling without injuring anyone. The two men ran away still carrying the gun, and as they left a piece of paper fluttered to the flagstone floor. Written on it in black pencil were the words 'Hand over one hundred pounds and your life will be spared'.

The farmer went to bed and the following morning reported the attempted robbery to the Gardaí and gave them the piece of paper. The farmer could not identify the two men. But their *modus operandi* was familiar to the Gardaí and brought the names of two suspects to mind. One of them was an employee of the farmer.

In a search of the employee's home, Detective Sgt Lawlor found a copy book hidden behind a picture on the wall of the bedroom which the man shared with his brother. In the book he kept an account of his wages, and on closer examination George Lawlor saw that the middle pages had been ripped out from the stapled notebook. The remaining centre pages bore indentations identical with the words which appeared on the piece of paper handed by the farmer to the Gardaí.

'It was necessary to give this evidence in court,' wrote George Lawlor, 'and to produce the piece of paper to the judge and jury and show that the indentations in the copy book bore the same words as appeared in pencil on the demand note. I accomplished this by obtaining a cardboard shoe box from a shopkeeper. It measured approximately thirteen inches by six inches by five inches. I cut a slit in the front near the bottom through which I was able to throw a beam of light from a flashlight. The beam of light was thrown obliquely on the paper which bore the indentations by placing it lying flat inside on the bottom of the shoe box. From a square hole which I cut in the lid of the box I was able to view the illuminated surface of the paper bearing the indentations. The oblique light had the effect of throwing up the indentations clearly and in this way the words were easily discernible. The case in Galway was the first occasion in An Garda Síochána, and probably in any other police force, in which indentations on paper were successfully demonstrated in court to a judge and jury.'

It was in 1931 the Garda Commissioner, General Eoin O'Duffy sent out a circular to the force requesting 'constructive ideas' from members of the force in any area of police work. A cash prize and gold, silver and bronze medals were offered to the writers of the best essays.

George Lawlor grasped the opportunity, and sat down to write an essay that was to become the blueprint for the establishment of the Garda's Technical Bureau — the teams of experts in ballistics, fingerprints, photography, mapping and investigation who ranked equally with their counterparts in the other enlightened police forces throughout the world. Into that 4,000-word essay the detective poured his self-taught scientific expertise and pointed to the failings of the Garda's current investigation methods.

Under the title 'crime detection' and its four sub-divisions — training for recruits, training of members serving in the country, appliances and present detective unit — he stressed the need for training in all types of crime investigation — from the simple scene of a car crash to a system for regularising descriptions. The practical side of crime detection was ignored in recruit training, he wrote. 'I hold that the practical side, if not totally disregarded, is dealt with superficially. Except for an occasional lecture or a paragraph in a police manual, the recruit is left to work out his own salvation. It will be argued that he has experienced comrades to assist him at his first station; perform duty with him and take the initiative when necessary. It, however, often transpires that he has to depend on himself. Furthermore, a fair number of Gardaí with service have had very little experience in crime detection.'

Fingerprinting had been introduced to Ireland in 1900 and the system was operated by the prisons department which took prints of convicted felons until the system transferred in 1929 to the Gardaí. Experts in fingerprinting had been appointed to the Force shortly before George Lawlor wrote his essay — but, he said, what was the point if an inexpert Garda destroyed potentially vital prints at the scene of a crime through lack of expertise?

'It must be admitted that lack of a little practical experience has resulted in cases being messed, or at least the subsequent investigation hampered, with resultant heavy expenses to the State. Indeed, I might add, in no small way it has reflected on the Force at times.'

Turning to the detective section he wrote, 'A detective is held to know more about the investigation of a crime than an ordinary Garda, but does he? It must be admitted that in a great many cases he does not. Why? Because he did not get proper training. Certainly a detective must carry a revolver but until lately very little effort was made to have him proficient in its use. After undergoing a course he must have practice at least once a quarter.

'He is required to investigate murders and all serious crime or assist therein. How is he to be successful without proper training? I hold that all members of the detective unit who are fitted for their positions by their aptitude for such work and their present and past ability should undergo a special course of instruction at the Depot. If this course is deemed too expensive then a Special Branch should be formed, attached to the Depot, members to be despatched to any division where a serious crime occurs, and assist therein or take charge of an investigation as necessity arises.'

The *Garda Review* magazine, which was circulated to members of the Force and included divisional news, a woman's section, Irish lessons and training advice, was also lobbying for a change through its editorial columns. The magazine, which carried letters critical of the often poor conditions Gardaí worked and lived in, pointed out the lack of expertise in the Force. 'Sending a man out armed with a revolver and a detective's identification card to investigate a big forgery case is as incongruous as giving an ambulance man a medical degree and scalpel and directing him to operate on a patient,' it commented scathingly.

George Lawlor's essay was read with interest in the Phoenix Park headquarters where Assistant Commissioner Cullen attached a note to the circulating essay which read : 'It makes one glad to find men thinking along these lines. This is a practical and useful production. Many points therein should have been attended to by Headquarters some years ago. There is scarcely a point with which one may disagree and that says a good deal.'

In October 1934 the three existing Garda specialist units — the photographic section established in 1926, the fingerprint unit and the ballistics section established just two years earlier — were brought together to form the nucleus of the Garda Technical Bureau in St John's Road near Kilmainham Hospital, Dublin.

The Technical Bureau was to serve two purposes, to provide instructors for the school of criminal investigation and to provide a team of investigators who had an impressive array of technical back-up ready to be despatched to any division in the country where a major crime had been committed.

The Bureau was made up of Gardaí with particular aptitudes for fingerprinting, photography, ballistics, map making and sketching, model making, forensic chemistry, microscopy and use of the violet ray.

George Lawlor lectured to Gardaí, customs men and military policemen and drew up training courses and lecture notes. Outside the force he was much in demand as a public speaker about scientific developments and their use by the Gardaí. When he wasn't writing these lectures, he was involved in daily investigations, and internally seeking regular expansions in the manpower of the Bureau.

He also lectured extensively, on invitation, to the public and to societies, about the application of science in crime detection. He admitted to his diary and the occasional audience that he gave up ending his lectures with the phrase, 'Crime does not pay', after a man on the platform behind him muttered in a loud stage whisper, 'It pays you anyway'!

One of the Technical Bureau's most famous cases, the body in the street murder, was widely reported as an example of the benefits of science to police forces throughout the world. This case alone prompted police forces from all over the world, including Israel, India, Britain, France and America, to visit Supt George

Lawlor for information about the latest developments in scientific crime detection aids.

Supt Lawlor's own files take up the story. 'The case opened by the discovery of the dead body of a young married woman on the footpath, in Hume Street off St Stephen's Green, Dublin, shortly after 6 a.m. on 18 April 1956. The body was covered by a lady's black overcoat which was identified as the deceased's property. On taking the coat off the body it was observed that the deceased's skirt had been removed and lay around her head, while her knickers were pinned to a piece of cloth which appeared to have been used as an aid to drag the body by the legs. A nylon stocking and head scarf were tied around the neck.

'It was clear from the position of the body that it had been dragged by the legs for a short distance to the place where it now lay — an opening leading down stone steps to an unoccupied basement.

'Before the post mortem was begun, each article of clothing, on removal from her body, was placed immediately in a separate envelope. The post mortem showed that the deceased had died from heart failure due to air embolism. This condition had been brought about by an attempted abortion which had allowed air to enter the circulation through the blood vessels of the placenta. The two articles tied about the woman's neck had no bearing on the cause of the woman's death, and were apparently placed there after death with the intention of deceiving those engaged in the investigation.'

Miss Mamie Cadden, a qualified nurse and convicted abortionist, lived in a flat on the same side of the road not far from where the body had been found, and was a suspect in the case. A search of her bedroom led to the discovery of several surgical instruments which could have been used to perform an abortion. When she was questioned she denied all knowledge of the woman's death, as she had remained indoors all evening, going to bed at about 11.30 p.m. She claimed that the first she knew about the woman's death was the morning the body was found when she went to her front door.

Mamie Cadden advertised in the daily newspapers extensively, offering cures for dandruff and other minor ailments, and kept a diary in which she made entries to identify her customers by their clothes, but never by name.

'An entry she admitted she made on 17 April 1956 read: "2 p.m. Blue coat". An attempt had been made to alter the original writing,' said Supt Lawlor who headed the investigation. 'At the Technical Bureau filters were employed in photographing this entry and it was established that the original entry read "8 p.m. Black coat". This was significant since enquiries revealed that the dead woman had been wearing the black coat she was discovered in, all day on 17 April.

'Her explanation for the alteration of the entry in her diary was a lame one. She said that she had made the first entry "2 p.m. Blue coat" in red ink, but as it was not legible she went over the original writing in blue ink.

'Examination of the footpath revealed a small bloodstain and a drag mark extending from the deceased's head for about three feet in the direction of the suspect's house about fifty feet away. In the hall of the house where the suspect had a flat, and on the stairway leading to it, minute traces of blood were discovered.

'The result of the investigation established that the woman's body had been dragged along the footpath apparently with the intention of disposing of it in the basement and placing with it all the woman's identifiable property, thereby avoiding the possibility of identifying the operator and where the illegal operation had taken place.

'Our major difficulty however was to prove that the deceased had visited the suspect's flat. In endeavouring to do so we were well rewarded by the care taken in the initial stages of the investigation because it provided the physical evidence, without which, I venture to say, it would have been exceedingly difficult, if not impossible, to secure a conviction,' he wrote.

Mamie Cadden's flat was searched and samples of dust, hair and fibres were taken from the stairs; two coconut fibre mats were removed from her bedroom floor and five of her head combs were seized in the same room, also a red dressing gown which she was wearing on the night of 17 April, and again on the morning of the 18th. On a subsequent visit a grey/brown rabbit fur cape was also taken for forensic examination by Dr Maurice Hickey the State Pathologist.

'From his examination,' continued Supt Lawlor, 'the following facts emerged. On the deceased's black overcoat and other garments several human hairs, animal hairs and fibres were found. The human hairs were grey hairs dyed a golden yellow colour and were exactly similar in texture and colour to the human hairs found on Mamie Cadden's five head combs.

'The rabbit hairs from the fur cape were exactly similar to the rabbit hairs found on the deceased's black overcoat and to the loose rabbit hairs found adhering to the coconut fibremats on the floor of Cadden's bedroom.

14

'On the heel of the dead woman's shoe, found in the parcel on the steps leading to the basement near the body, two hairs were found. One of them was a rabbit hair which compared exactly with hairs from the grey/brown fur cape. This hair was adhering to a cigarette end and was not damaged.

'If the dead woman had been wearing the shoe and had walked on any hard surface one would expect the hair to have been crushed. Apparently before the dead woman removed her shoe in the accused's bedroom she crushed the lighted end of a cigarette on the mat and thereby picked up one of the loose rabbit hairs shed by the grey/brown cape. The human head hairs of the dead woman were similar in texture, colour and wave to hair found on the accused's red dressing gown. Red wool fibres found on the dead woman's black overcoat were similar to the fibres making up the accused's red dressing gown, and were dissimilar to wool strands from the dead woman's red woollen cardigan.

'I think the most striking physical evidence emerged from an examination of the two coconut mats taken from the accused's room. In all, 89 coconut fibres were found on the dead woman's clothing and amongst them the same seven colours were found which matched the seven colours in the mats. One of the seven colours — the blue fibre — was faded and similar fading was noted in the blue coconut fibres taken from the dead woman's clothes. Micro-photographs of the fibres were taken and prepared as slides and photographs for the benefit of the judge and jury at the trial.

'All the evidence in this case was circumstantial and that portion which resulted from the comparison of the hairs and fibres forged a strong link in the chain of evidence which resulted in the conviction of the accused woman on a charge of murder,' concluded Supt Lawlor.

Three years earlier, the Bureau had solved and obtained a conviction in an unusual crime, by using a painstaking process. Two men had driven their lorry from one phone kiosk to another on the north side of the city, from the North Circular Road to Parkgate Street, where they had ripped out the phones and money boxes, broken them open and thrown them into the River Liffey after extracting a total of £7-3s-3d. When they were traced, tiny pieces of bakelite were found in the cab of the lorry, and subsequent investigations turned up a record of the men paying for a variety of goods with coppers. The phones were eventually retrieved from the Liffey, and after a painstaking jig-saw puzzle the pieces from the cab and the phones were matched and photographed.

One of the proponents of this art was Detective Garda Eamonn O'Fiacháin in the Bureau's ballistics department. In November 1953, a pedestrian was killed by a hit-and-run driver near Wicklow Town as he walked home around midnight.

Broken fragments of glass were found at the scene, and from the make-up of the glass it was concluded it belonged to the head-lamp of a Simca or a Fiat car. A local farmer was questioned the following day, but he denied involvement in the accident, saying his windscreen and headlamp had been smashed six weeks earlier by a flying stone.

Not so, concluded Detective Garda O'Fiacháin after examining a total of 1,565 tiny fragments of glass found at the scene which he compared with a fragment of glass taken from the broken head-lamp. He was able to identify these as the same type of glass and also match a fracture mark common to both exhibits. Micro-photographs were taken of the fractured sides which showed up the irregular markings common to both, thus allowing the Gardaí to take a successful prosecution against the driver of the car for his involvement in the hit and run.

Supt George Lawlor was a shrewd investigator and an idealist. A strict but kindly man, he took a close interest in the well-being of his family and colleagues. He set high standards for both his colleagues and his six children. His work hours were erratic and long, making his holidays and Sunday trips to County Laois and relatives all the more memorable.

Supt George Lawlor was the head of the Technical Bureau for a number of years. He argued for increased staffing, a special pro-motions systems for detectives within the Bureau so that they would not transfer out of it solely for promotional opportunities and have their skills lost to the Bureau. In 1951 he had a break-down due to overwork, but continued his practice of working up to twelve-hour days, six days of the week, and was continually on call.

His obituary was published shortly after his death on 12 January 1961 in the *Garda Review* magazine. It noted that he had been working on the day he died advising the Assistant Inspector General of the Punjab police who had travelled to Dublin specifically to visit him.

'The extent to which officers of the Force relied on George Lawlor for guidance and advice, not only in connection with the investigation of crime, but in administrative matters of diverse kinds was phenomenal, and those who mourn his loss will find consol-tion in the knowledge that his colleagues never failed to recognise and appreciate his great personal and professional qualities. What a tragedy that those in whose power it lay to reward those great qualities by the promotion he so uniquely merited, failed so lamentably in so obvious a duty. His death concludes one more sad chapter of neglect of the men whose lives of sacrifice and dedication to their work will live on.

'Personally he was unassuming and one of the friendliest of people, but in his work he was not only astute and painstaking but he brought to it a quality which for insight and deductiveness was very akin to genius. He was essentially thorough in building up an investigation and in preparing the case for prosecution. The story his life has to tell us is, in its own way, of the birth and development of a nation. He participated actively in the building of an independent nation, giving, as he did to that nation's police force, an incomparable tradition of service.'

2.

The Rosmuc Murder

IN May 1928 Rosmuc was a barren desolate place. Its inherent character had changed little, emigration was a feature of growing up, and there was little prospect of a job in the area. Farmers scratched a livelihood out of poor ground in harsh conditions. All the farms were small, their holdings rarely stretching beyond a ten-acre horizon. Living conditions for most people were poor, and life had changed little in the past hundreds of years.

On the morning of 31 May 1928 a turf cutter, Mark Connelly of nearby Turlough, passed by Padraig Pearse's picturesque thatched cottage and crossed a small footbridge. As he walked over it towards the bog he saw the body of a man lying face down in the bed of a stream in a crouched position. The man was dead, an excited and breathless Connelly told the sergeant in charge of the local Garda station. He didn't know the man, but the name of the stream was Sruthain-na-Muillean (Mill Stream), he said.

Connelly returned to the spot with Sgt Dan Gallagher and Garda McBride and they recorded the details of the body's location. The field in which it lay was similar to those around it. The land was rough, and strewn with stones, and the ditches were populated with sturdy squat bushes capable of withstanding the ravages of Atlantic gales and harsh winters. The man was lying in the water about five feet from the little stone bridge with his head towards the mouth of the stream. The water was only about four inches deep where his face lay, and before moving the body they noted that the man's eyes, nose and mouth were covered by water.

A cloth cap lay in the stream on the left of the corpse. A stick, cut from a bush and common to those used by working men for walking, lay on the bank of the stream about nine feet from the head of the corpse.

There were no signs of a struggle. There were a few scrape marks on the soles of the man's boots as if he had slipped off a stone. The two uniformed Gardaí rolled the body out of the stream for a closer examination. There was a mark over the man's right temple, a small cut that had bled slightly. His hands were rough, calloused and, like his face, were weathered, but there were no other marks on them.

In the right-hand coat pocket of the loosely cut jacket there was a black five-naggin bottle which was later found to contain about a glass of 'poitín'. The sewn patch-type pocket also contained a smooth stone weighing about half a pound. In the left-hand pocket there was a brown paper packet, which contained two pieces of buttered bread. In the right-hand trouser pocket there was a small purse which contained some papers, but no money. There was no money in any of his pockets. His left hand trouser pocket held two small lengths of twine.

The Gardaí who were stationed at Rosmuc knew the dead man to be Daniel Walsh, a local farmer, known as Sonny, or Sonny Dan. He was aged about 52, and lived with his wife Anne, who was seventeen years his junior, and six children. Three of the children, Donal aged six, Thomas four and Annie aged two years, were the product of their marriage, while Mary, Katherine and Rita Kelly aged 14, 13 and 10 years respectively, were from Anne's previous marriage.

Annie Joyce was born in Lettermore, Co. Galway. Work was scarce and emigration was a way of life, and at nineteen years of age Annie left for America. She met an Irishman there, Coleman Kelly, and they married in 1914 in Boston, and she gave birth to three daughters before her husband died in April 1919. Annie returned with her young family to her father's house in Lettermore. She had known Sonny Dan for four weeks when she married him and moved to his home in the village of Rosmuc, some miles away. Annie would recall the date of her wedding as the '15th of the first month of the harvest of 1919'.

Sonny Dan was a man of small build and height. His family was known as 'respectable' and his sister was a matron in the Oughterard Union, or workhouse, for twelve years. She had lived with Sonny Dan, cooking and cleaning for him for a year before he married. She stayed with him and his new wife for another year after his marriage before leaving for America. Sonny Dan had been badly burnt in an accident at his home when he was just three years of age and the shock of the burning — which left a mark on his face — had affected him leaving him 'a simple man', his sister Kate would explain later.

Sonny Dan had a liking for strong drink, and Kate often complained to him about his excesses. His wife Annie would make the same complaint. She tightly controlled the household purse strings, and gave him an allowance. This he spent at local fairs, getting drunk once a week.

A post mortem was carried out on the body of Sonny Dan by two local doctors. Five days later on 5 June the Deputy Coroner for Galway, sitting without a jury, opened an inquest into the farmer's death.

One of the doctors gave evidence at the inquest of the injuries he had found on the skull and on the right side of the forehead. There was froth on the mouth and nose and some clay inside the teeth. There was no fracture or injury to the skull or the brain. The wounds on the head would not have caused death, but might possibly have caused slight concussion, but they would not have been sufficient to deprive him of the power of movement. Death was from asphyxia due to drowning and the marks on his face could have been caused by a fall against the small stones lying on the bed of the shallow stream. His colleague gave corroborative evidence.

Annie Walsh, a widow for the second time, wrapped in a black shawl, gave her evidence in a deposition in Irish. She told of Sonny Dan's final day, a day like others when he had worked on the farm and made arrangements for his small carting business. Sonny Dan had been moulding potatoes all day Wednesday 30 May. The evenings were long, and he stayed working late, returning home at 9 p.m. He took his supper which she had prepared and he washed himself from the water stored in buckets in the house which had been drawn from the well. He checked to see the children in bed, and at 11.30 p.m. he left to go to Oughterard (some miles away) to have the body for the chassis of a cart made to order. Annie Walsh gave him a one pound note and an orange ten shilling note. The one pound note was to pay for the crib for the cart, and six shillings and six pence was interest on money due to the Bank of Ireland, Oughterard. She watched him put the two notes into his pocket rather than his purse which was his usual custom. She had not known he was going to Oughterard until shortly before he left the house carrying a walking stick. When Sonny Dan left the house she bolted the door on the single-storey cottage and went to bed. He had no drink on him that night as far as she knew and she saw no signs of it. The next day she was told he was dead. He had had good health, but a few weeks earlier he had been laid up in bed for two days with a pain in his back, she said. The rest in bed seemed to have cured him as he did not complain any further.

The stick found lying near Sonny Dan's body was produced and Annie Walsh identified it as her husband's walking stick. That concluded the evidence at the inquest. The verdict, death from asphyxia due to accidental drowning was recorded, and as death had been accidental the police discontinued their inquiries.

Sonny Dan was waked and buried. Then tongues began to wag in the area, and rumours spread. It was hinted that a young man from South Shore, Rosmuc, named Martin Joyce, a second cousin of Annie Walsh, was on more than friendly terms with the twice widowed woman. The 25-year-old man was rumoured to be a frequent visitor to the house at night, and it was said that he had often stayed later than other visitors and had been seen leaving the house alone in the early hours of the morning.

'When the Gardaí endeavoured to probe these rumours,' wrote George Lawlor, 'they found some truth in them. Martin Joyce was in the habit of visiting Walsh's and would join with some other boys from the neighbourhood in an innocent game of cards or talk of the day's events. A rather strange feature was that Annie Walsh used to join in the fun, while her husband, who slept in a room with his youngest child, usually retired to bed early.

'It was not possible to clarify the position regarding the rumours that Martin Joyce had been seen leaving Walsh's in the early hours of the morning and in this connection, beyond rumours, nothing definite could be established. In fact the police inquiries in the Rosmuc area only sealed the lips of those who might have been in a position to give useful information. Eventually the inquiries concluded and the police were led to believe that there was little in the rumours.'

But the file on Sonny Dan's death had not been closed. A nephew of the dead man, an attorney in the USA, wrote to the Department of Justice stating that his mother Mrs Gavin and her sister Miss Kate Walsh who both lived with him were convinced that Sonny Dan had 'met an untimely death'.

The Department of Justice wrote back seeking evidence and reasons why the two women believed there was foul play involved in the death of the Rosmuc man. However, no satisfactory explanation came by return post. Instead Kate Walsh herself returned to Ireland. She was adamant in her allegation that her brother's death was not accidental, 'and she stated so in no uncertain terms,' wrote George Lawlor, 'indeed so much so, that the Minister for Justice directed that investigations be re-opened. Thus in November 1928 I found myself on temporary transfer to Rosmuc station.' A senior and experienced Garda, Superintendent James Hunt, attached to headquarters in the Phoenix Park, was also despatched to Connemara to head up the new investigation, which opened approximately six months after the death of Sonny Dan.

George Lawlor looked forward to the temporary transfer, his first big case, which had the extra bonus of being situated near the occasional home of one of his heroes, Padraig Pearse, who had come to Rosmuc to perfect his knowledge of his native tongue and learn more about his culture.

The body of the dead man had been found within a short distance of Pearse's tiny whitewashed cottage, a wildly picturesque spot. One of the first rumours the new investigation team checked out was a persistent one that surfaced regularly. It claimed that the two young doctors had not carried out the post mortem correctly and had failed to establish the correct cause of death. Some people, who refused to repeat or substantiate their gossip when approached by the Gardaí, claimed that Sonny Dan had been poisoned. To end the rumours the Gardaí had the body exhumed, which inevitably caused a stir in the area. The State Pathologist, Dr A.R.J. Duggan M.D., travelled from Dublin to carry out the examination. He took the major organs from the body in large sealed jars to the State Analyst in Dublin, but the examination proved negative, showing no traces of poison or other contaminant. The State Pathologist was unable to arrive at an opinion as to the cause of death.

'Our difficulty at this stage,' George Lawlor explained, 'was to decide whether we were investigating a murder case or an accidental death. In support of an accident we had to consider that the unfortunate man had been found in possession of a bottle containing a small amount of poitín, which on analysis was found to contain 90.2 per cent proof spirit. In comparison, brandy and whiskey contain about 43 per cent proof. The marks on the soles of his shoes were consistent with his having slipped on the stones and fallen heavily into the stream while in a drunken state. His hazel stick was found on the inclined bank near him. He had been out in the dark of night and he had died from drowning, and the suggestion that he had been poisoned had been proved untrue. His body was found on a short cut leading from his home to Oughterard.

'On the other hand we knew that the maximum price of a bottle of poitín in Connemara at the time was about five shillings and as his wife had stated that he had thirty shillings when he left home, where was the remainder of the money? Was he robbed or did he lose it? Could he have consumed almost five naggins of poitín himself — which was almost physically impossible — or had he companions with him? Where was the poitín purchased? These were questions, amongst others, for which we had no satisfactory answers and which required explanation,' wrote George Lawlor.

The next step was to go over all the available evidence, and that included a re-check of all statements taken at the time of Sonny Dan's death. Martin Joyce, who had been questioned and asked to account for his movements on 30 June, had denied meeting Sonny Dan that night. He said that he had attended a funeral on Illaunmore Island, and that he returned about nightfall and was very drunk with the poitín he had taken and did not remember his exact movements on the night. He had gone to a townland called Snabo where he had taken a boat and crossed to Camus. He said that he slept on the side of Shaun-na-Curka mountain that night. He had gone there looking for work. The following morning, 31 May, the day the body was found, he said he had tea in Martin Ridge's house in Muckan-agherdaughaliha (which probably boasts the longest name in the country), and had then returned home by boat to South Shore at about 3 p.m.

In the light of the rumours surrounding Martin Joyce, the investigation team checked his statement. He had gone to a wake, but it had been held on the 29th — twenty-four hours earlier than he said in his deposition. He had stayed at a house next to the wake house. He was drunk and fell into a fitful sleep staying there until shortly before 6 a.m., when he left. Extensive house-to-house calls were made throughout the area, and eventually a Mrs Grealish of Muckanaghederdaughlin confirmed that Joyce had called to her home at 6 a.m. on the morning of 31 May and she had given him a cup of tea, and that he was sober at the time.

'Here we had a discrepancy in Joyce's statement' said George Lawlor, 'which directed all our attention to his movements around that time. Despite the most extensive inquiries which we made at this stage we were unable to establish his movements between 6 a.m. on 30 May and 6 a.m. on 31 May, which was the time within which the murder had been committed. According to the deceased's widow her husband had left the house about 11.30 p.m. on 30 May and the body was found about 8 a.m. on 31 May. Therefore if we were to eliminate Joyce it was necessary that his movements during that period be accounted for.

'We continued our inquiries which were rather difficult as we were working in an all Irish-speaking district and our knowledge of the language was not good enough to carry us through, without the assistance of a native speaker. Six months had elapsed since the death of Sonny Dan and apart from a time element which naturally prevented people in the area from remembering clearly dates of occurrences, the consumption of home distilled spirit — poitín — in the area dulled the memory of many people. Eventually our efforts were rewarded and we got the break for which one waits in every case, and which is often referred to as luck. I have met Mr Luck several times in other cases, but I have always been introduced to him by his friends, Mr Persistence and Mr Hard Work.'

That break was the discovery of a new witness. John Walsh, a nephew of Sonny Dan, was able to tell the Gardaí that he heard his dog bark on the night of 30 May. It was about 11 p.m. and he got out of bed to investigate. He went to the small bedroom window, and looking out saw Martin Joyce and his uncle passing by. It was a bright night and he had no difficulty recognising either man.

John Walsh was a frequent visitor to his uncle's house. One night his father and Martin Joyce swapped words with each other, tempers flared and they fought on the kitchen floor. Annie Walsh intervened holding a kettle blackened from the turf fire, threatening to throw scalding water over anyone who gossiped or 'carried stories' about her.

As the Garda team continued their inquiries they discovered that Martin Joyce was making plans to emigrate to Canada. The Gardaí decided to move fast and decisively. Joyce was arrested.

'The evidence for a charge of murder against Joyce was very weak, but our hands had been forced by the likelihood of his flight from the country,' wrote George Lawlor.

When he was arrested a Garda wrote down his reply to the charge. 'If the man that is dead were alive there would not be much talk about me,' said Joyce.

Annie Walsh's statement about her husband's last movements, and what she knew of Martin Joyce now came under scrutiny as the investigators began collecting their files of evidence. Three new statements were taken from Annie and her two eldest children, Mary and Catherine. The statements were of little evidential value the team agreed, but they showed up something they had been unaware of before — that the children, aged fourteen and twelve years of age, were both terrified of their mother, and that they were lying.

Mary let it slip that her mother had been out of the family home on the night Sonny Dan had died. The two girls were both able to say she was out of the house on the night of 30 May, but neither could say who she was with or where she had gone, or how long in total she had been missing.

'At this stage' wrote George Lawlor, 'the mother, fearing that the net was tightening and also that Rita, the youngest daughter, might divulge some useful information, sent her away to her grandmother in Kilronan on the largest of the Aran Islands. This provided another break for us, as it put the girl outside her mother's influence and we decided that she should be questioned. On 19 December we crossed the 40 miles from the mainland to the island and, although we were only an hour and a half there, we found out from Rita that Joyce had been in her house on the night of the murder.'

In the meantime the eldest girl, Mary, left her home to take up a position as maid to a publican in the east Galway town of Tuam. Again the Gardaí interviewed her, believing that she would feel free and independent enough to reconsider her first statement which had been prepared for the inquest. Supt Hunt questioned her but she stuck to her original statement except for one major point.

She said that Annie Walsh, her mother, had beaten her after the death of Sonny Dan. If the Gardaí came to question her she was to tell them that she got up from the bed she shared with her mother during the night he had died in order to warm milk for the baby, and that she remembered seeing Sonny Dan sitting by the fire.

The continual Garda attention rattled Annie, and she was becoming short-tempered and nervous. George Lawlor noted:

'She was showing obvious fear that her daughter was in a position to give damaging information against her, because when she heard that the Gardaí had visited Mary she wrote to her insisting that she must come home immediately. When Mary did not return she sent her a telegram. Mary's employer responded to the telegram, saying the girl had no money to return home, and Annie Walsh replied to that by sending a money telegram for ten shillings to cover her fare home.

'When we learned of this it was decided to arrest Annie Walsh immediately. It was 29 January 1929 when Annie Walsh was charged with the murder of her husband. On 17 June she and Martin Joyce were put on trial for the murder of Sonny Dan over twelve months previously.'

Annie Walsh was arrested by Supt Tom Collins from Clifden on 4 February at her home in Turloughbeg. She said nothing after the charge was read out to her.

Mary Walsh was one of the first witnesses called to give evidence in the Central Criminal Court. The trial was conducted in English with the aid of an official interpreter.

Martin Joyce never said anything to her about his relationship with her mother, Mary told the court. But her mother, Annie, often asked her would she like Sonny Dan to be gone and maybe Martin in his place. Martin Joyce was always shown favouritism by her mother, even in simple things like giving him larger helpings than any of the other men at the table, even Sonny Dan, when she ladled out the food.

On one occasion she had watched as Martin Joyce mixed up a concoction of seagull droppings he had gathered with milk and water which he then put into the milk her stepfather subsequently poured into his tea. Her mother, she said, had watched Joyce carry out his operation. When her stepfather complained, her mother said there was no taste in the tea and he drank it. This was some time before he died, said Mary.

Guano was easily gathered from the rocky outcrops around the area and was widely used as a manure and was also believed by some to be a poison. The Gardaí had also linked the sale of a phial of iodine from a chemist to Annie Walsh, and they believed she may have tried to doctor his food with the chemical.

The picture of life that was to emerge through the testimony in the trial was of a hard and often miserable one. Sonny Dan's cottage was a standard thatched house, with entry through the kitchen which was the breadth of the house. There was a room behind the chimney breast, and a second at the other gable. A small lean-to extension looking out over a muddy yard contained another small room, used as a bedroom by Sonny Dan. There weren't enough beds or rooms to go around the large family. The cottage snuggled up to a wall with a large overgrown bush providing the only shelter, there were no trees hardy enough to grow in the area, and the paths were merely worn tracks strewn with large stones. Prosecuting counsel Cecil Lavery S.C. described Sonny Dan's cottage as a 'hovel'.

Continuing her evidence, Mary said that, like the other children, she had been sent to buy presents for Martin Joyce — she had been despatched to buy him a pair of boots.

Her sister Katherine told the court that her mother had sent her to buy a pullover for Martin Joyce — 'the nicest one in the shop' was how her mother described it. She told how she had picked out one she liked and returned home with it. Her mother gave it to Martin, but he refused to wear it or even try it on for size, saying it was a woman's jumper as the neck was too low. The shop also sold Annie Walsh a neck-tie which she gave Joyce as a present.

In comparison to her sister, Katherine said Martin Joyce had asked her would she like Sonny Dan to die. Katherine said she replied, yes, and Joyce said that he would marry her mother if Sonny died and they would all have a good life together.

Thirteen-year-old Katherine said Sonny Dan and her stepbrother Donal slept in a small back bedroom, while her mother shared a bed in another room with Mary.

Martin Joyce was always 'hanging around the house', and he never did any work, she told the court.

He slept frequently in the house, sometimes staying there every night of the week and other times for one or two nights. Sometimes he slept in her mother's room, other times in the 'big room' — the kitchen — by the fire.

There was a row one time about Martin Joyce. Sonny Dan had come back from cutting turf in the bog, and he spoke to both Martin Joyce and her mother, she said. Someone on the bog had spoken to him while he was working and told Sonny Dan: 'Take care of yourself, Martin Joyce is going to your house.' Her mother repeatedly asked Sonny for the name, and it wasn't until later that evening that he told her it was a neighbour, Martin Conroy. Annie went to put on her coat, telling Katherine and her younger sister Rita to start crying. Sonny had missed this advice from Annie, and alarmed, asked her where she was going when he saw the girls sobbing. 'To choke Martin Conroy,' she said dramatically and rushed out of the house.

Mary corroborated her sister's story in the witness box. The day before her stepfather was found drowned she was sent to the island of Illaunmore to buy poitín and Martin Joyce gave her six shillings for a bottle. When she returned, Joyce poured some of the poitín into another bottle and heavily diluted it with water. Rita said that it was about 3 o'clock that afternoon when she got home, and Joyce was drunk and she could hear him with her mother in the bedroom. He had spent the previous two nights with her mother in the bedroom, but was sober and sitting by the fire with her mother when Sonny Dan returned home that evening.

Sonny Dan was immediately poured a large measure of poitín from the undiluted bottle and he sat down with them. Martin Joyce didn't drink any more and instead watched and encouraged Sonny Dan to get progressively drunker. Annie Walsh told Mary she was going to visit her father's home and that Sonny was going to Oughterard, twenty miles away, that night. There was no need to run across to ask their neighbour Bridget Conroy to milk the cow as she'd return herself to do it.

Before they left, Mary was told to look out and see if there was any light in Mrs 'Head' Walsh's public house which was just across the road. Mrs 'Head' Walsh, who was no relation to Annie and Sonny, was so called because she was the widow of a Head Constable of the Royal Irish Constabulary, the forerunner to the Garda Síochána.

When Mary pulled her head back in to report there was no light, Sonny Dan was helped to his feet by Martin Joyce. Katherine was then sent outside to check again that the Head Walsh was in bed, and when she returned to say she could see no light, Martin and Sonny left through the back door followed by Annie Walsh. Mary bolted the door behind them. Mary and Katherine then went into the bed in their mother's room, and it was some time next morning — daylight was streaming in — when Mary woke up to find her mother and Martin in the room. She had bolted the door behind them and the front door was locked, so she asked how they had got into the house. Through the window, replied her mother.

Rita asked how Sonny Dan was as he had been very drunk the night before, and her mother told her that they had left him 'out abroad there'.

'Why?' asked Mary as her mother and Martin got into the bed with the two girls.

Sonny had his knife out and opened it saying he was going to stick Martin Joyce, said her mother. Sonny wouldn't even let her go half way to Oughterard, he had been mad drunk with poitín, and they had left him on the roadside as they were afraid of him. Both girls were warned not to tell the Gardaí or anybody that Martin Joyce had been in the house the previous night, or had returned to the house that morning. Mary also noticed that her mother's skirt, stockings and shoes were dirty and wet. Joyce's stockings and heavy boots were also muddy.

Later that morning Annie went into the fields with Kate where they worked moulding potatoes — flattening the drills to keep weeds down. Mary, who had stayed in the house, came out to the bog to tell them that a Garda had called to say they had found the body of Sonny Dan who had drowned in a stream near the house. Mary was crying, and her mother asked her where Sonny had drowned, but Mary didn't know.

The body was laid out in the large kitchen of the cottage, surrounded by candles and with two pennies resting on the eyelids. Large bottles of porter, poitín and port wine as well as a supply of snuff were bought in, with extra food to cater for the ensuing two-day wake.

28

Martin Joyce called to pay his respects on the second day. It was a month later that he again came to the house, and he stayed both day and night using the same rooms as before, sleeping with Annie Walsh.

One day the Gardaí called to the house on a routine matter and Joyce hid himself in the loft. He lived continually in the house at this stage, and whenever he thought that the Gardaí might call he would retreat to the loft, taking a blanket with him. Sometimes he stayed hidden under the unruly thatch for hours on end — even when there was no sign of a Garda. The children estimated that he spent about three weeks in all in the loft immediately after Sonny's death, only coming down from his hiding place during darkness. On a number of occasions immediately after Sonny Dan was found, Annie Walsh would send the children out to see if they could find out why the Gardaí were calling to Mrs Head Walsh's house.

Joyce told Annie Walsh's six children that he had married their mother, and they would all be going to Canada soon. He intended going first and he would send for them in the time-honoured manner of poor emigrants.

In response to questions from the defence counsel, Mr Brereton Barry, Mary admitted to having told untruths at the previous District Court hearing which had resulted in the couple being sent forward on the murder charge for trial in Green Street. She had lied because her mother had beaten her before and told her what to say, but now she had made up her mind to tell the truth. She had been upset and cried when Sonny Dan died, she said. She also said that Sonny didn't know her mother and Joyce slept together, even though he saw them together in the house late at night as he left them to go to his own bed, and again early in the morning.

Three witnesses were able to tell the court that Joyce had not slept out on the mountain as he had claimed in his statements to the Gardaí. That statement to the Gardaí about his movements, which was part of the investigation before the inquest, worried Joyce. He had told Thomas Canavan who lived on South Shore that he was afraid the Gardaí would 'find him out a liar'.

He was afraid that Annie Walsh would give the Gardaí a statement that didn't tally with his own, and specifically referred to the thirty shillings which Sonny Dan had on him before his death. 'That is what will play havoc with me if we don't agree to the same thing in our talks,' he said, referring to Annie's statement, Canavan told the court.

Martin Conroy from Rosmuc said that he had met Joyce after Sonny Dan's death and they too had talked. 'Nothing can be said to me when nobody saw me do it,' Joyce had told him, Conroy repeated to the court. Conroy also denied that he had had an argument with Joyce and was spreading stories about him.

Both Martin Joyce and Annie Walsh gave evidence on their own behalf. Annie told how she was born in Lettermore, was forced to emigrate to America, married and had three children, was widowed, returned home and met Sonny Dan. She had not known him before her return, and was home for three months when she first went out with him. Four weeks later they married. He was 'a bit queer and strange' she admitted to the court. He gave her his money, and he was drunk on average once a week, sometimes he had to be carried into the house unconscious with drink. Neighbours came by most nights, and Sonny Dan was on good terms with them. She had earlier told the Gardaí that she stopped sleeping with Sonny Dan after the birth of the third child.

Martin Joyce was her second cousin and he used to work for her husband. Part of his wages included his meals at the house, but she denied having ever given him better quality food than that given to her husband. She also denied having ever put guano into his milk, saying it was poured from the one jug for everyone. Sonny Dan knew that Joyce slept in the house, and he had no objections to that. Annie estimated that he stayed in the house just two nights in total before her husband's death.

'Do you deny that you had any special friendship or relations with Martin Joyce?' asked Mr Cecil Lavery K.C., in cross examination.

'Yes. He was no more than any other neighbour who used to come in and out of the house. He was a hired hand, and he was paid two shillings and six pence a day,' Annie responded.

'Martin Joyce was nothing to you?' he pressed.

'He was something,' she conceded.

'And had you any special reason to protect him?' he asked.

'No,' she said.

Martin Joyce was in the house the night before her husband's body was found. There was no drink in the house and one of the girls brought some in. Joyce poured some for Sonny Dan. Later Sonny appeared to be drunk, and he told her he was going to Oughterard to a first cousin to buy a crib for the cart. She gave him some bread to eat and thirty shillings for the cart. He was sitting over the fire with Joyce: it was about nine o'clock at night at the time and she put the children to bed.

30

She went to bed at about ten o'clock, and Martin Joyce said he was going and would go along with her husband to Oughterard. The two men left the house by the back door, and she went outside with them.

She saw them leave and walk into the darkness and then she came back into the house. She bolted the door and went into her own bed, in which Mary, Anne and Thomas were sleeping, and she fell asleep, waking at about seven o'clock. She couldn't tell if they were awake or whether her clothes were unusually dirty. Annie said that when she got up she prepared the children for school, milked the cow and then she and her daughter Kate went to the bog to collect turf.

Annie Walsh denied ever having had a row with her husband, or ever asking the children if they would prefer to see Joyce in place of Sonny Dan, and had certainly never mentioned going to Canada. She had no 'hand, act or part' in her husband's death and estimated that Joyce had only come to the house about three times since Sonny Dan's death.

In response to questioning by Mr Lavery, she claimed that her statements to the court were exactly the same as those she had originally made to the Gardaí: he said they weren't. She didn't believe Martin Joyce would have had anything to do with the death of Sonny Dan, and if he did, he should be punished, she said. The statements made by her two children Mary and Kate were untrue, and there was no reason they should do her any harm, she said.

'Are the children speaking false when they say you slept with Martin Joyce?' asked Cecil Lavery.

'They are. I had no reason to sleep with Martin Joyce,' replied Annie.'

Are the children speaking the truth when they say that Martin Joyce was frequently in your room?' asked Lavery.

'They are. I would not go with him, having a man of my own,' she said with emphasis. Asked why she had given Joyce the pair of boots, she said it was because she had no money to pay his wages. The following day she was again called to the witness stand, and said she gave him the boots because she did not want Joyce to go barefooted.

To a series of brief and blunt questions, Annie Walsh replied that she had not told the Sergeant who called to her home to tell her about her husband's death, who was with him that night. 'I did not because I did not think that there was any reason to do so. I thought there was no reason to tell him that anyone was with him,' she said.

31

'And what business had he there?' he asked.

'He did not say why he came,' replied Annie.

Annie said that Sonny had thirty shillings when he left the house, and she presumed he had lost it when his body was found without the notes.

She again denied that Joyce had spent any part of the night in the house after the pair had left together, nor had she coached Joyce in what to tell the Gardaí.

'Was Joyce in your house day after day for weeks after the death of Dan?' asked Lavery.

'No, I never saw him there more than once or twice after my husband's death,' replied Annie.

'Is there any truth in the statement that Joyce would hide in the loft?' he continued.

'No; what use would there be for a man to go up to a loft like that?' she questioned in reply.

Martin Joyce was called to the stand to give evidence. He lived about one mile away from Sonny Dan, and yes, he had sent the child to buy poitin, and had poured out drink for Sonny, he said. Sonny Dan said he was going to Oughterard, and Joyce told him he'd walk part of the way with him. Later, Joyce turned east towards Strabogue, and Sonny turned in the opposite direction west. Joyce said he took a boat and rowed to the island where he slept rough, and the following morning visited some houses. He too denied the children's story, saying they had no reason to invent it.

Joyce also denied that he was in the house with Annie Walsh several times after the death of Sonny Dan and had hidden in the attic. The evidence given by Annie's daughter Mary was also untrue, he said.

Mr Brereton Barry, summing up on behalf of Joyce, said they should not rely on the statements of impressionable young children. The circumstantial evidence was capable of being explained away innocently and the testimony was full of contradictions and discrepancies, he said.

There were unquestionably rumours about the relationship between Annie Walsh and Martin Joyce but this was not a matter for the jury, said Mr Barry. Instead, they had to decide whether or not the death of Sonny Dan had been brought about by murder or was the result of an accident.

Mr Diarmuid Fawcett, for Annie Walsh, then rose to address the jury, saying the State had not 'a scintilla of evidence of guilt' against her. In fact, he told them, the circumstances of the case as detailed and even the photographs of the scene produced by the Gardaí all pointed to a death brought about by accident. The medical evidence also backed this up, and the State had only managed to produce thirty witnesses to envelop the case in an atmosphere of suspicion.

In response, Mr Lavery for the State said that there was no reason whatever put forward by the defence, why the children would perjure themselves to take away the life of their mother and another person, and in so doing fabricate a story which, however, remained unshaken by cross examination.

Recalling the case almost thirty years later George Lawlor wrote that 'today the use of science would have been employed and the investigation could have been much easier.

'The contents of the stomach would certainly have been analysed in the early stages and not after the body had been removed. It might have been possible to tell whether the stomach contained alcohol, and/or salt water. No doubt the finding of the former would not mean as much as the latter; which would have established definitely that Sonny Dan was not drowned in fresh water, and thus point to his having been placed in the mill stream after perhaps being drowned in the nearby Atlantic. There was a theory held locally that he was drowned in the small inlet of the sea, close by the stream and on the route leading from the back of John Walsh's house where, it will be remembered, Walsh saw Joyce and Sonny Dan pass at 11.30 p.m. on 30 May 1928.

'The dark clay in the deceased man's mouth would also have been analysed.

'The Rosmuc case marks one milestone in the employment of photography and its application to crime. I took eight photographs of the scene itself and other places figuring in the evidence, and for the first time in a court in Ireland, photographs were provided for judge and jury in album form showing the important positions and the scene.

'Photographs of the body should have been available to the investigation, and I would not have had to resort to dressing up a dummy in the dead man's clothes and placing it in the stream months after the killing in an effort to get some idea of the real position. Another point in the investigation would have been the undoubted examination of the five-naggin bottle found in Sonny Dan's pocket.

'Nevertheless, it was obvious that Joyce and Annie Walsh had entered into a conspiracy to murder Sonny Dan. It was a deliberately thought-out murder. How well it was planned and the care which they took to avert suspicion can be easily appreciated. The fact that no money was found on the body was a blunder which they could not subsequently rectify.

'The Rosmuc case was not spectacular in the sense that the evidence which was adduced to prove the guilt of the accused was, while circumstantial in itself, based on the evidence of local witnesses without any scientific aids. There was no recourse to the use of the microscope or even the magnifying glass. It was hard solid digging for three months and the recording of the results on paper, eventually to be sworn into court by the various witnesses. There were many thorny paths strewn with major and minor difficulties, but by dogged perseverance all were overcome,' he concluded.

On the fourth day of the trial Mr Justice O'Byrne addressed the jury, thanking them for the attention they had given the case. Every ordered community was based upon recognition of the fact that crime must be punished. But it was a recognised principle of the law that it were better that one, two or three guilty persons should go unpunished than even one innocent person be penalised and punished, he told them. This made it all the more important that the jury should have 'earnest regard' to the great obligations placed upon them, and remember that if they entertained a reasonable doubt they should give the accused the benefit of that doubt, said the judge.

'You may come to the conclusion, and I should say upon the evidence, you probably will come to the conclusion, that for a considerable time prior to the death of Daniel Walsh an intrigue had been carried on under his own roof between his wife and Martin Joyce. You ought not to be influenced by that in considering the evidence against the accused. They will not be tried for having carried out that intrigue,' said Mr Justice O'Byrne.

The case had been put that the unfortunate Sonny Dan, being drunk, had slipped on the rocks and fell into the stream and was drowned in three or four inches of water. But the Judge said that appeared an unlikely type of suicide bearing in mind the position of the dead man's limbs. In his pocket was a bottle of poitín, and some yards away lay his stick. Was it possible the body had been placed there in such a way as to suggest that it was an accident? And what had happened to the thirty shillings he was proved to have had on him when he was leaving home, he asked. There was 'grave significance' in the child's statement that on the morning Sonny Dan's body was found, her mother's clothes were soiled and wet, and that Joyce's boots and stockings were muddy. Particularly, it was emphasised, when Annie Walsh had maintained in her statement that she had never left the house that night.

Martin Joyce had similarly made a very significant observation: when speaking about the crime he had said to a neighbour, 'What can they say to me when they did not see me do it?'

The jury spent an hour in conference before returning to ask a question. They retired again and forty-five minutes later brought in their verdict.

Martin Joyce was the first prisoner called into the dock. He was shaking and a terrible look of shock crossed his face when the verdict of guilty was delivered. He appeared to be on the point of breaking down as the judge reached out and took up the black cap. Asked if he had anything to say, Joyce tried to speak, but there were no words.

The Court remained totally silent as the judge spoke the words that rang across the packed courtroom but echoed darkly from another age: 'It is ordered and adjudged that you Martin Joyce be taken from the bar of the court where you now stand to the prison from where you last came and that on Thursday, the 18th day of July in the year of Our Lord 1929 you be taken to the common place of execution in the prison in which you shall then be confined and that you be then and there hanged by the neck until you be dead and that your body be buried within the walls of the prison in which the aforesaid Judgement of Death shall be executed upon you.'

Martin Joyce stumbled down the stairs, a Garda at each arm. As he disappeared from view, he screamed and screamed, his shouts gradually dying away as his voice faded further and further underground.

Annie Walsh was then called up, and she too was found guilty by the jury. She stood pale and erect, and when asked if she had anything to say, she replied, 'Not guilty'.

The judge said that he 'entirely agreed' with the jury in both cases, and sentenced her to be hanged on 18 July. She was quickly and silently escorted to the cells below the court.

Sitting in the public benches, Miss Kathleen Walsh who had returned from America after voicing her fears about her brother's death, sat quietly in a bench amidst the uproar in the court as the tears rolled down her cheeks.

Both the accused, Martin and Annie, were subsequently reprieved and their sentence commuted to life imprisonment.

3.

The Two-timing Killer

IT was a bitterly cold day in October 1928 when a well-built man, John Fleming, first went into the Central Café, in Dublin's D'Olier Street, for lunch. The pretty seventeen-year-old waitress who served him attracted his attention. His good looks had attracted her too. He worked as a shoe salesman in Hickey's of North Earl Street, a three-minute walk away across the Liffey. Over the next twelve months he was to have his lunch in the café every week-day except Wednesdays, and their friendship was to grow. Almost a year to the day he had first noticed Rita Murtagh he asked her out.

She was impressed with him; he was twelve years older, a man of the world who was renting his own house in Drumcondra, and he spoke of his plans for the future with her on an increasing number of dates over the next three years.

They went to the pictures, for walks around the northside of the city, particularly the Whitehall area, and they visited the theatres when they held music hall nights, and restaurants.

He had brought her to his home at Carlingford Road where, he told her, he lived with his aunt, almost two years after their first date in January 1930. He had walked arm-in-arm with her past the rows of two-storey red-brick houses whose front doors fronted the footpath in pairs and opened directly onto the footpath.

'When we're married we'll live here together, and all this will be yours,' he said as he flicked on light switches and showed her around the modest but well-kept house.

They had been going out for over two years before John made his first call to Rita's home to meet her parents and six younger brothers and sisters.

Three years after they first met, Rita and John spent their first night together. They subsequently spent nights together in his aunt's bed in Carlingford Road, and it was in January 1933 after several nights of lovemaking that she told him she was pregnant.

John was thrilled, 'It was always my ambition to have children,' he said and solemnly pledged that they would be married before Lent. John was her first serious affair, and the only man she had ever made love to.

Prior to her pregnancy they had got around the problem of spending nights together by John asking her father's permission to take her to all-night parties. He spoke well and was courteous during his visits, which lasted for about fifteen minutes, and her father had no qualms about letting his daughter out.

Sex outside marriage was frowned on and a single mother was a social outcast. Although John had often spoken to her of marriage he had never proposed. It was in January 1933 that she told him she was pregnant and they would have to get married. The impending birth was a cause of terrible worry to Rita who still lived at home with her parents. She was slightly built, and it wouldn't take long for the pregnancy to show, she thought, with real terror.

The following month, John formally proposed. She accepted, and it was with a spring in her step that she went with him to Benson's jewellery shop on O'Connell Street on 6 February. Rita took some time selecting an engagement ring: she liked a number of designs, but the one she really liked was too large for her slim fingers. The shop assistant, David Ginsberg, assured her this was not a problem and measured her finger, saying they could easily reduce the 15 guinea ring to fit her. The couple also selected two wedding rings for £2 10s 0d each, and John said he would return the following day to collect all three rings.

A week later he still had not collected the rings, and when Rita asked why, he said he was waiting for some money from the bank, but this was delayed as he was awaiting a signature for its clearance. John Fleming never returned to buy the rings as promised, and they were eventually returned to the window.

In March, Rita gave up her job to avoid scandal and John told her that they would marry as soon as his aunt left the house in Drumcondra. He expected her to leave within a few weeks, he said. As spring turned into summer they were no closer to being married, and the baby was due in September. As she fretted about her single state, John reassured her saying he had bought a house in Galway where they could live when they were married — but he could not get possession of the house for another two months. He reminded her that his aunt had had a stroke, and speculated that she was unlikely to live much longer.

He also told her that seventeen-year-old John Berry who lived in the house at Drumcondra was being moved on too. He had written

to another aunt who was coming to Dublin to seek new accommodation for him. He later told Rita that she had arrived, and had found
him a post with Mooney's and he would be moving out shortly as he
would be living in accommodation over the shop.

By July, Rita was a bundle of nerves, her parents were still unaware
of her advanced pregnancy, and a rumour had reached the Murtaghs
that John Fleming was married.

On Thursday 20 July, Rita met John and questioned him bluntly.
What was the truth? Did this explain all his delays in getting married,
she asked. He denied the rumours as a ridiculous story, laughing it
off. But Rita's temper was short. The pressure of her secret was telling.
'If you can prove you are not married, you should prove it to my
Mammy and Daddy,' she challenged him angrily.

'Look, there are two Flemings living on my road, and the other
one is married, and they've mixed him up with me,' he said. The
explanation calmed Rita, and John said he'd meet her father and
explain it all to him.

He called to the Murtagh home on the following night, and
asked to see Tom Murtagh but he was out at the time, and instead
John chatted briefly to Rita's mother. 'A desperate state of affairs is
going on about me being a married man, and it's all lies. I'm very
upset about it,' he said.

'It has upset me and the family too,' said Margaret Murtagh.

'As far as I'm concerned I'll marry Rita in August,' said John.

'Well now, that's a question for the girl's father,' she said, and
John replied he'd call back when the 'boss' was home. The following
night Rita's father, a worker with Dublin Corporation, and his pros-
pective son-in-law were tucked up in the bar of a pub in Stoney-
batter with pints in front of them.

The conversation soon got to the point when the barman moved
out of earshot. What was the truth of the rumours about him being
a married man? Jealousy, pure and simple, said John Fleming. He
lived with his aunt, he said, and the only thing he could put it all
down to was jealousy. 'I have an aunt who keeps house for me, and
cleans the brasses and so on. I take her out sometimes for walks.
When I am out walking people actually stand on the streets and
look at me as much as to say — "Surely he's not married to her".'

The talk continued, with Fleming doing his best to reassure Rita's
father. 'Look, I know the anxiety of a father's mind about these
things. We've never been bad friends, have we?'

'No, and we won't be either if you can prove to me that you are
a single man,' said Tom Murtagh gruffly.

Fleming said that he had a suspicion about neighbours on his road who might be spreading the marriage rumour, and that he had a plan to draw them out from cover. Tom Murtagh promised, 'I'll go back to the person who told me you were a married man to find out where the information came from.'

'It's terrible to accuse a person of anything except you can prove it against him. I hope to find out who's been accusing me in a few days,' said Fleming.

On Monday around midday the phone in the shop rang for John Fleming. It was Rita arranging to meet him that evening. 'What has Daddy said', she asked him, almost bursting with curiosity. He told her that her father was pleased that they had talked about the rumours. He had been impressed by her father's concern for her, and he'd feel sorry for anyone who would do any harm to her as they'd have to answer to her father. Everything was being taken care of, he said, and they agreed to meet two days later, on the following Wednesday evening at her home, at 6.30. They still had not told her family about her pregnancy.

On the sunny Wednesday afternoon, John Fleming returned home promptly from work and immediately began tidying up the garden, using a pair of clippers to cut the grass, in preparation for a visit by his house guest's mother and a family friend who were coming to stay in Dublin for a short while. He had left the house by the time they arrived at 7.30 p.m. in a taxi from the railway station.

John Berry, who had returned from his holiday in Mount Temple, County Westmeath, with them, knocked at the front door and received no reply. Thinking his aunt had gone to meet them at Broadstone railway station but had missed them, he went to Mrs Catherine O'Rourke, their next door neighbour, who held a key for them. He then opened the front door, entered through the small hall, but was unable to open the door to the kitchen as there was some obstruction. He called his neighbours for assistance, and eventually Eddie Brophy from No. 52 and P. J. O'Rourke who was pushing with him against the jammed door managed to force it open a few inches at the top. Peering through the gap they could see a woman's foot and large pools of darkening blood on the floor. Shocked, Berry sent one of the group to call for the local doctor John Shiel, in nearby Drumcondra Road, and ran to a corner shop himself to telephone the Gardaí. A priest was also called to the scene.

By the time Eddie Brophy returned, Dr Shiel had already examined the body, and it only took him a moment to realise the woman had been murdered.

She was dressed to go out. Her hat was still partly on her head, even as she lay stretched out on the floor. There were a number of large cuts in the felt hat that corresponded with cuts in her head. Her jumper and skirt were soaked with blood. While alive she had been badly beaten, and Dr Shiel estimated over twenty wounds had been inflicted on her. Her upper dentures had been knocked from her mouth and lay on the floor beside her, her spectacles had been knocked off one ear and lay askew on her face, a necklace around her neck was broken on her chest. She had not been sexually assaulted.

Any one of three major injuries to the head — on the left brow, on the top and back of the head, and a fractured skull — could have been fatal, he said. He was also to say later that it was possible a specific type of hammer, with a blunt head and chisel projection at the back, could have inflicted the deadly blows. The attack was so ferocious that even if she had not died from any single or combination of blows, she would have bled to death within fifteen minutes.

The ferocity of the attack was underlined by Dr Shiel's belief that many of the blows were inflicted as she lay on the living room floor. He estimated, by touch, as he did not take temperature readings, that the woman was dead for up to three hours when she was discovered. There were no blood spurts around the room, except where the blood lay in two pools on the floor, and if the injuries were inflicted while the woman lay on the ground, it was likely that the killer would have large bloodstains only on his shoes. There was a considerable amount of bruising on the woman's arms and these were most likely defensive injuries, sustained as she tried to ward off her attacker, Dr Shiel concluded. He was later to perform the post mortem on the body.

The dead woman was known to everyone in the locality. She was Ellen Fleming, wife of John Fleming, the woman he had told the Murtaghs was his aunt.

John Fleming was a native of Tuam, County Galway. He had left school aged 13 and was apprenticed to Mr James McGarry, a general draper and merchant in Claremorris, County Mayo. He spent three years there before going to Ballina, then Ballinasloe, and on to Cahill's outfitters of Talbot Street in Dublin. Ellen, who was a niece of the shop owner, also worked there. Not long after he joined they began dating and married shortly afterwards in October 1921.

He went into partnership with his brother-in-law, Edward Berry, after the wedding for about two months, but subsequently returned to Cahills. He again left the shop, going to Australia for two months before returning to Dublin and his wife, to a new job in Hickeys where he worked for seven years. Ellen Fleming became pregnant early in the marriage, but the child was stillborn. There were no other children. Despite suffering occasional dizzy spells when she would collapse, Nellie continued to work at Cahill's and shared the same Wednesday half-day as her husband.

The couple were on good terms with their neighbours, and were good tenants, according to their landlord. John Fleming had recently met him to ask about the possibility of buying the house they had rented for over seven years. Mrs Catherine O'Rourke, their next-door neighbour, was one of the last people to see Ellen, or Nellie as she was known, alive. Nellie had said she had intended going to her aunt's for lunch but Jack (John) had insisted on cutting the grass that afternoon, so she bought steak for lunch at home instead. 'When I tidy up the house I'm going on to meet my sister from the 7 o'clock train. If she doesn't come I'll go on to Cahills,' she said.

Michael McHugh, at number 58, lent a pair of garden shears to John Fleming at about 3.30 p.m. Mrs Martha Carolan, from number 46, saw John Fleming busily clipping the grass in his own back garden between 3.30 and 4 p.m. when she looked over her own garden wall. She was on good terms with the Flemings and even though she kept a springer spaniel in the back garden, there had never been any complaints about the dog barking or making noise at night. At 4.30 p.m. she was chatting at the front door of number 48 with Nellie, the two women wearing housecoats over their clothes, when twelve-year-old Olive O'Rourke called to say she was going on her holidays to her sister May, and wanted to say goodbye before being put on the bus by her parents.

Nellie sent her out to the back garden through the house. Olive was a regular visitor to the house and both the Flemings had a soft spot for the vivacious child. John Fleming was wearing a brown striped shirt, his sleeves were rolled up and the grass had been cut. 'Goodbye, and enjoy yourself, and remember me to May,' he said, before pressing a shilling into the child's hand.

Another neighbour, Elizabeth O'Brien, recalled seeing Mrs Fleming at her own front door talking to an insurance agent at about 4.55 p.m.

But Terence McParland, assistant superintendent with Prudential Assurance Co., who was doing the rounds collecting weekly premiums in the area with his agent John Cunningham, insisted it was 4 p.m. when he called to Mrs Fleming. There was a joint policy on the lives of John and Nellie Fleming for £250. The premiums were collected quarterly and the policy was fully paid up.

41

At about 5 p.m., Nellie, still wearing her housecoat, crossed the street to chat with Mary and Stephen Dowling on the street outside their house. By 5.10 p.m. she had returned home.

Gardaí who were called to the scene carried out a detailed examination of the house. Both the scullery door and the garden gate leading to the laneway were unbolted, and this was the most likely escape route as the fallen dead woman blocked the front entrance. There were no signs that the killer had tried to clean himself by washing in the scullery sink as bloodstains were not found either in the scullery or bathroom sinks or in the waste pipes. And the kitchen window was bolted shut.

The room was tidy and neither milk nor water, stored in vessels to keep them cool, had been spilt and there was no sign of a struggle. An open handbag containing £4 was lying on a table near the body.

Sgt Mark Byrne was one of the first detectives on the scene. The fact that the victim's handbag was still in the room and contained a large sum of cash, and the absence of any of the hallmarks of the twenty or so robbery cases he had investigated in recent weeks, ruled out robbery as the motive to murder.

It was not until almost two hours after Nellie Fleming's body was discovered that her husband John could be traced by the Gardaí. Det. Sgt Byrne, accompanied by Det. Gardas Tumbleton and Monahan, traced him to friends of the Flemings who lived on the Clontarf Road, and where he was a regular visitor.

Bridget Wynne, the maid servant for Stephen and Charlotte Ryan at 128 Clontarf Road, saw Fleming come to the house by the back door at about 7.45 p.m. He came into the kitchen and said that he had had a 'great dip' at Dollymount Strand and subsequently sunbathed in 'blinding weather' at the Bull Wall. He wore no hat and was dressed in a dark blue suit with a white shirt. He carried a copy of the *Evening Herald* in his hand and had neither bathing costume nor towel.

Fleming apologised for being late for tea, and afterwards went into the garden with their son who was his godson, and continued work he had been doing the previous evening.

He had cut his right index finger the previous evening, which bled profusely, and Mrs Ryan helped him bandage it. It bled again that evening, and he rewashed it, but didn't bandage it. He mentioned the cut to two of his workmates the following day. He spent the night of the 25th with the Ryans, going straight to work the following morning, and home then at lunchtime.

Fleming was in the Ryans' garden on that long summer evening when the three Gardaí arrived.

Det. Sgt Byrne noticed a number of small bloodstains on John Fleming's left cuff and sleeve and on the front of his shirt. He asked him about them, making no reference to the murder of his wife. John Fleming said he had got the bloodstains from a cut on his finger, and stuck out his finger for the detective's inspection. When Stephen Ryan saw the three men in his garden he wondered what was happening, and when he went outside to ask if there was any trouble, one of the detectives drew him aside, whispering that Nellie Fleming had been murdered. John Fleming never asked the Gardaí why they had come to see him, why they were so interested in blood on his clothing, or what they wanted.

Det. Sgt Byrne cautioned Fleming and asked him to accompany him to Mountjoy Garda station.

'What did you say? Murder?' asked Fleming. 'Oh, my God I will go with you sir,' he added, failing to ask who had been murdered.

Before they left Ryans the Detective Sergeant asked Fleming to strip off his shirt, collar and tie. These were subsequently given to the State Pathologist, Dr John McGrath, for examination. Stephen Ryan gave Fleming the loan of a fresh shirt.

In the station on Dublin's North Circular Road he was asked for his shoes, socks and suit. A Garda, sent to his home, brought back replacements in a suitcase.

At 1.20 a.m. the following morning, John Fleming was charged with the murder of his wife. It was the first time the Gardaí had told him who had been murdered and during the four hours he was in the station, he never once asked who had been killed.

'I know nothing about it because I was not home at that time,' he said in a short statement when charged. 'It was between 4.30 and 4.45 p.m. when I left home. At the time I left home my wife was waiting for Mr Cunningham, insurance agent of no. 7 Dargle Road, to call. He usually calls on Tuesday evening,' he added.

Detectives carried out a thorough search and examination of the house. Measurements of all rooms and the layout of the back garden and adjacent lane were also taken. Gardaí believed the assailant had left by the back door, and that door was specifically examined. However, fingerprints could not be found on the back door because of its rough surface.

The State Pathologist, Dr John McGrath, received John Fleming's clothing for examination two days after the murder. Two days later again he examined them.

There were no bloodstains on the soft collar, tie, braces, socks or a pair of shoes. However, there were six spots of blood on the left side of the waistcoat and three on the right. There were nine small blood spots on the front and on the left leg below the knee of the trousers. On the shirt there were four small spots, some four inches from the collarband, seven on the left cuff and one on the left sleeve approximately five inches below the shoulder. There were about thirty small spots spattered over the front of the left sleeve of the coat from the elbow to the wrist. All the stains were of human blood.

His examination showed that the spots of blood seemed to have got on the clothes from sprinkling or splashing. The spots on the cuff of the shirt were consistent with being caused while the coat was being worn over it, but the spot on the upper part of the shirt could only have been caused when the jacket was off. One of the blood spots on the coat was on the inside of a buttonhole. The body of the button was clean, but there was some blood in the holes made for the thread. That suggested that some attempt had been made to wipe the button clean. There were signs that attempts had been made to wipe off spots of blood from the coat sleeve and the trousers below the knee. The cleaning was superficial, as the attempt had smeared some minute bloodstains. However, because the Pathologist had not been given a sample of either Nellie or John Fleming's blood he could not say whose blood was on the clothing.

Nellie's nephew, John Berry, who had lived with the Flemings for the past six years was intensely questioned. He had helped Gardaí to check the house, and noticed that one of four hammers was missing from the coal house. It had a rounded head on one side and chisel edge on the other. It was not missing before he went on holidays just two weeks previously and it was the only item missing from the Flemings' home. He found the key to the coalhouse in the kitchen, and had to unlock it to check its contents. If the hammer had been used as a weapon which seemed likely, the killer had taken it and then locked up the coal house and returned the key to its original position.

A team of forty Gardaí under Superintendent Richard O'Connell carried out exhaustive searches of the neighbourhood, searching all the gardens in Carlingford, Richmond and Hollybank Road, their adjoining terraces and lanes towards Glasnevin and waste spaces in the area, the Tolka River and the foreshore along the Bull Wall out to and beyond the low water mark.

However, the hammer was never found although it didn't take long for the investigating Gardaí to turn up the stories about the

44

other woman in John Fleming's life. Relationships with his wife had gone through a rough patch in the past fifteen months. Nellie had lived away from him for six months in the previous year, only occasionally returning to the house.

One morning when she was away John Berry had discovered Fleming in his bedroom when he awoke. There were two cousins of his staying overnight in the main bedroom where Nellie and John usually slept, Fleming told the boy.

He saw a fur coat on a hall stand when he went downstairs to make his own breakfast, Berry was to tell the Gardaí. Later that morning he saw Fleming having breakfast with a girl in the kitchen. He subsequently found a card in the bookcase in Carlingford Road, with the name Rita Murtagh and her address printed on it.

He didn't know her at the time, but at a play put on in the Claude Hall, in Drumcondra, in October nine months earlier, he saw John Fleming enter, and sit down beside and talk to a girl he was later to know as Rita Murtagh. Suspicious or just curious, the teenager followed them after the play as far as the nearby canal bridge.

Rita Murtagh came home with Fleming a number of times during the six months Mrs Fleming was away from the house but stayed only occasionally.

Delving into the background of John Fleming the Gardaí were also to investigate an incident that took place at midnight sixteen months earlier that seemed to be directly linked to his wife's murder.

At midnight on 31 March 1932 John Fleming woke up John Berry, telling him to get their neighbour as Nellie had had 'a stroke'. Berry banged loudly on the wall dividing their two houses. Awoken from her sleep and alarmed, Catherine O'Rourke called out, 'What's the matter, John?' and heard young John Berry shout back, 'Come out, Auntie is very bad'.

She dressed quickly, and John Fleming opened the door for her saying Nellie had had a stroke. She could hear Nellie moaning upstairs, and when she went into the bedroom saw her in great pain, her eyes wild and staring, while she continually opened and clenched her hands, rubbed her jaws and moved her legs up and down.

Catherine O'Rourke immediately began massaging the joints of Nellie Fleming's legs and her jaws to ease her pain. Her brother-in-law P.J. O'Rourke entered the bedroom shortly afterwards. He worked as a medicine compounder and knew she wasn't having a stroke; he too did his best to help, massaging her as her body was racked with spasms. He shouted out to her husband who was still downstairs to get a doctor. A few minutes later John Fleming entered the bedroom with a glass of hot milk, which he offered to his wife. She refused to drink it, 'Why do you insist on my taking it, Jack?' she asked.

He left the room, and returned again a few minutes later with a wine glass which contained coloured liquid which when she asked what it was, he replied was port and whiskey. 'It's not, there is none in the house,' she said as the spasms eased.

'There was a little in the bottom of the bottles,' he said. She took the glass, sipped from it, and then spat it out across the rumpled bedclothes.

'It tastes like the chocolates you gave me, bitter with a taste of aspirin,' she said.

'Did you put aspirin in it?' asked Catherine O'Rourke eyeing him suspiciously.

'I might have,' he replied.

'How could you do that when I got the aspirin from the back room as soon as I came in and have it in my pocket?' she asked.

Fleming made no reply, but instead picked up the wine glass she had put on the bedside table and went downstairs, saying he was going for a doctor.

P.J. O'Rourke followed him into the kitchen where Fleming stood at the sink washing the glass under the running tap.

'I'll hold you responsible if anything happens to Mrs Fleming,' said O'Rourke. 'I can get a doctor in the wilds of Connemara in half an hour, and it's queer you can't get one in the city of Dublin in an hour and a half.'

P.J. O'Rourke's suspicions had been aroused. He had previously seen three cases of strychnine poisoning when he served as a trained nurse, and had again just witnessed the classic symptoms of strychnine poisoning. The convulsant has a bitter taste, and within fifteen minutes of a fatal dose being administered the muscles of the body start to twitch and the victim's breath catches, while the chest feels tight. The victim's back will arch suddenly and the face fixes with a grim smile as the jaw muscles become drawn back and rigid. The body will relax after a minute or two, and then the convulsion starts again until the exhausted victim dies, all within two hours.

The victim's mind remains clear throughout the spasm attack until the moment of death.

'I'll get a doctor,' replied Fleming as he went out.

Fleming left the house twice to find a doctor, and said he failed. The second time, he returned to say that Dr Cotter's maid servant had spoken to him from an upstairs window of his house, which was only a few minutes away, and he knew from the way she spoke that he must have been drunk. This story further upset his wife, who said the doctor must have been 'terribly drunk' not to able to call to help her when she needed him.

It was now just after 2.30 a.m. and John Berry was despatched to get medical help as Nellie Fleming was still suffering.

P.J. O'Rourke, although suspicious of a poisoning attempt, never reported his fears to the Gardaí. 'That responsibility was taken off my shoulders when a doctor arrived,' he was to say later.

Nurse McDonagh, a midwife and psychiatric nurse, was called to the house and arrived fifteen minutes after P.J. O'Rourke sought help. She was to stay for the next six hours, applying hot towels on Nellie Fleming's legs and jaws to ease the stiffness. Fleming had told her his wife had taken 'a bad turn' and he came into the bedroom two or three times to ask if there was anything he could do to help. He never asked the nurse what was wrong with his wife.

Catherine O'Rourke remained in the bedroom until about five o'clock that morning. She stayed a further two hours in the house and then went home. She returned an hour later, with her husband. John Fleming was in the kitchen.

'About this poisoning,' said Fleming. He told them that when he was down the country he had got Nellie's brother Joe Berry to get strychnine poison from the chemist to poison Carolan's dog. 'Some of it might have got loose in my pocket on the chocolate. I buried the rest in the back lane. For the life of you don't tell Nellie,' he pleaded.

They heard this statement in stunned disbelief, and O'Rourke could only tell him that it was dangerous to carry and keep strychnine close to any foodstuffs.

Dr Cotter arrived around midday, unaware of P.J. O'Rourke's fears that Nellie Fleming had been the victim of an attempt to poison her.

'I have seen your wife. She is suffering from nerves and needs tonics and building up. I will take her in hand,' said Dr Cotter. Fleming agreed with him, saying he had pretended to go for him the previous evening to ease her worrying. He was convinced, he said, that there was nothing seriously wrong with her, just her imagination. Dr Cotter was to confirm subsequently that no one had contacted him, or roused his maid, the previous night. A few days after this event, which was not reported to the Gardaí, Nellie Fleming left to live with her family in Co. Westmeath, returning only occasionally. It was obviously not the first time she feared for her safety as Fleming had struck her only a short time before when she complained that he had failed to fulfil his Easter duties by not attending Mass.

It was during a holiday in Mount Temple, Co. Westmeath in March 1932 that Fleming asked his brother-in-law Joe Berry to buy some strychnine for him as he wanted to get rid of a neighbour's dog, and wouldn't be given the poison in Dublin.

Joe agreed, and a third man bought the strychnine on their behalf from a chemist's shop in Moate. The purchase was traceable, as the man had to sign for the purchase of sixpence worth of the deadly and controlled poison. The amount purchased was more than double a fatal dose.

On Tuesday 14 November that year, John Fleming appeared in Green Street court charged with the murder of his wife. Hundreds of people were to be turned away from the courthouse over the next seven days as the trial unfolded, and space for the public was at a premium.

Early into the trial, the judge, Mr Justice James Creed Meredith, K.C., ruled that the alleged assault on Mrs Fleming could not be considered by the court, but the attempted poisoning could.

John Fleming, wore an immaculate suit, collar and cuffs and his hair brushed back in a quiff. His well-set build but mediocre looks were nobody's idea of a callous killer or latter-day Lothario.

He was to spend seven hours in the witness box. Calmly and deliberately he answered all questions put to him, by his own counsel and the prosecution. He denied he had ever intended to poison his wife. 'She was a breadwinner the same as I was,' he said.

'I mentioned about poison having got into chocolate in my pocket. I had poison in my pocket which I wished to lay down with sandwiches for a dog. I had the chocolate in my pocket and I gave some of it to my wife,' he said.

He laid the poison on his return to Dublin, ate one chocolate himself and gave his wife two chocolates — she subsequently suffered an attack, the fourth in recent months, he told the crowded court in Green Street.

He also denied that he had put poison into either of the drinks he had brought his wife, the night she had suffered 'a stroke', claiming that P.J. O'Rourke had to be lying when he gave his evidence about the whiskey and port. He claimed that he had not emptied the mixture down the sink and washed the glass, but had given it to Mr O'Rourke, saying, 'There you are, have a look yourself.'

He had promised Joe Berry not to bring the poison for the dog into the house, and he had kept that promise, he said.

Rita Murtagh and her family were 'good, decent, respectable people', he admitted, and he had deceived her and them by pretending he was single, he told the court. He had met her four years earlier, and never knew her age, admitted she was young, and guessed at one stage that she was perhaps 21 years of age. A friendship had grown up between them, they had discussed marriage, and he had taken her to a jeweller's to get her fitted for an engagement and wedding ring. But he had continually put her off. He had mentioned the possibility of buying a house in Galway, but had never been to Galway at any stage to follow up his suggestion.

'Friendship grew between us and we liked each other, and I did not like to tell her,' he said when questioned in the dock about his refusal to tell the girl he was married.

'Had you any affection for her?' asked prosecution counsel Mr M. Maguire S.C.

'I rather liked her. I had no particular reason for not telling her. I suppose it is a case of the weakness of human nature,' he said, brushing aside any suggestion of coldness. But Mr Maguire hammered away at the point. 'I am asking you did you have any genuine affection for the girl? Don't mind about human nature.'

'No, I had not,' said Fleming.

As the cross-examination continued he admitted he liked the girl, had seduced her, but never had any intention of marrying her. He maintained also that he had 'always had' an affection for his wife, and reconciled that with seducing the girl in his wife's bed through the 'weakness of human nature'.

He admitted that he 'never had any real great affection for her', but apparently contradicted himself later saying that if he was single he 'probably would have' married her. In response to his own counsel, Sean Hooper B.L., who even then, as a relative newcomer to the profession, was carving out a noteworthy and successful career in the courts, Fleming denied any intention of marrying Rita Murtagh.

'Had you any intention of marrying Miss Murtagh?' his counsel asked. 'I had not,' he replied.

In response to the judge, he said that he had never complained about the dog to Mrs Carolan because she was a good friend. He had not made the sandwich with the poison in it in his own house because he had promised his brother-in-law not to bring the poison into the house.

'Are you always as careful about not breaking your promises?' asked Judge Meredith.

'In a case like that, I did not want to have any dealings with poison in the house,' said Fleming.

'Was this the only occasion on which you were so careful about your promises to people? Especially when you did not worry about your promises to Rita Murtagh or the faithful promises you made on marriage to your wife. Why should you attach such importance to this faithful promise to Joe Berry?' asked the Judge.

'My principal reason,' Fleming replied, 'was that I did not want to have any transactions with the poison.'

On the day of the murder John Fleming said he had arrived home at 1.30 p.m. They had their lunch at about 2.15 p.m., and then he cut the grass in the back garden. He finished trimming and tidying the garden at about 4.30 p.m. He locked the shears and the lawn-mower back into the coal shed, and did not notice whether the hammers were in the shed or not.

He went into the house, took £4 in cash from the wardrobe in an upstairs bedroom to buy a new overcoat while in town, and tidied himself up in the bathroom. He admitted he was wearing a blood-stained shirt, but it wasn't noticeable. 'One shirt every week,' he explained. The bloodstains on his clothing were caused by the cut on his finger which had re-opened and bled profusely, he claimed.

That afternoon his wife had asked him to go and see some new houses with her that were on the market in nearby Mobhi Road, but he said that she wasn't ready to leave as she wanted to meet the insurance man. He said that he couldn't wait for her and left the house, arranging to meet with her later in Ryans in Clontarf.

Rita Murtagh's life had been hellish since she had been told John Fleming was married, and stood accused of the murder of his wife. In September of that year she gave birth to a baby boy. In November, at Fleming's trial, she was to faint twice and had to be carried out of the courtroom and receive medical attention as she gave evidence.

She gave her name and address in a barely audible voice, and within a few moments was sobbing uncontrollably. 'Try and be calm, Miss Murtagh; everyone has great sympathy with you,' said Judge Meredith in a soft voice leaning down from his bench towards her.

Rita described how they had first met when she served Fleming his lunch in the D'Olier Street café. But it was twelve months later before she agreed to 'walk out' with him. They went to the pictures and for walks, and he took her to his home once, promising her it would be hers when they were married. Asked if she believed his promise of marriage, she nodded yes, and burst into tears. People in the public gallery shifted in their seats uncomfortably, embarrassed as the girl's wails rent the air. The Judge asked her if she wanted to leave the court, and she sobbed out 'Yes, I want to go.'

Rita was taken to an ante-room, and a doctor was called to attend her. In her absence the trial continued. On her return an hour later, the prosecution counsel asked if she could be allowed to give her evidence from the seat she was sitting in rather than at the witness table in order to ease her anxiety and upset. 'Try, like a good child, to come to the witness table,' said the Judge. Rita Murtagh wept violently, tears splashing down to her lap as she sat with her head bowed. The Judge agreed to let her give her evidence from her seat — a place which ensured she kept her back to her former lover.

She gradually calmed and resumed giving evidence in the court, answering questions about their growing romance. She told how she had stayed in Fleming's aunt's bed one night, and how he had come into the room and slipped into the bed beside her, how he had told her of the house they were going to buy in Galway, the visit to the jeweller to purchase the engagement ring, and how she had told him that they had to get married.

Mr Hooper, the defence counsel, cross-examined her. 'Did you ever hear it suggested before July last that Fleming was a married man?' 'No,' she replied in a whisper.

'And was it ever suggested, even as a joke?' he persisted. 'No,' she said again, and as he put another question to her, she broke down into wild sobs. The Judge, alarmed, said she should be taken outside into the air as she appeared hysterical. As she was being helped out of her seat, she fainted and had to be carried.

Outside, Dr Shiel, who was in court to give evidence about his post mortem on Nellie Fleming, attended to Rita Murtagh.

The court had adjourned, and when it resumed thirty minutes later, Dr Shiel returned to say Rita was unconscious and couldn't give evidence. The court adjourned for another half an hour, but Rita was still unconscious. Dr John McGrath, the State Pathologist, had also lent his assistance, and said that although the girl had regained consciousness, she couldn't possibly answer questions. Rita Murtagh returned to the court the following day. Only a few questions were put to her about the last time she had seen Fleming, and about his intended house purchase in Galway.

'You have had a very trying time and you have been a very good girl. Now go home to your mother and father and try to forget this place,' Judge Meredith counselled her. As she stood to leave, she fainted again, and was caught before hitting the floor by Supt Richard O'Connell, the first senior officer at the murder scene, who carried her out of the Green Street courthouse.

John Fleming had given a perfectly reasonable explanation of his conduct on the night in question in March 1932, and his evidence was just as likely to be right and more so than that of the inconsistent and forgetful witnesses upon whom the State relied, his defence, Senior Counsel Sean Hooper, said as he opened his address to the jury. There was no proof, only an opinion that strychnine had been administered to Mrs Fleming. That opinion came from Mr P.J. O'Rourke , who had not contacted the police about his suspicions. Also Dr Cotter had contradicted his belief after examining the woman, saying she had suffered from a bout of nerves. 'There was not a single fact produced that could point inevitably and only to Fleming. Most of the evidence pointed to his innocence, and there was nothing that pointed to his guilt,' he said.

There was nothing significant in the disappearance of the hammer, in fact a hammer may not have been the murder weapon at all. He said the case against his client was flawed, that blood spatters found on John Fleming's clothes were never tested to see was it his blood or his wife's blood, and, he said, the exact time of death had not been fixed either.

Having recounted Fleming's trip to the Bull Wall, his swim and sunbathing, and his visit to Ryan's house that evening, Mr Hooper asked, 'Would not any man, no matter how callous or brutal, show some effect in his appearance, with this terrible crime blackening his soul?'

He addressed the jury for almost four hours, concluding, 'I have made no efforts to appeal to your pity, credulousness or fears. All the evidence which could indicate one way or another whether he is guilty of the offence of which he is charged is consistent with one thing only — his complete innocence, and I demand that of you.'

Counsel for the State dismissed suggestions that a mystery assailant could have attacked Nellie Fleming. On the contrary there was an overwhelming mass of evidence against the accused, and beyond all doubt robbery was not a motive for the attack.

The evidence about the poisoning attempt had been introduced to show a systematic course of action by Fleming against his wife and to show a previous murderous intent in his mind, and that in 1932 he was a potential killer who had failed.

Fleming had realised that his first attempt to poison his wife had failed. He offered her the glasses of milk and the mixture of port wine and whiskey in a desperate effort to complete the crime. He possibly believed his wife would have died before the O'Rourkes arrived, and that they would believe his story of a stroke. No one would then learn of his intrigue on the other side of the city, and he would then be free to marry the girl concerned.

The story about using a doctored sandwich to try to poison Carolan's dog, which he had never complained about before, was 'incredible' said Mr Haugh. It was a clumsy effort at an excuse, almost as clumsy as his attempt to poison his wife. 'If Fleming had a motive for doing away with his wife in March 1932' said Haugh, 'he had a still stronger motive in March 1933, when Rita Murtagh's condition compelled her to press him to marry her, and when her parents were beginning to show uneasiness on account of the reports that he was a married man.'

Mr Justice Meredith began his charge to the jury at 8.20 p.m. on Monday 21 November, the sixth day of the trial. The 'natural revulsion' that arose from the account of the accused's conduct with regard to Rita Murtagh would practically settle the matter as far as the outside public was concerned, but, as a matter of law, the fact that the accused did those acts and admitted them should not create any presumption whatever that he was guilty of the crime with which he was now charged.

Even if the jury was satisfied that in March 1932, the accused had attempted to poison his wife that would not constitute, according to law, any ground whatever on which they could presume that he had committed the offence for which he was being tried. The evidence was wholly circumstantial and the jury were not entitled to convict the accused if the evidence was only sufficient to arouse suspicion, said Judge Meredith.

Fleming had never made any statement about the route he took to the Bull Wall until he got into the witness chair, 'when all the cards of the prosecution were on the table'; instead of making a determined effort to find a witness who may have seen him, by previously describing his route.

The jury had to consider the number of lies he told to Rita Murtagh, and also whether, in order to get himself out of that difficulty, he told untruths. They also had to decide if they were to place much reliance on his statements now, as to the route he took that day, and if they would accept them, just because he said so and that there was difficulty in disproving it.

The jury retired to consider its verdict at 10.45 p.m. At 12.25 a.m. they returned to a hushed and expectant crowd who had remained packed into the gallery running around the wall at the back of the courtroom.

The foreman of the jury listened as the charge was read out again, and in response to the question, he said they had reached a verdict of guilty.

John Fleming stood motionless in the dock, his eyes fixed on the Judge. Mr Justice Meredith asked him if he had anything to say why sentence of death should not be passed upon him. He replied, 'I wish to make an appeal.'

Mr Justice Meredith then put on the black cap, and delivered the death sentence, saying the prisoner should be hanged in Mountjoy jail on Tuesday 19 December 1933. 'May the Lord have mercy on your soul,' he said.

Fleming remained standing, expressionless, in the dock, until a prison officer touched him on the shoulder, to lead him from the courtroom to the cells below.

Leave to appeal was sought and granted, on the grounds that the evidence relating to the administration of strychnine was inadmissible.

His appeal was dismissed, and despite a petition presented to the Minister for Justice on his behalf, he was executed at Mountjoy jail on 5 January, 1934.

There could not have been, at any time, any doubt about the guilt of John Fleming of the murder of his wife, wrote Supt George Lawlor:

'Fleming showed himself in his true colours by endeavouring to throw suspicion on the insurance agent when he was arrested and was charged with the murder of his wife. However, this was merely wasted effort on his part. His clothing, on examination, showed many small stains of human blood. There were also signs that an effort had been made to remove these bloodstains.

'From the investigator's point of view there were no difficulties in procuring the evidence and in bringing his guilt home to the accused man. Motive was there too, in the strongest possible form, in his association with a young girl whom he had actually arranged to marry at a later date than the murder.

'Yet there was one aspect to this case that has never since been solved: the receipt of a letter by Fleming when he was in Mountjoy jail awaiting trial.

'The letter arrived after depositions had been heard at the District Court, and while Fleming was in custody in Mountjoy Jail awaiting trial in the Green Street courthouse. It was obviously written by someone who knew the facts behind the case. It could have been, and read as, an anxious helping letter, but on the evidence one is forced to the conclusion that it was not a bona fide letter intended to help Fleming, and that it was written for the purpose of drawing attention to a previous attempted poisoning incident which would be damaging to Fleming. Who the letter writer was is still unknown and will probably never be known, though it is possible to suggest a reason for its writing. It was a strange feature of the case, and it read:

Dear Jack,
I was stunned when I read in the paper on Thursday night that they knew all about the strychnine. For God's sake don't give in about it. If you do you will only damn yourself and then they will not be satisfied until they find out where you got it and then I would be for it. I know you would not let me down for anything. Keep your head and everything will be OK. I can let you into a secret, but for God's sake don't breathe a word to anyone or you will ruin it all. You will be a free man soon. We got men out of the 'Joy' under worse conditions and we will have you out soon. Rita sends you her love. She says she forgives and will marry you when you are free. Burn this in case any of the warders get it.
Yours only pal,

PH.

'Up to this stage' continued George Lawlor, 'no mention had been made at the District Court proceedings of where the strychnine had been obtained. It had been mentioned that proof would be forthcoming of an attempt by the accused man to poison his wife with strychnine.'

'Had Fleming obtained poison by another source or was this a deliberate attempt to compromise him falsely by someone who was afraid that he might escape unless this matter of the strychnine poisoning attempt was brought to light? Whatever may have been the explanation, to this day, the writer of the letter bearing the initials "PH" was never traced.'

4.

The Caravan Killing

JAMES Redmond was a bachelor who lived a primitive life in a caravan in a muddy field and was reputed to have money. He had been to Canada twice and had also worked in England before he returned home in 1934.

Aged forty-three he worked locally as a farm labourer, was single and kept to himself. He excited no controversy in the area, there was no one to say a bad word about him although his behaviour was considered a little odd, as he was a recluse. One of a family of seven, his only regular contact with his family, all of whom lived locally, was his sister Mary who lived about one mile away. She called regularly to his caravan, visiting him at least once a fortnight. On 10 January 1937 she bumped into him on a lane near the caravan. They swapped a few words as they were both on errands. She said she'd call on him later that week. It was the last time she saw him.

Three days later Mary called to the lonely field where he lived but discovered his caravan was locked, and her brother's bicycle, which was normally left leaning locked up against one of the four large wheels of the caravan, was missing. She wasn't particularly worried as he had told her earlier in the month that he was thinking of returning to England. Even if he hadn't left the country, she thought he could have cycled to the village for his shopping. James wasn't working at the time and was drawing approximately six shillings a week in unemployment insurance. She was to call three more times, but the caravan remained locked, and there was no response to her persistent knocking. There was still no sign of the bicycle. On Monday 25 January she again went to the caravan, and saw the field gate was open. There were donkey tracks leading through the gate, into the field and away to the right of the entrance.

56

'I followed the tracks to a wall, and there I found the body of my brother. I did not recognise him immediately, but I recognised his clothes,' she told Gardaí.

The body was fully clothed, Redmond's cap was missing, and his overcoat had been pulled up around his neck. The body was lying on its back, stretched out against the muddy earth. Redmond's hands were thrown up, as if protecting his head. The left hand lay outstretched almost touching a pool of water surrounded by bushes, the right hand was thrown across his face.

Mary Redmond rushed back to the gate where she had left her own bike, and cycled to her brother Patrick, a small farmer who lived half a mile away. She met him walking along the roadway with his eight-year-old daughter Maggie. Mary dismounted, and so as not to upset the child, whispered the news of her dreadful discovery. Patrick said it was almost a month since he'd last seen his brother. There wasn't much he could do but get the Gardaí, he said, with shock in his voice. He sent his daughter home with his sister, and told her to fetch a priest. He took her bike and set off to the Garda station in Carrigbyrne.

It was 7.40 p.m. when Sgt Con Coughlan and another Garda arrived at the field. Without instructions as to where to find the body it took them almost five minutes to discover it partly hidden under the bushes.

Neither member of the Gardaí knew the dead man, but they recognised foul play; the man's head had been severely battered. The dead man's waistcoat, jacket and overcoat were open and pulled back, suggesting the pockets had been rifled. When Gardaí searched his pockets they found a small purse in his trousers containing £2-11s-6d in notes and small change. But there were no keys to the still locked caravan. In the top left-hand pocket of the dead man's jacket was a watch. It had stopped at twelve minutes to three.

The local Garda Superintendent, from New Ross, was called to the scene, and a search of the field beside an old disused mill and the caravan was organised. The Technical Bureau was also telephoned that evening.

The dead man's cap was found and later identified by his sister, lying in the wet field about six yards away from the body.

The horse-drawn caravan was of traditional design, a rectangular timber base on a four-wheeled wooden chassis. A canvas was stretched around an almost circular framework to form the ceiling, and the entrance was through a door set high above the shafts.

That door was still locked, and Gardaí had to force it open to gain entry. It was untidy, but there were no obvious signs of a struggle although the small stove stood at a tilted angle. A torn envelope lay on the floor of the caravan near the bunk opposite the entrance door. It was marked, 'Ulster Bank, Wexford, Deposit receipt'. Unlike many country people, and old folk in particular, who mistrusted banks, James Redmond appreciated their value. However, the torn envelope was empty and the small portmanteau, which Redmond kept under his bed and which was used to store the envelope, had been prised open.

The dead man's body was rolled onto a door that had been lifted off its hinges to provide a makeshift stretcher, and was taken to outhouses owned by the Kellys who farmed nearby, at approximately 10 p.m. that evening. Garda inquiries were to reveal that he was last seen alive exactly fourteen days earlier when he cashed his six-shillings allowance postal order in the Taghmon post office. He then bought groceries and small items of clothing in Bridget Reville's shop, and went on to Rocheford's pub in Camross and had a bottle of stout.

The State Pathologist, Dr John McGrath, carried out the post mortem examination of the body. It had begun decomposing, rats had attacked the dead body as it lay in the open field, gnawing away at the face, the legs and one of the arms. However, there were more serious wounds and damage to the body. On the head alone there were nine different wounds, and each, he believed, was caused separately. The jaw was broken, and four teeth were smashed into the mouth as a result of a number of blows. There was a stab wound which had punctured the skull above the right eyebrow. The left side of the face was severely bruised. The jaw and the skull bore severe fractures and it was quite clear that Redmond had been clubbed to death with some heavy blunt instrument, and in endeavouring to protect himself, he had received severe injuries on his hands. Death would have taken place between one and fifteen minutes of the attack commencing, he estimated.

Dr McGrath also examined the caravan, but found no blood marks or other clues. However, when he examined the ground around the entrance to the caravan he found traces of blood. There were also a large number of minute blood splash marks around the door of the caravan, particularly the base, which would have been about shoulder height for a man standing on the ground, indicating that the initial stage of the attack had taken place there.

Mr F.M. O'Connor, a solicitor and the Coroner for South Wexford, conducted the inquest shortly after the body was discovered. Speaking at its conclusion, he made a heartfelt and long-winded plea to 'maintain the crime-free name of Wexford', saying: 'I don't think — and I am sorry to have to say it — that there can be any doubt that this man was, as described, murdered. There is no evidence before you to show who did it, and therefore, you have no evidence whatsoever before you upon which you can bring that crime home to any person. If any person had been charged with the crime, we would not have been asked to adjourn this inquest pending the completion of any criminal proceedings that might follow. No person has so far been arrested, therefore, it is the duty of every citizen who has any knowledge whatever regarding as fact which might in any small way lead to the apprehension of the person responsible for this foul murder to come forward at once and give the Gardaí and those in authority every possible assistance which may be in their power to give.'

'Looking back over the past thirty years I think the murder was the most audacious one committed and that it provided us (the Gardaí) with the most complete chain of circumstantial evidence,' George Lawlor was to write later.

A time-consuming and painstaking search of the caravan and the field where the man was found was carried out the day after the body was found. A variety of special tasks were issued to a large team of Gardaí drafted in from the surrounding stations to help Detective Inspector Lawlor's team for the Bureau. Garda Dan Leahy from the local station was given the task of chopping down the gorse bushes that lined the ditches surrounding the field. As the day wore on he gradually cleared the field, searching through the prickly branches and rough roots of the bushes for possible clues. About eighteen feet from the entrance gate to the field he discovered a portion of a shotgun stock. Another piece was discovered near the gate. They fitted together, but despite an intensive search of the area around the caravan and the vehicle, the rest of the broken shotgun could not be found. To the investigating team it looked as if the dead man had been beaten with the shotgun. The firearm had undoubtedly broken into pieces in the ferocious attack and the bits were then discarded.

Heavy rainfalls during the previous week had washed out any chance of getting foot or other prints from the now muddy ground surrounding the caravan. The interior of the caravan was also checked for fingerprints, but none of evidential value were found.

The investigation team was also making progress on the theory that Redmond had been robbed. The Ulster Bank in Wexford had a few surprises in store for the investigation team when they arrived in the town branch. James Redmond did have an account with them, the bank confirmed, and in fact it had contained a considerable amount of money, a total of £318, with a further £11-11s due for interest. The account had been opened in July 1931 with an initial deposit of £200 and had been steadily increased since.

However, two days after the dead man was last seen, a man who claimed he was James Redmond had visited a branch of the Ulster Bank in Dun Laoghaire and had withdrawn £280, saying he needed the money as he had bought some horses in County Dublin. The trail was still hot, and Detective Inspector Lawlor immediately went to the Ulster Bank branch office in Dun Laoghaire.

Corwell Orr was the conscientious cashier who recounted what had happened on the morning of 13 January. The man who called to his desk presented a deposit receipt and said he wanted £280. The cashier said he could not give it without the authority of the Wexford office, and the man said that he would 'wire' Wexford, and Orr helped him draft the telegram. Orr also told him that he would need someone to identify him in Dun Laoghaire once the clearance came through, but the man said he knew no one in that part of the country.

The man went to the post office, and when he returned at midday Orr telephoned Wexford, checking the man before him against the telephoned description he was receiving. His customer was then put on the phone. The cashier heard him say, 'I have bought horses and I want about £250 to pay for them.' Hugh Maguire, the cashier in Wexford, was at the other end of the line. 'Is that you, James?' he asked. 'Yes,' said the man. 'Will they not give you the money there?' asked Maguire. 'No,' was the reply. The two cashiers then spoke for a moment or two, and the Dun Laoghaire cashier asked the man if he had ever been in Canada or Australia. The man said he had been in Canada. The answer satisfied the bankers, the phone receiver was replaced in the cradle, and the cashier paid out £240 in ten and five pound notes, and a further £40 in one pound notes. The man then signed a bank cash docket in the name, James Redmond. A full description was then taken, including an approximate age of 42 and the general impression that the man conveyed an 'agricultural look'.

Using the bank premises as a central radial point, teams of detectives visited shops in the area hoping to match the description to a customer.

Descriptions were also circulated to Garda stations throughout the country. A description of James Redmond's bicycle was also sent out at the same time, as it had not turned up in any of the searches around the caravan. It was assumed that the bicycle had been used by the killer to get away.

As local enquiries continued it was learnt that someone who answered the description of the man who had presented Redmond's deposit receipt in Dun Laoghaire had tendered a deposit receipt at the Munster and Leinster Bank, the Bank of Ireland and the National Bank, New Ross, on the morning of 12 January. This was a fair day in New Ross, and while the cashiers in all three banks refused to cash the receipt, they were able to recall that it was in the name 'Redmond' or that the amount was for over £300. One of the cashiers was able to describe the man with the deposit receipt; the description matched that given by the Dun Laoghaire bank. The seasoned hands on the investigation team could feel the draw lines of the net closing tighter around their quarry.

By this time enquiries were being made very widely as employees of all sea ports, railway stations, bus depots, hackney car owners — particularly those along the route from Wexford to Dublin — were contacted to see if the description rang a bell. A check of rail ticket sales was also carried out at the Great Southern Railways head office. This check showed that three excursion tickets had been purchased at New Ross on 12 January. The investigation switched back to the south east again, as detectives confirmed the sales with the ticket clerk, Patrick Magennis, in the railway office.

There was a train from New Ross to Dublin's Harcourt Street station at 3.45 p.m., and about 3.40 p.m. a man came into the booking hall and asked for a return ticket to Bray. Then he asked would it be cheaper to buy a three-day return ticket, and return to Wexford on it. Magennis said no, he'd have to buy another ticket for the extra part of the journey.

Two other people bought three-day tickets that day, both of them women. Magennis gave a description of the man to the Gardaí — and the description matched those given by the two bank cashiers.

The next step was an interview with the ticket inspector who travelled on the train to Wexford. He was able to recall that on 13 January, the day after the ticket had been purchased, he checked a return ticket to New Ross. He said that he'd told the man that he should have taken the bus at Enniscorthy, but his passenger had replied that he wanted to get off the train at Killurin, as it was nearer his home. 'I was at the fair in New Ross yesterday, that's how I have the New Ross ticket,' he explained.

Again, his description of the roughly dressed countryman matched the three already collected along the trail. The ticket inspector was also certain that only one man had got off the train at Killurin station and he was the man who said he'd been at the fair the previous day.

Supt Farrell from New Ross then led his team of local Gardaí in a massive house-to-house inquiry in the area, a trawl that might identify the man.

John Hornick from Kilgaran had travelled to Dublin on 12 January and returned the following day. He had told his wife and relatives that he was visiting his sister in Dalkey who had just got out of hospital on the 12th. Hornick was arrested on 7 February. Supt J. Farrell, of Wexford, questioned Hornick and wrote down what he said. Hornick told him that he was at New Ross fair on 12 January, and that the following day he was at home. The superintendent said that he understood Hornick had gone to Dublin that day. 'Oh, yes, quite right,' said Hornick, 'I went up to see my sister.'

Hornick later made a statement after being charged and cautioned. He farmed 45 acres which he had inherited from his uncle. He married in July 1933 and received £400 on his marriage, which he used to build his house. They had three children and he was just making ends meet, he said. There was no money to spare and he had none at the moment. He dealt in cattle and purchased them at local fairs. On the 12th he went to New Ross fair as he had some money. He carried out his business as usual, canvassing various sellers for their prices before settling on four heifers which he bought for £7 each, except for one he got for £6. He paid for them with money he had made on the sale of lambs two days earlier, and drove them home himself.

On the following day, he said, he set out for Wexford on his bicycle to get fittings for a plough. When he had bought them he decided to visit his sister in Dalkey, who had been ill. He stayed and chatted with his brother-in-law and his sister on his arrival at 2 p.m. until his departure at 6 p.m. that evening, when he returned to County Wexford by train.

He said he sent a telegram to his brother to meet him when he got off the train that evening. His brother Philip met him at Killurin station and brought him to their father's house, where he picked up his bicycle and went home.

He said he knew the deceased man James Redmond, and he knew where he lived. He'd heard Redmond intended going to Birkenhead in England, but he'd never had any transactions with him and did not know he had any money. The last time he saw him was before Christmas, he said. In his statement he also denied that he was in Dun Laoghaire on the 13th, or that he had ever cashed a deposit receipt in the name of James Redmond, and said he never sent a telegram from Dun Laoghaire.

Hornick was placed in three identification parades, held in Mountjoy Garda station in Dublin. As was the practice Hornick was allowed to choose any position he wanted in the line-up. He chose to stand fourth in a line of eight people, as the post office clerk, and two shop assistants from Woolworth's stores in Dun Laoghaire were asked if they could see the man who had called to their business establishments. All three separately identified Hornick. Both the cashier in the Ulster Bank in Dun Laoghaire and the ticket clerk in New Ross also identified Hornick as looking like the man who had cashed the receipt and bought the return ticket.

Hornick was charged with the murder of James Redmond between 11 and 25 January. He said, 'I did not kill him anyhow.' Hornick was also charged with uttering a forged document, and when charged said, 'There is one thing, I did not take it anyway. That is all I have to say about it, thank God.'

Hornick's house was searched by the Gardaí, and it was discovered that his single barrel-shotgun, for which he held a firearms certificate, was missing. He had been seen by a labourer he employed and neighbours on both Sunday 10 and Monday 11 January carrying the shotgun on his lands near Redmond's caravan. Sgt James Millane, who was in charge of the search at Hornick's house, found the single barrel of a shotgun, with part of the stock broken but still adhering to the barrel, concealed in a hayrick on the farm. The remains of the gun had blood marks on it and when it was compared to the other section of shotgun found in furze bushes in Redmond's field it fitted perfectly. Patrick Fox, who had worked for four years as a labourer on Hornick's farm, identified the gun as belonging to his employer. He had made a new hand-grip for the gun and carried out other repairs on it which made it easily recognisable.

The State Pathologist, Dr McGrath, also examined the piece of shotgun retrieved from Hornick's hayrick, and said that the blood-stains found on both the barrel and stock were human. The search of Hornick's lands also turned up Redmond's bicycle. It was discovered in a large patch of furze and ferns, unlikely to be found in a casual search of the area. It was examined for fingerprints but none were found.

On Tuesday 12 April the trial opened with more than eight witnesses ready to give evidence. Only one person called to serve on the jury was told by the State to stand down when he said that he had a conscientious objection to capital punishment — the penalty for murder.

Mr Kevin Haugh prosecuted the case, which he told the jury, was 'a calculated and most deliberate murder, committed purely for the sake of gain'.

Hornick had been in severe financial difficulties; six months before Redmond's killing he had owed the bank £271. His family had had to try and bail him out as the bank cashed a life insurance policy on Hornick which they had held as security.

On Sunday 10 January he was seen going across the fields with a gun in the direction of the caravan. Redmond had been beaten to death. The person who attacked and killed him must have taken the key from the body and and the deposit receipt from the caravan, said Haugh.

His colleague, who continued, said: 'The accused man must have waited for a considerable time at the gate through which the deceased must enter on his way to the caravan, and having waited there in ambush until the deceased came along, the accused, from the shelter and shadow of the bushes suddenly attacked him.' There was no doubt, he said, but that the shotgun had been used as a bludgeon.

In the Dun Laoghaire branch of the bank there was carried out as cool a piece of effrontery as had ever been transacted in the bank or elsewhere, he said.

On his return home, Hornick surprisingly began buying items and paying off debts. They had come to the conclusion that the accused had taken the bold step of cashing the receipt by the grossest form of fraud and cunning and, when he got the money, began spending it as quickly as possible without raising undue alarm. Even if he had not gone to Dublin, said Mr Haugh, there were his movements on Sunday and Monday and the fact that the deceased man's bicycle was found on Hornick's land and the stock of the gun near the caravan, while the barrel was found near his house.

One of the first witnesses called for the prosecution was Samuel

Willis, the ticket inspector on the train on 13 January. He identified John Hornick in the courtroom and confirmed that he had got off the afternoon train from Dublin to Wexford at Killurin.

A string of witnesses, including a shop assistant and a bank cashier, climbed into the witness box to contradict his statement that he hadn't been in Dun Laoghaire on the 13th.

His brother Philip said that he met John Hornick from the train after receiving his telegram on the 13th, and he drove him from the station back to his father's house where he stayed the night.

The assistant in the post office at Killurin, John White, said he recalled writing out the telegram to Philip Hornick, which had arrived in Killurin at 1.50 p.m. on 13 January.

Extensive Garda investigation showed that Hornick had spent a small fortune within a very short time — all monies were spent after 13 January when £280 was withdrawn from John Redmond's bank account.

A total of twenty-two witnesses from the New Ross area gave evidence of Hornick making them payments for a variety of items in cash on 14, 15, 16 and 19 January and on 1 and 2 February. Included among the payments were: £42 outstanding for a debt, £15 for overdue land rental payments, £31-1s-0d for heifers, £15-11s-0d for sheep, £4 for an account in a shop, £8 for clothing, and £7-15s-0d for farming implements.

Mr Maguire S.C., prosecuting for the State, said that a total of £230 had been spent by Hornick within a week of the murder. John Hornick gave a number of samples of his handwriting to the Gardaí after he was arrested. Captain J.A. Quirke, a handwriting expert, later told Green Street court that he classified as the writing of the same individual the signature of 'John Hornick' on lodgment forms produced from the Ulster Bank, Wexford, and the signature 'James Redmond' on the deposit receipt. He then produced enlarged photographs of portions of signatures which showed similar characteristics in the signature on the lodgment forms, the deposit receipt, the Dun Laoghaire lodgment form and specimens provided by John Hornick.

Counsel for the Defence, J.L. Esmonde, decided not to call Hornick to give evidence. Putting the accused man in the witness box would also open him up to cross examination by the prosecution. A strong feature of the case was that James Redmond was murdered some time on the evening of 11 January and if the jury had any doubt that Redmond was alive after that date, they must acquit Hornick, he told them.

In the indictment, the accused man was alleged to have murdered Redmond between the 11th and 25th. Not one piece of evidence had been given that the murder was committed on any date other than the 11th. Did it not mean that the State had placed this case before them in some doubt as to the date, he asked? On the day the murder was said to have taken place Hornick had engaged a new workman, and the following day he went to New Ross fair and transacted his business in a perfectly normal way, argued Mr Esmonde. There was also the fact that the body was not found until the 25th. In the post mortem the State pathologist could only give his opinion as to the date of death, that it occurred between one and three weeks before his examination, and more likely between two and three weeks. He contended they must be satisfied that Redmond met his death on 11 January, otherwise that was the end of the case against his client.

Mr Esmonde also criticised the evidence of identification, and said that it was possible that Redmond had visited the Ulster Bank in Dun Laoghaire himself. If the jury thought that, he told them, the whole prosecution case fell. In addition, he said, there were no signs of combat or traces of blood on Hornick when he returned home at any time during January. The man who had committed the murder and carried the body from the caravan to where the body was found must have been covered in blood, yet Hornick returned to his kitchen fire that night without so much as a drop of blood on him.

His life had continued as normal during that month, Hornick had paraded himself before his family, his employees and members of the public as a man who had not a thing on his conscience, said his counsel.

Mr Justice O'Byrne took two hours to charge the jury. There were, he said, two questions of paramount importance which they had to decide on.

Firstly, was James Redmond murdered; and secondly, if that was so, was that murder committed by the accused man, John Hornick? They had to have moral certainty, mathematical certainty wasn't good enough. A lot of people were inclined to be frightened when they heard that a case depended on circumstantial evidence, he warned. 'Do not allow yourselves to be frightened or misled in any way by hearing that this is a case of circumstantial evidence. Murder is, from the very nature of it, a furtive crime. It is a crime that is usually and naturally committed in private, and the person

66

who has determined to commit such a crime naturally tries to commit it at a time and in such a place that no human eye will see it.' Justice O'Byrne reviewed the movements of Redmond, and said that, based on Dr McGrath's evidence, he did not think they could escape the conclusion that he had been murdered. Also the 'reasonable inference' from the evidence was that he was murdered in or around seven o'clock on the night of 11 January.

There was little evidence as to where the accused man was on the afternoon of 11 January. There was no explanation given for his disappearance, and there was no account given for the missing five or six hours.

On the next day he went to New Ross fair. There was evidence that he was in Dalkey, but he was absent for some time, and where was he during those hours which were of such great importance in the case? Turning to the gun, he said there was no doubting that the gun belonged to Hornick. It had been seen in his possession shortly before the death of Redmond, but he had given no account of the missing gun. On the question of Hornick's sudden purchases and his payments against debts, the judge said no explanation had been offered as to where the money came from. If the money represented payments from any member of his family, what was the difficulty about proving it?

Mr Justice O'Byrne said he thought it necessary to refer the jury to portions of the statement made to the police at Taghmon by the accused man. Many parts of that statement were untrue. Why were these statements made? Was it to put the Gardaí off his trail, he asked.

The jury retired for exactly one hour, and returned with a verdict of 'Guilty'. When asked if he had anything to say Hornick rose slowly to his feet and stood emotionless. 'No, sir,' he said.

'You have been convicted by a jury of your fellow countrymen of the murder of James Redmond,' said the Judge, 'Not only do I entirely concur with the verdict but it seems to be the only verdict at which any reasonable jury could arrive. According to the evidence the crime was one of a very deliberate and cold-blooded character, committed for the purpose of possessing yourself of money belonging to this unfortunate man. I cannot hold out any hope of mercy to you, and I can only implore of you to utilise the short time you have at your disposal in this life for the purpose of making your peace with God.' He then put on the black cap and sentenced him to death. Leave to appeal was refused. On 17 June 1937, John Hornick, aged 36 years, was hanged in Mountjoy jail.

5.

The Dohertys

ON the afternoon of Saturday 20 April 1940, a telephone message was received at Garda Technical Bureau, Kilmainham from Superintendent Heaphy, the officer in charge of the District headquarters at Buncrana, Co. Donegal. The body of a woman, Miss Hannah Margaret Doherty, aged 29, had been found on the mountainside at Ballyhillon, Malin Head about three hundred yards from her parents' home.

She had been missing since 9 o'clock the previous evening. The body was lying face downwards on the ground and there were several wounds clearly visible on the back of the dead woman's head, and an investigation into her death had commenced, he said.

The phone line was busy throughout the evening as further details of the girl's death were communicated to Dublin, and the following morning a photographer, Det. Sgt Michael Wall and a fingerprint expert were despatched to Donegal. The State Pathologist, Dr John McGrath, was also contacted and he too left independently for the Inishowen peninsula.

The post mortem took place in a disused house at the foot of the mountainside after the two Gardaí had carried out their initial investigation at the spot where the dead body lay.

There a woman had been strangled, and there were sixteen wounds on her head. Her skull had been fractured in a number of places from the blows, which could have been inflicted by a bloodstained stone found near the body. Her face had been beaten in during the attack and the bridge of her nose had also been broken. The body had been fully clothed and pieces of grass were found sticking in dried blood on the body. These were likely to have been transferred there either by the weapon or when the woman had been beaten to the ground.

The woman had been forty days pregnant, and had had a previous pregnancy, Dr McGrath's post mortem report concluded.

The inquest was held without delay. The body was cleaned and re-dressed, and was laid out in the same house in a coffin resting on two chairs.

Mr Michael J. White, the acting coroner for Inishowen, adjourned the hearing after Dr McGrath told the sworn inquest that death was due to shock and haemorrhage and certain specimens were being removed for further examination.

The State Solicitor, Mr M.T. McMenamin, appealed to the public to help the Gardaí find the killer, and went some way to expressing the widespread horror felt at the killing. 'This crime has appalled the people of this country,' he said, 'and it is of such a nature to be absolutely foreign to this country and to all of us. It is unthinkable that the like of it should occur, but unfortunately it has occurred, and all the energies and resources of the State will be kept at full pressure until this mysterious occurrence is unravelled and the perpetrator brought to justice.'

The brief inquest also heard how the dead girl's brother, Dan Doherty, had left home on the Friday night at about 8.15 and returned at 11 p.m. He had been at the parochial hall, and when he returned his sister was not at home. A search was carried out that night and her body was found the following day, which he identified.

Hannah's young brother broke down and wept uncontrollably at his sister's funeral as he knelt by her grave.

The curate in Malin Head, Fr Meehan, who celebrated the funeral Mass said that the sympathy of the whole countryside went out to the girl's relatives. He had not known her by name, he told the congregation, but he had known her devotion to the Church for she had shown more than ordinary fidelity to the Faith. 'She was indeed, outstanding among the whole parish.' he said. Hannah had been in church the morning before she met her death, and throughout the bitter winter mornings during Lent she attended the whole series of Lenten services.

'Malin Head, on the Innishowen peninsula, the most northerly point in the Republic, is a very sparsely populated district, peopled by an industrious farming class. The holdings are small, averaging between five and ten acres of arable land or semi-arable land,' wrote Supt George Lawlor. He had arrived back in Dublin on Monday 22nd after investigating an attempted murder in Co. Meath, typed up his report, submitted it to the Assistant Commissioner in charge of crime branch and was immediately despatched to Co. Donegal to investigate the Hannah Doherty murder.

'In addition to their holdings,' he continued, 'each farmer possesses a section of the rough mountain on which sheep are grazed. They live a hard precarious existence. Owing to the complete absence of trees in the area and since there are no turf bogs available, they are dependent to a great extent for their fuel supply on drift wood which is swept up onto the beaches by the Atlantic. The whole area is windswept and barren.

'As I climbed the steep mountainside to examine the spot where the body had been found, the house in which the deceased girl lived, though directly below me, was difficult to distinguish from the many similar whitewashed homesteads which caught the morning sunshine. Further away and to the left I could see the masts of Malin Head wireless station, and still further ahead on all sides, were the broad stretches of the North Atlantic.'

Examination of the area by the detectives showed that Hannah Doherty had been killed at a spot less than 200 yards from her home. The killer had then carried the dead and bloodied woman approximately 130 yards further up the mountain before dumping her. The grass beneath the body had been soaked with blood, and the body had lain partly concealed in the bracken at Ardmalin, before it was discovered by her father.

Hannah normally left her home, a single-storeyed thatched cottage, which was protected from buffeting winds by a stone wall, to visit friends after the evening meal. It was about 9 p.m. that evening when she left. Her brother Dan returned home at about 11 p.m. and there was still no sign of Hannah. Her mother left the house and walked down part of the roadway expecting to meet her, but fifteen minutes later returned alone.

Hannah's father, Thomas, then left the house, pulling on an overcoat against the cold night air. He searched around by the shoreline, fearing the worst, and called to neighbours who made up an impromptu search party whose ranks swelled as the night progressed and more houses were alerted. Dan was also calling to neighbours' houses, some of whom returned with him to his own house where they organised search parties; even the local priest was called out to help the search teams. They searched throughout the night, and the next day. It was the following day after a relentless search that her father found her partly hidden body. 'Blood-stained stones about 200 yards from her house and bloodstained grass clearly indicated the spot where she had met her death,' George Lawlor concluded after examining the hillside. 'The absence of tracks or marks of dragging through the grass and heather,

70

coupled with the condition of her clothing, clearly demonstrated that her body had been carried up the mountain from the actual place where she had been attacked. Her facial injuries were very severe and since there was extensive bleeding it was only natural to conclude that the person who carried her body must have got blood on his clothing,' he added.

Hannah Doherty was a strikingly good-looking woman with a fine head of chestnut hair and an equally attractive disposition. She had no enemies in the district and the sixty Gardaí assigned to the murder hunt reported that the local people 'found it difficult to picture anyone in the neighbourhood who could have been so base as to be guilty of this terrible crime'.

The daily conferences held by the murder squad team, where information was pooled, quickly drew up a list of suspects. It was apparent from where she was found that she must have met somebody by appointment, and equally likely that her attacker was from the neighbourhood or at least familiar with the territory. In view of her secret pregnancy she may still have been having a clandestine affair, so close male friends topped the list. Hannah was a popular local girl, and although she never attended the local dances she had many admirers in the locality — all of whom had to be checked.

'In crimes of this nature there are three main lines of investigation,' Supt George Lawlor wrote. 'These are the examination of the scene, the movements of the deceased and those of the suspects.

'The scene was examined thoroughly, and in the immediate vicinity of the killing several cigarette butts and burnt matches were found and from these, and the nature of the ground at this spot, it was quite obvious that the deceased and her assailant had remained there for some time, that there had been a struggle and that, eventually, she had been overpowered and beaten to death with the large stones which lay around the mountain slope. The second phase was not difficult to establish. Any cry she might have uttered had apparently gone unheard. This was quite understandable owing to the great height of their position on the mountain and due to the few people who would be out of doors at that time.

'The questioning of all likely suspects narrowed down this line considerably after a few days, and, as enquiries were intensified, a man called Daniel Doherty, a second cousin of the dead girl, came in for particular attention.'

Daniel Doherty lived at the end of Inishowen peninsula, with his wife and his aged mother. Just over eight miles from Malin

71

village the road forks, and at the end of the road on the right fork was Doherty's. Daniel Doherty was a small farmer who had been married for the past six years; his wife was forty-four years old. They had no children, and the only other occupant of the house was his aged mother.

The left-hand fork in the road would take the road user around the base of the mountain and on to Hannah Doherty's home at Middletown. Five houses lay between the two Doherty households on the road. A Garda walked across the top of the mountain from Daniel's on the east side to Hannah's on the west side, a distance of approximately one mile and 300 yards and timed his walk at seventeen minutes. There were no houses between the two points on the mountainside.

'Despite the most exhaustive enquiries from persons who had been on the road that night and from the occupants of the houses in the area none could be found who saw Daniel Doherty on or near the road between his own home and the dead woman's on that fatal night. It was not too much to assume, therefore, that if he were the culprit he must have crossed the mountain. This, however, did not simplify matters since it would be almost an impossible task to check his movements over the unfrequented sheep track,' said George Lawlor.

It was Saturday night when Supt Heaphy and Det. Sgt Tuttle called to Daniel Doherty's house. He was in bed at the time, saying he was ill, but got up and dressed himself at their request. Doherty appeared uncomfortable when asked by the Gardaí to make a statement detailing his movements on the previous night when Hannah was murdered, but he willingly co-operated.

He said he had heard Hannah had been killed on the mountain but he didn't know where it had happened. He knew her and had been in her house on a few occasions.

'I last saw her yesterday morning when I was leaving the chapel at about nine o'clock. She bid me the time of day and passed on. I said "Good Morning". I went to Confession and received Holy Communion yesterday morning,' he said in his statement. He had changed into his good clothes to go to Mass in the village and hadn't changed back into his working clothes. He had remained working around the house that evening until about 7.30, when he went to a neighbour, Mickie Houdon's, a few hundred yards away for milk. On the way there he met a young fellow, Pat Douglas, and they chatted for a moment before he sent him on an errand to the local pub to buy him some rum. Doherty continued on his way, and got the milk from Houdon's. On his return with the milk he met young Douglas and took the rum from him and continued home.

It was about 9 p.m. when he got home but he didn't go in as he was distracted by the sound of their mare 'rattling' in her stable — a sign of the horse's sickness with cramps. He took the mare out of the stable and walked her down the lane and into a field bordering the main road to ease her suffering. He walked the animal up and down for about half an hour and as the pain eased he brought her back up the lane and put her in the stable. No sooner was the animal in the stable than she began 'rattling' again, so he shouted into the house, calling out for a light. It was about ten o'clock at that stage, he estimated, and his wife, his mother and a friend of the family, Owen McLoughlin, came out. Owen held up a lighted lamp and helped him walk the mare up and down the lane.

At the top of the lane they met another neighbour, Cassie McLoughlin, who was coming to visit them that night. They walked back down to the yard and she took the lamp, and held it aloft, as the two men poured a dose of medicine down the mare's throat. Shortly afterwards Doherty put her back into the stable and the visitors left. He went to bed at about 11 p.m. as did his mother and his wife, although he drank the rum purchased earlier that evening and smoked a cigarette first.

Det. Sgt Tuttle, who was based in Letterkenny, asked Doherty for the clothing he was wearing that night and the bottle from which he drank. Within a few minutes Doherty produced a pair of pinstriped trousers and a matching waistcoat and a half-pint glass bottle.

In reply to a question, Doherty explained that a cut on his upper lip had been caused the previous day when he was shaving. 'Hannah Doherty was a second cousin of mine. I didn't go up to her house today as I am not well. My wife and I are to go up there tomorrow. It was about six o'clock this evening when we heard she was dead — Cassie McLoughlin told me at my own house,' he added.

'Statements taken from the other two members of the household bore out Daniel Doherty's account of his movements that night,' wrote Supt George Lawlor. 'Owen McLoughlin, a deaf mute and of weak intellect, could give little corroboration of the night's happenings. Miss Cassie McLoughlin corroborated Daniel Doherty's account of her meeting him at the top of the lane, and her subsequent assistance in holding the light. Daniel's statement in accounting for his movements was a simple alibi and bore a ring of truth.'

The trousers Daniel said he was wearing were pin-striped and there were two different types of staining on them, bog mould and what appeared to be blood. Det. Sgt Tuttle took the trousers from the bedroom into the brighter light in the kitchen and asked Daniel what caused the staining.

Nothing much, just blood, said Daniel. He had only recently been visiting Carndonagh and had taken the bus home. On the bus he had a row with another man who hit him. As he sat in his seat his bloodied nose dripped onto his trousers, he said. The Garda investigators traced the bus conductor, James J. Coyle, who remembered a dispute on the bus that ended in a row. He knew Daniel Doherty to see and remembered that his nose had in fact been bleeding. The incident had taken place on 18 March, a hotel assistant in Malin Head, Mary B. Douglas, clearly recalled. She had seen Doherty receive the blow which bloodied his nose, she told the Gardaí.

Daniel Doherty had also told the Gardaí that the mare had nipped his right hand when he dosed it. It wasn't much of a bite but it explained the three cuts on his hand — two under the thumb and one on the third finger — which had bled slightly and probably onto his trousers, he said.

The blood-stained trousers were given to the State Pathologist, Dr John McGrath, for examination. 'Daniel Doherty's story about the row was investigated and there were several people who witnessed the row and saw his nose bleeding profusely. Thus, unless the blood of the murdered girl differed from his, the finding of blood on his pin-striped trousers was of minor import,' wrote George Lawlor in his casebook.

A sample of blood was taken from Daniel Doherty and this was tested by the State Pathologist, Dr McGrath. It was the same blood group as that of the dead girl, Hannah Doherty.

'Daniel Doherty's alibi was to an extent corroborated, and, considering its simplicity and all the surrounding circumstances — the isolated scene, the possible manner of approach and other factors — the alibi if false was a difficult one to break down,' Lawlor wrote later. 'However, perseverance, patience and methodical checking of the movements of Daniel Doherty and practically every other person in the locality eventually succeeded in establishing that the alibi was false and provided some of the most important evidence in the strong case which was to be presented against Doherty.'

The statements taken by the Technical Bureau's detectives were being cross-checked and cross-referenced, a painstaking and tedious task that was often unrewarding except in the matter of Doherty's clothing. In a number of statements witnesses said they saw Daniel Doherty on the night Hannah Doherty was murdered, wearing a pin-striped trousers and a matching waistcoat. These two items were in Garda custody. But some witnesses had also seen Doherty that evening when he wore his pin-striped trousers, a woollen pull-over and a brown coat. A relative of Doherty's described it as a 'working coat'.

'Undoubtedly he had worn the suit that day, but we now had irrefutable evidence that he was wearing an old brown lounge coat and pullover on the evening of 19 April, and that he had it on him when attending to the horse that night, afterwards removing the coat when he entered his own home,' wrote Supt Lawlor.

Gardaí then required Doherty's coat and pullover for examination. Doherty denied he had either item of clothing, and the farmhouse was searched. However, neither jacket or pullover were found in the house and the search was widened to the outhouse and an ash heap at the rear of the cottage. Burnt fragments of cloth, a piece of woollen material and one button were unearthed from the ash heap. A short distance away another piece of cloth was found which had been washed down into a drain. The small amount of ash covering the pieces of cloth indicated that they were recent additions to the ash pile.

Doherty and his wife had watched the Gardaí search and saw the pieces of cloth being unearthed. Sgt Patrick Flanagan asked Daniel to account for the cloth and the button. 'They are the clothes of my brother that died of consumption of the flesh. We burned them a short while after he died,' he said.

The dead man's bedclothes were burnt at his house, and when asked where his clothing had been burnt, Doherty walked away, calling back over his shoulder that he had already made a statement.

The Gardaí caught up with him and showed him the piece of charred material taken from the drain. 'I can give no explanation as to the garment or as to who placed it in the drain. I did not place any coat or any other piece of cloth in that drain,' he said as Sgt Flanagan took notes.

The county records office was queried about Michael Doherty's death, and a death certificate was forwarded to the investigation team. Michael had died on 7 April 1939, almost a year earlier, of chronic bronchitis.

George Lawlor recorded: 'We established that the brown coat which was missing, was made up from a piece of material purchased from a pedlar some two years before, and that another neighbour had bought a piece of similar material, and that both pieces had been made up by the same tailor, Andrew Logue from Carndonagh. Doherty's neighbour still had his complete suit and a sample of the cloth was obtained from him. This, with the burnt portions of cloth found at Daniel Doherty's house, was sent to a textile expert for examination. He stated that from his examination of the burnt pieces of brown cloth, they originally formed part of a lounge coat. He referred to two button holes and pointed out that the smaller one at one time was the button hole in the lapel of a lounge-type coat. He also found that the specimen piece of cloth and the burnt pieces of cloth were similar in all respects. The piece of woollen material had once been used in making a knitted article, such as a sock, cardigan or pullover.'

Meanwhile another avenue of investigation was being explored. The empty bottle Daniel Doherty had given the Gardaí was shown to the youth, Pat Douglas. He couldn't remember what type of bottle the publican had given him to pass on to Doherty, but the publican could. He told the Gardaí that it wasn't the same bottle. He had given the boy a naggin bottle which he had filled with rum. Doherty had given the Gardaí a half-pint bottle. Another simple test also threw a question mark over Doherty's story. The bottle smelled of whiskey, not rum as he had told the Gardaí.

An extensive search was immediately started on the mountainside, and Gardaí carried out a sweep from Daniel to Hannah Doherty's house. The search took several days, and resulted in Gardaí finding a naggin bottle near the beaten track across the mountainside. It contained a small amount of rum, although a test for fingerprints was unsuccessful.

On 27 April, eight days after Hannah had been murdered, Doherty was again asked to make a statement detailing his movements. He adhered to his original statement with a few additions. 'I knew Hannah Margaret Doherty well and had great regard for her. It was my custom to go to her house a couple of times a week.'

He said that he had walked down the lane that night with the mare and onto the main road before calling in to his home. He had walked the animal about 300 yards and had tried to walk her in a field adjoining the lane but she had tried to lie down. He stated that he walked the mare up and down the main road for twenty minutes.

'One neighbour who passed the main road at Doherty's house and had met Miss Cassie McLoughlin as she was calling to

Doherty's home that night, failed to see or hear him walking the animal either on the main road or the laneway,' George Lawlor wrote. 'A neighbouring farmer who was attending to cattle close by corroborated this evidence. After parting with the youth who fetched him the rum, Doherty said in his second statement that he turned to the right across the 'brae' towards his own home. Fortunately for us, the youth was more observant than the ordinary country boy and like Lot's wife he was rather an inquisitive type. On looking back he observed that Doherty, instead of turning to the right, had swung to the left in a direction which would, if continued, take him over the mountain to the scene of the crime. 'On checking and rechecking times it was established that at this time it was 8.30 p.m. and that Daniel Doherty had not arrived at his home earlier than 9.50 p.m., that Miss McLoughlin was only five or ten minutes after him, and that he had only removed the mare to the lane at this time with Owen McLoughlin,' he concluded.

Investigations further afield brought a very significant fact to light. On two occasions Daniel Doherty had gone to Carndonagh to obtain abortifacients. On one occasion he had cycled there and returned home on the bus with the bike saying he wasn't feeling well — but sat by himself although Hannah Doherty was also on the bus.

Dr Robert McLaughlin from Malin Head said that on 7 April, two weeks before Hannah was killed, Doherty had called to his house and said he needed a bottle of medicine for a girl who was 'in trouble' with a soldier. The doctor said he couldn't do that and told Doherty he should send the girl to him. That can't be done, replied Doherty. Being 'in trouble', he was to explain, was an expression used in North Donegal to describe the situation of a pregnant single girl. Doherty had left the surgery, in the words of the doctor, 'more or less displeased'.

'On that fatal date,' wrote George Lawlor, 'while it could not be established by evidence in court, we were satisfied that he had communicated his failure to Hannah Doherty. The meeting that night apparently developed into an altercation which culminated in the unfortunate girl's death. This theory is borne out by the fact that Doherty did not go to the scene armed with a weapon, but used the stones which lay convenient on the mountain slope.

'A strange feature of the case was the fact that it could not be established that Hannah Doherty and the accused had been having clandestine meetings. There was, of course, evidence that the accused visited Hannah's home at night, sometimes on three nights of the week, but so did other neighbours. Several nights during his visit Hannah was absent. Doherty had, however, been seen loitering in the vicinity of houses where Hannah had been visiting. On two occasions he was known to have met her in what appeared to be an accidental way.'

Eight days after the death of Hannah Doherty, and after he had given a second statement to the Gardaí, Daniel Doherty was arrested, charged with murder and remanded in custody to Sligo jail. His trial opened before Mr Justice Martin Maguire in Dublin on 30 November 1940.

Cassie McLoughlin was unable to write and told the court that she had gone to Doherty's house on the night of the 19th to get his wife to write a letter on her behalf. She met Daniel Doherty there and was 'afeared' of him because of his 'dark look' that night and ran all the way home.

'In what way did Doherty make you "afeared" on the night of 19 April? Was he wild looking?' defence counsel, P.J. Roe, S.C., asked.

'He was queer looking. He was upset,' replied Cassie.

Evidence was given at the trial by prison doctors from Sligo and Mountjoy jails that Doherty had displayed signs of insanity while under lock and key. Conflicting evidence was tendered by independent medical experts on the question of his insanity and one of them expressed the opinion that Doherty might be faking it. The experts all agreed, however, that he was sane at the time of the trial.

The defence claimed that if he had committed the murder he must have lost his head completely and suffered from 'mania', which condition passed away when he realised the terrible consequences of his act.

The prosecution, however, pointed out that his actions after the crime were consistent with those of a sane person and referred to his ability to prepare an alibi, account for his movements, and offer an explanation for his bloodstained clothes.

Summing up the case, Mr Justice Maguire said the jury might have taken the view that the people on the distant peninsula of Innishowen were of a savage type. But that was not so, he said. They had seen during the trial sturdy, hard-working people. They had heard of the ceilidhe — some of which were held in Hannah Doherty's house, of the cups of tea and the bottles of milk, of the friendliness that made life possible in a harsh place. They had also seen the dignity of the lives of these humble people living in the outposts of the country whose sole protection was the law, he said.

The medical evidence ruled out both suicide and accident.

It was the case put by the prosecution that a 'brown telltale coat' which Doherty used to wear had been destroyed by him because it bore bloodstains. Doherty denied this and that he had gone near Hannah on the night she was killed. But there was no evidence to corroborate his statement relating to the missing time, and if he had been in his house at the time when the murder was committed, nobody had been brought forward to say so, said the judge. Doherty was now perfectly sane, he added.

The jury considered their verdict for more than an hour and a half. Doherty was guilty of murder they said. Asked if there was anything he wanted to say as to why sentence of death should not be passed on him, Doherty, who had gone pale, hesitated, said 'Yes', and muttered something.

The trial had lasted for five days. It was Mr Justice Maguire's first murder case, and he reached for the black cap and sentenced Doherty to death, fixing 29 December as execution date.

Doherty's wife who had been in court throughout the trial, collapsed. Court attendants carried her to a side room where a priest and one of the doctors who had given evidence in the trial attended to her.

Before leaving the dock Doherty turned to the court and speaking clearly said, 'I have only once to die,' and was then led away. An appeal failed, and Daniel Doherty swung from the gallows on 7 January 1941.

Detective Superintendent Lawlor concluded: 'We can never know now if the murder of Hannah Doherty was premeditated. There are certain significant facts pointing towards the conclusion that it was. For instance, why did Daniel Doherty fortify himself with a naggin of rum drunk in a short space of time while crossing the mountainside to keep a tryst with Hannah Doherty? Again, he did not waste a lot of time in her company before his murderous attack. Most important of all, he had a pressing motive. On the other hand there is one telling factor against that conclusion and that was the manner of the killing. It was senselessly crude. It was that crudeness that was eventually to be his undoing: it left on him evidence that he had to destroy and that in its destruction proved his guilt.'

6.

The Mystery

IT was Christmas Eve 1941. The Collins family lived in Abbeyfeale East, Co. Limerick just over a mile from the centre of the town. Mrs Mary Collins had been to town and had completed the last of her Christmas shopping. Laden down with bags and bundles, she returned home at about 2 p.m. with her second youngest son Richard. He was 22 years of age, with a brother Patrick, 33 years old, and a sister Mary Ita, 23 years old. The tradition of lighting the Christmas candle signifying the Holy Family's journey to Bethlehem was reserved for twenty-year-old James, the youngest in the household.

Christmas Eve was a busy time for housewives, and Mary spent the next four hours preparing the following day's feast and cleaning the sparsely furnished but already spotless kitchen. Richard was pressed into service stocking up on turf for the open fire. Mrs Collins's other three children arrived home at about seven o'clock and as they did so she served them their tea in the kitchen of the single-storeyed thatched cottage. Patrick was the first to finish and he left the house at about 8.15 p.m. to attend to the cattle which were in a barn across the yard at the front of the house.

Denis Collins, the head of the family, arrived home at about 8.30 p.m. having stopped for a drink after work. He sat reading the local newspaper with his back to the front kitchen window. An oil lamp was attached to the wall over his head, and the open fire was to his left. The shutter on the kitchen window was still open and the Christmas candle placed on the sill shone onto a cardboard crib placed beside it.

When James had finished his tea, Mrs Collins, who wished to have the nightly Rosary recited early, asked her husband to sit up at the table to have his tea. James and his father swapped places, and James took up the discarded newspaper and began reading. 'He was only reading a few minutes when I went to pour out his father's tea,' said Mrs Collins later.

'Mary Ita was at the table doing something to collars she was about to iron. Just as I walked from the fire to the table with the tea pot in my hand, I heard a loud report at the front window. I said: "What's that?" and I looked towards the lamp as I thought it had burst.

'Just as I looked I heard my husband say: "Jamesie, is there anything wrong with you?" and I saw my husband holding my son James, and I saw blood coming from his head. I looked towards the window and I saw the bottom of the blind turned up and the glass broken. I screamed and I heard my husband say: "Jamesie is dead" and I then rushed out of the house for a priest and a doctor.'

Mrs Collins returned shortly, in a hysterical and distressed state, with some neighbours. As she entered the kitchen she saw Jamsie lying on the stone-flagged floor in a pool of blood, and fainted.

'For several days she was in a most distressed state, and was it any wonder?' asked George Lawlor. 'Her son, a quiet inoffensive young man full of life a few moments before, had been killed before her very eyes. He was a great favourite with everyone and no motive whatsoever could be assigned to his murder. The same could be said of all the Collins family, who were a highly respected, industrious family. The local doctor and curate were called to the house, and the following day Dr McGrath, the State Pathologist, and a photographer from the Technical Bureau travelled to the Co. Limerick town.

'I picked up Detective Inspector Donovan on St Stephen's morning and we spent our Christmas holidays in Abbeyfeale. It was not a pleasant way to spend the holidays, working a fourteen to sixteen hour day, but we had several companions and in the height of a murder investigation one soon forgets the many good things one can have and enjoy at this festive time,' admitted Supt Lawlor.

An examination of the scene showed that it had been a reckless shooting. The blind had been drawn on the window and the person who discharged the gun could have neither seen nor known who was sitting by the window.

The dead man's head had been just above the window sill. A hole in the lower pane of glass on the right of the window, about eight inches in diameter, and a corresponding hole in the blind showed where the charge of shot had entered. A number of stray pellet markings found on the opposite wall of the kitchen established the line of fire. The shotgun had been discharged from a close range, only feet from the outside of the house. The post mortem examination showed that by far the greater part of the charge, including the cartridge wad, had entered the dead man's head behind the right ear. The examination showed that death was instantaneous. His family had come to the same conclusion, as Jamesie had made no sound after the shot was fired.

Patrick Collins was still in the barn when his brother was shot. He was coming across the yard to the house when Mary Ita rushed out of the house. He had heard a loud bang when he was in the shed with the cattle, he said. He went to the door of the barn to look out, but neither saw nor heard anyone. He went back into the barn and a few seconds later heard screaming coming from the house. Patrick said there had been no sound of footsteps either coming or going in the yard.

'The movements of the entire Collins family were gone into in detail' wrote George Lawlor. Their associates and all contacts which they had with persons, particularly during their visits to Abbeyfeale on Christmas Eve, were traced.

'People who had travelled the road by the Collins home that evening were traced and questioned and it was learned that two people had heard a gunshot in the vicinity at about 8.30 p.m. No suspicious person was seen at or near the scene at the crucial time.

'From a re-checking of the movements of people who had passed the Collins home after 7.30 p.m. we were satisfied that the culprit could not have taken the main road or the avenue to the Collins's home, up to 8.15 p.m. that night, and that if the culprit returned by the road after 8.30 p.m. he should have been met by the persons we had interviewed travelling on it.'

A murder conference was called by the local Chief Superintendent the day after Supt George Lawlor arrived to review the facts of the case. Because of the varied times everyone had returned to the house from the village and the closed blind, it was clear that the culprit could not possibly have known if someone was sitting at the window. That left two possibilities, the first that the shot had been fired into the house intending only to serve as a warning of some sort. The second was that the culprit could have approached the house from the rear, which actually faced the main road, through the fields. There was no blind pulled or shutter drawn on the back window. It was possible that someone had looked in through the window, saw the father sitting at the window, and then moved around to the other side of the house and fired the shot, intending to kill the father. Only, the gunman wasn't to know that as he moved around the house the father and son changed places.

'It was logical to assume that the intention was to shoot the father and not the son and that changing his position had saved the old man's life,' said Supt Lawlor.

Churchgoers on Christmas morning had been surprised to see a number of freshly-painted slogans on walls in the town of Abbeyfeale on Christmas morning. They had obviously been painted overnight. The slogans posed a question that was to trouble later generations, and significantly, at the time to distract manpower involved in the investigation of James Collins's death. The slogans read 'Who shot Collins — Up the IRA'.

'These slogans lent a more or less political tinge to the crime,' wrote George Lawlor, 'but the deceased young man never had any connection with this or other organisations, nor had any other member of his family. Nor was he a member of the Local Defence Force, but cognisance had to be taken of the slogans and for a time it rather confused investigations.

'Soon, however, we were able to satisfy ourselves that the IRA had nothing to do with the death of James Collins, and the local organisation, like all the people in the neighbourhood, condemned the outrage.'

Another lead was meanwhile being followed up by investigators as they continued checking the movements of the members of the Collins family.

When the dead man's father had been having a drink in a local public house on Christmas Eve, shortly before his return home, a man in the bar had made some threats and rude remarks about him. The argument had gone no further, but it was a reminder of the lasting bad feeling between the two men, Denis Collins and Larry O'Connor, a former British and National soldier, a court messenger, a widower and father of nine children. Two years previously the two men had had a row which resulted in court proceedings being issued. The intervention of a neighbour resulted in Collins paying over a small sum of money in compensation, and this pre-empted any court action but did not result in them returning to speaking terms with each other.

Larry O'Connor lived on a 24-acre farm at Abbeyfeale east. His farmhouse was two fields away from the Collins's farmhouse and the Gardaí noted that he would have had no difficulty going to the Collins's home without being observed.

On 28 December a statement was taken from him in which he detailed the events of Christmas Eve. He said that he had gone into the village and had visited four pubs, but denied meeting Denis Collins or using any threatening language.

Other witnesses were sought out, and two men who had been drinking with O'Connor said that he had been a bit unsteady on his feet because of the drink, and they had given him a lift home on the back of a cart. It was about 7.30 p.m. when they dropped him off at the side of the road and saw him walking up the fields to his cottage.

O'Connor said he had his tea when he arrived home, sat by the fire for a while and then went to bed. His two eldest daughters aged 17 and 16 more or less corroborated their father's story, noted Supt Lawlor.

'While the investigations and searches of the area were proceeding' wrote Supt Lawlor, 'other lines of investigation were being pursued and eventually we got that lucky break in the guise of "an earful". It was to the effect that O'Connor had left his house soon after his return on Christmas Eve and had taken a gun with him. This was alleged to have been told by one of O'Connor's young children to a friend coming from Mass on Christmas morning. It took a whole day to sift the information, but we were satisfied, after questioning six people, as to the truth of it.' On the evening of the 30th O'Connor was met by Gardaí in Abbeyfeale as he was shopping. They asked him to come to the Garda station and he was then cautioned and questioned.

Simultaneously his children were being questioned about their father's movements on Christmas Eve. This resulted in one of the children admitting that her father had left the house at about 8 p.m. that night carrying a gun.

A search of O'Connor's house turned up a long timber box by the fire which had a false bottom in it. Marks and oil stains in a secret compartment suggested that a single-barrel shotgun had been stored there . However, O'Connor, who was now being held by the Gardaí, denied that he ever owned a gun and repeated his previous statement in more detail.

The following morning when Supt Lawlor arrived at the station, the Garda sergeant in charge of the Abbeyfeale station said that during the night O'Connor had said he wanted to speak to the Superintendent as he had hidden the gun in the thatch of his cottage. Lawlor had an avuncular air. A strict disciplinarian who demanded high standards from his staff, he could empathise with criminals but never condone their actions.

O'Connor was again cautioned, and Supt Lawlor asked him if he had anything he wanted to say: 'I want to tell you Sir, I put the old gun in the thatch.'

O'Connor volunteered to show the Gardaí where the gun had been hidden. The stock and the barrel of the shotgun were taken from the thatch. There was no sign of a cartridge case and O'Connor said he had thrown it into the fire. The brass end of a cartridge case was subsequently discovered when the ash heap in the field at the back of the house was searched. It bore unmistakable signs of the heat.

A pair of wellington boots were also discovered hidden in a hedge on O'Connor's land. The boots were his own, and he had been wearing them on Christmas Eve. On Christmas day he had gone to his brothers and taken the loan of a pair of boots which he subsequently continually wore. However, this admission could not be substantiated as casts of bootprints taken on land around the Collins's farm proved to be useless for comparison.

On 31 December 1941 O'Connor was charged with the murder of James Collins. In reply he said, 'All I have to say is that I was in a bad state of drink that night and when I came home and saw my little children without their mother, I got mad. I took out a gun and fired a shot and don't know what happened. The next day when I realised I had done something I took out the gun and hid it in the thatch.'

'Laurence O'Connor never stood trial at Green Street,' Supt Lawlor wrote. 'The prison doctor and an independent mental specialist certified that he was insane while in custody and at Abbeyfeale District Court on 14 January.

'Subsequently by order of the Minister for Justice he was removed to Limerick Mental Hospital, there to be detained pending further instructions. On 17 January 1946 he was certified by the mental hospital authorities to be of sound mind and by order of the Minister he was removed to prison. On 28 January 1946 he was brought before a special court at Newcastle West, and the Attorney General's views were made known to the District Justice. He refused informations and discharged the accused.'

7.

Friends Turned Enemies

'SMALLIE', the black and white collie dog owned by Moss Moore, a Kerry farmer, returned home to Reamore on Saturday 29 November 1958. The return of the small dog to its home caused a minor sensation, the *Sunday Independent* newspaper reported the following day. Why? Because the dog had walked eight miles from its new home, to return to the house of its dead master, Moss Moore, who had been murdered three weeks earlier.

It was a murder George Lawlor had spent a number of weeks investigating. It was a murder that had shocked the local population, and it was a murder that playwright John B. Keane was to subsequently use as the basis for his work, *The Field*.

It was a dark, moonless, wet night when Moss Moore waved goodbye to his friend Tim Sugrue at Reamore Cross to walk the 200 yards up a narrow muddy bohreen to his cottage. It was the last time he was seen alive.

Moss was a 46-year-old bachelor. He owned 25 acres of land on the side of one of two 1,000-foot hills at Reamore, seven miles from Tralee. Half of his land was boggy and useless for agriculture, while the other half was poor and barely productive. Moore also owned four cows, two pigs, a horse, a collie, a greyhound and a kitten, as well as several chickens. He eked out a living by supplying milk to the local creamery, selling turf from a bank which he shared with several other local farmers on the mountainside bog, and working an occasional day for other farmers.

It was a tough life, and for Moss, a gentle-mannered soul, his games of cards at Mrs Julia Collins's and other neighbours' houses were his main pleasure in life. He had been playing '31s' at Julia's home, about three quarters of a mile away from his house on the night he was last seen alive. He had been lucky that evening, the stakes were sixpence a time and he had won a few shillings.

Another regular card player, Paul Reidy, had been unable to make it to Julia's house on the Thursday evening as his car was being serviced. Paul normally saw Moss pass his gate each morning on the way to the creamery, but missed him on the Friday morning. When there was still no sign of Moss on his pony and cart the following day, he wondered if Moss was ill and decided to call on him. When he arrived at the cottage the door was shut, and the two dogs, which Moss always kept locked up, were loose. Unless he locked up the dogs, Smallie and Spring, they'd follow him wherever he went, Moss would tell neighbours, with a simple pride in their faithfulness.

Paul Reidy was concerned, felt something was amiss as the dogs whined, and went back down the bohreen to return with neighbours Tim Sugrue and Tim Gainey. They were about to remove the staple from the door lock to get into the cottage when they realised it was already loose, as though it had already been pulled free and replaced. The trio went into the cottage but found no sign of disturbance, or of the missing farmer.

Paul drove into Tralee, where he met Detective Garda Pat Kavanagh. He had cut turf with Moss Moore, and knew him as a quiet man, and he launched immediate inquiries in the Reamore area. A search was organised as there was a dark foreboding among locals in the area that Moore could be dead. The best that could probably be hoped for was expressed by Dan Foley, Moore's nearest neighbour — that he had taken 'a weakness' and fallen somewhere on the boggy mountainside. As the winter rain sleeted down on the mountainside a large search party, using sticks, ranged across the rough, boggy terrain.

The following morning Fr Michael O'Donoghue and his curate Fr O'Murchu appealed to their congregations in Ballymacelligott and Clogher churches to help with the search. By afternoon over 200 people, wrapped up against the harsh winter rain, had joined the search. Their numbers swelled the following day as volunteers from Killarney and Listowel joined the search which was directed by the Gardaí.

That Monday and the following day Radio Éireann broadcast an appeal for help as part of the efforts to find the missing man. The radio bulletin described him as being 5'8" tall, slightly built, dark hair going grey, wearing heavy nailed boots, a brown belted overcoat, and most likely carrying a walking stick and bicycle lamp.

Chief Supt Pat Cronin who headed up the 32-station division in Kerry was to say later that he had a hunch. By the following

Saturday he felt that the area had been searched and searched again without success and that as such a large area had been covered, the body was still probably close to the cottage.

Between Dan Foley and Moss Moore's cottage ran a rushing stream through a narrow gully about six feet deep, bordered by rushes and weeds. The searchers had passed the gully each of the past nine days, and could see every inch of it from the bank except for two feet, a spot which was densely screened with rushes.

Chief Supt Cronin and Sgt Michael Costelloe waded into the stream, whose level had dropped as the rains of the past week had eased, and began an inch by inch search. It was Sgt Costelloe who felt something give on the bottom of the stream under pressure of his stick. He had found Moss Moore's cap. Approximately 40 yards upstream, hidden from sight of the bank, a boot and part of a head became visible. The body was bundled up and wedged into a hollow which the stream water had worn into the bank. It had been so tightly wedged into the bank that Gardaí had to dig it out. It was the corpse of Moss Moore.

A post mortem examination was carried out the following day at Tralee's County hospital by State Pathologist, Dr Maurice Hickey M.D.

The five-hour examination built up a picture of Moss Moore's final moments. There had been a confrontation between Moore and his killer. Moore's nose was broken and had bled extensively before death. The right side of his jaw and his vocal box were fractured. His fists were found to be clenched and he had received a heavy beating. Moore had not been drowned, however, as no water was found in his lungs. He had been strangled and his body then placed in the stream, hidden from view by anyone passing by on the bank.

Detectives investigating the murder and led by Supt Lawlor were also probing the dual puzzle about Moss Moore's death. Why were his dogs, which he always locked into the cottage when he left home, loose, and what was the significance of the loose staple in the padlock hasp on the front door? Had it been removed and later replaced, and if so why?

The banks surrounding the spot where Moore's body was found were searched thoroughly and his stick was found, broken and hidden by overgrown briars, rushes and long grass.

During the search Gardaí had the unenviable task of sifting through more than eight tons of manure stored on the farm in the hope of finding the missing bicycle lamp or Moss Moore's purse, which was not discovered on the body and might give further clues. A bicycle lamp was discovered in a ditch a few miles from Reamore, but examination showed this was not Moore's. It was some weeks later when a mine detector was introduced into the search by the Technical Bureau that Moore's missing bicycle lamp was found buried in the cabbage patch by his cottage.

On Tuesday 18 November Moss Moore was buried in O'Bhraonain graveyard in Ballymacelligott at the foot of the mountain where he had lived. It was the biggest cortège in living memory in the area, and the line of mourners in cars, traps and carts stretched for over a mile and a half.

Moore's cattle were later sold at a fair in Castleisland. His nephew, John Moore of Gortalea, took the collie, while Jer Hogan of Tylough took the greyhound. The black and white kitten which Moss had added to his household shortly before his death was given to a woman in Tralee.

The Gardaí inquiry received mixed support from the people. Some would say nothing, and information was often difficult to come by as an understood code of silence operated in the area and outsiders were told nothing. The clergy appealed to their congregations to come forward with information to the Gardaí. Some people refused to speak about Moss Moore. Others spoke about his relationship with his neighbour Dan Foley who lived just forty yards away from him.

Foley was almost twenty years older than Moore, and both men had been good friends and would cut turf together until a row blew up between them. Foley lived with his wife Nora and his disabled brother Mikey. He was a broad-shouldered man, with clean-cut features and a reserved manner. Unlike his neighbour who was noted for his witty tongue, Dan's words were few. He was a hard-working man with the skills of a handyman and a strong back that he used to make his home comfortable for his wife and brother.

In the summer of 1957 the men discussed Foley replacing an old ditch which no longer acted as a fence to keep in cattle. Moore claimed that Foley had agreed to build the ditch in a certain place, and instead had moved the boundary when building the ditch. Foley said that Moore's placing of the boundary would cut him off from a traditional passage between his cottage and the bog where he cut his turf. The argument soured their long-standing friendship. They abused each other, and both vowed to go to court over the matter and hired solicitors in Tralee. But Moss Moore's body was found in the stream near his house before the matter could be aired in court.

Moss, who was a smaller man than Foley, told neighbours that he was being followed home from the houses where he played cards. He was taking no chances, he said, and took to carrying a stick in case he was attacked.

Dan Foley was interviewed a total of three times by the Gardaí about the night of Moss Moore's murder. He was at home with his wife and brother, he told the Gardaí.

The Gardaí prepared a file on the case and sent it to the Attorney General, Aindrias Ó Caoimh, but no charges were laid against the chief suspect, Dan Foley.

Although he never faced charges, and none were ever brought against anyone else, Dan Foley's life changed.

Many neighbours refused to speak or have any dealings with him. Foley, too, ceased to speak to many of his former friends and acquaintances in the community.

Shots were fired into the corrugated roof of Foley's cottage. No one was injured. Worse was to follow when in April 1959 a charge of gelignite was detonated against one of the gables of his single-storey cottage. Again, luckily, no one was injured.

On Sunday 20 March 1960 agrarian trouble at Ballyseedy, Co. Kerry and the murder of Moss Moore brought strong condemnation and the imposition of spiritual penalties on people in the area from the Bishop of Kerry, Most Rev. Dr Moynihan.

'Over a year ago there was the murder of Maurice Moore of Reamore, a townland not very far away from Tralee. Maurice Moore was a God-fearing, harmless man. On his way home from the house of a neighbour he was foully done to death,' Dr Moynihan said at the closing of the men's retreat in St John's Church, Tralee. 'That murder was denounced the following Sunday by the priests, and the people were asked to give to the Civic Guards any information that they possessed which could help in tracking down the murderer.

'Whether they had information to give or not I cannot say, but the murderer of Maurice Moore is still at large. Nobody suspects that the murderer of Maurice Moore came from miles away. Most people think, I suspect, that that the murderer is a native of that district somewhere, that he is one who knew the habits and movements of Maurice Moore and knowing his habits and movements waylaid him and did him to death. Now if it is not too late I make this public appeal to any people who can throw any light on the murder of Maurice Moore to tell what they know to the Civic Guards,' he said.

A year earlier Dr Moynihan had travelled from his palace in Killarney to Tralee to issue a threat to reserve certain sins. On that occasion he did not allow his threat to be published in the newspapers because, he said, he felt 'no anxiety whatever to bring a diocese or county of law-abiding people into public odium in the press because of the misdeed of a small but lawless band'.

In March 1960 he followed through on that threat, and reserved the sins of threats, intimidation, boycotting, spiking of lands, injury of persons and property, and attacks on persons. Dr Moynihan said that the reserving now meant that any potential penitent had to come to him or the Vicar General for absolution. 'Is it too much to hope that never again will it be necessary for the Bishop or the Dean to speak words of condemnation from this pulpit? At all events I hope so,' said Dr Moynihan.

However, despite the Bishop's decision, his actions and threat, the murderer of Moss Moore was never brought to court.

8.

The Real 'Quare Fella'

IT was known as the Murdering Bohreen. Some people referred to the overgrown muddy lane leading to the turf banks at Ballin-cloghan, Rahan, Co. Offaly, near the Grand Canal, as the Killing Bohreen. Folklore had it that a ghost haunted the narrow track at certain times of the year. However as the bohreen was the occa-sional haunt of courting couples, local wits claimed the 'murdering' was a slang reference to sexual prowess.

The nine turf banks which zig-zagged across the corner of Ballincur bog were owned by Patrick Leonard and rented to eleven families. John Dunne's sister had married Leonard who now employed Dunne and another man, Joe Bracken, as farm labourers. It was just twenty minutes before 6 p.m. on 29 May 1942 and quitting time was approaching fast. The men were still clearing a drain to take water away from the bank to allow for another year's harvesting. A cutting they had made the previous year to drain away the water had clogged because of an unduly wet winter. To release this water Bracken was given the task of re-opening a drain. Joe Bracken used his four-pronged fork to dig out the break, and as he did so he felt something pushing against the fork. 'While I was doing this the fork stuck into a corner of a bag at the side of the drain. I stuck the fork further into the bag and pulled it out,' Joe was to tell the Gardaí.

'I lifted the bag onto the bank with the fork. It hardly weighed four stone. One end of the bag opened and I saw white grease coming out of it. There was a heavy smell. I then saw what I thought were ribs and pieces of white skin, and what I took to be backbone,' he continued. He called Pat Leonard who looked at the grisly sight. 'It might be a sheep, I don't know what it is,' said Leonard, who was an arthritic cripple and was leaning on his two walking sticks watching them. Leonard thought it was suspicious that there was no skull bone, and told him to bury it to keep the dogs away from it.

That evening he hitched up his pony and trap to tell the local priest of the suspicious find.

The following morning the Gardaí arrived at the bog to examine the remains, and to take statements from the three men. As George Lawlor was to write: 'They had uncovered a coarse bag which contained the torso of a human body. Thus by an accident it was discovered. Were it not for the unusually wet season the old drain would never have been re-opened and the body might be there until doomsday. We had searched the same bog for weeks on end without discovering it, and we had the assistance of both the local security and defence forces. But anybody with a knowledge of bogs will readily admit that to search one properly is an almost impossible task.'

Photographs of the find, laid out on the bog, and of the spot where the bones were found, were taken before the remains were sent to the State Pathologist, Dr John McGrath, at the Department of Medical Jurisprudence, University College Dublin, Earlsfort Terrace. The sack was made of a coarse brown material, with the words 'Blue Seal binder twine' stamped on one side. It had been partly tied with a piece of rope.

Dr McGrath's 27-page report, set out on headed notepaper and including photographs, was a detailed examination of the remains which aimed to determine five points — whether the remains were human; and if so, the age, sex, stature and other details of the person; the cause of death; the time of death and the mode of disposal after death.

Using X-rays to help him in his examination, Dr McGrath reached a number of conclusions. Firstly, and without doubt the remains were human, comprising the upper part of the trunk of a human body, but the head, arms, pelvis, and legs were missing. It was a male body, aged between 25 and 45 years, of normal height, of strong build and with a shoulder width of about 16.5 inches. The body had been divided after death, and the manner in which it had been chopped up 'indicates that the operator had special anatomical knowledge such as that of a doctor, or a veterinary surgeon,' Dr McGrath's report claimed.

However, it was not possible to say what was the cause of death. It was also difficult to estimate the precise time of death, but it had occurred at some time between three and eighteen months before the post mortem examination, he said.

The discovery of the body had increased talk in the area about a missing man, a local farmer, who had lived less than one mile

93

from the spot where the remains were found in Ballincur bog. Thirty-one-year old Laurence Kirwan of Ballincloghan, Co. Offaly, had been missing for approximately six months. There had even been an SOS on the radio for him, but there had been no response.

The request for an SOS message had been relayed by telegram to the radio station by Bernard Kirwan, the brother of the man missing since 22 November. 'Before the news, there is one SOS. It is for Laurence Kirwan — will Laurence Kirwan please communicate with his brother Bernard at any Garda station.'

The Kirwans' parents had lived in Galway, where Laurence's father was a member of the Royal Irish Constabulary. They bought a small farm at Ballincloghan, Co. Offaly, and in 1912 Mary Kirwan was widowed and then raised her family of three sons and three daughters. Peter the eldest son was married and lived two miles away in Rahan village, where he ran a pork and mutton shop. Margaret had married and lived outside the village, Mary Kate worked in Dublin and the third sister Annie was in a convent in Ceylon.

Bernard and Laurence worked the farm. In February 1936 Bernard cut the barrels off a shotgun and held up a postman as he was delivering registered mail. Kirwan blasted the postman's bicycle tyres to avoid pursuit and capture. He hid his haul in the hollow tubes of his bicycle frame, and while the investigation into the hold-up continued offered the Gardaí all the assistance they required — and managed for a short time to send them off on a wild goose chase. He was eventually convicted of the crime and was sentenced to seven years penal servitude in Portlaoise prison. The following year Mary Kirwan died, leaving a will which purported to leave the majority of her assets to Peter her eldest son and his child. The will was never proved as it also stipulated that all debts had to be paid first. As there was approximately £1,800 due to the bank for repayment of a mortgage on forty acres of farmland, payment of the debt would liquidate all the assets, so the farm remained in Laurence's possession. Laurence had been left one eighth of the farm in the unproven will, and was by nature a hard worker, a good farm manager and noted for a mean streak — all of which explained how he amassed a bundle of money which he carried around in a purse during the day and hid under his pillow at night.

Bernard Kirwan was given a conditional release in June 1941, after serving four years of his sentence. He lived with his married sister for a short while before returning to the family home to live with his brother Laurence.

Laurence resented his brother's return, and refused to give him a bed in the house. This resulted in Bernard taking his meals at Ballincloghan, but cycling to his sister's each night for a bed. This lasted for about a week, and then Laurence allowed his brother to return. The two brothers and the farm labourer shared the one small bedroom. About a month or so later, Bernard took a short holiday in Dublin, staying in a small hotel and 'doing every show in the city at night' as he later explained. The holiday was funded by the theft of £15 from Laurence.

On his return relations between the two brothers were very strained, and a petty war broke out. Laurence locked up the food after each meal, forcing Bernard to provide for himself or go to his sister's house. Laurence suggested that the three of them would go to the bog to cut turf, but Bernard said he wouldn't do any heavy work and was only prepared to work around the farmyard or in the house.

Towards the end of August Bernard returned home in the early hours of the morning from a dance, to find the front door locked. He broke it in, and went to bed. Later that morning Jack Foran, the farm labourer, was woken by the sounds of an argument between the two brothers. The sound of shouting soon turned into a struggle as the brothers tussled, then Foran heard Laurence shout, 'Jack, get up , he is after stabbing me with a knife.' Laurence burst into the bedroom, with blood flowing from a deep wound in his right hand and said that Bernard had tried to stab him and he had received the hand wound when he tried to ward off the blade. Bernard disputed this version of events, saying Lar had started the argument. Bernard talked about the row on a number of occasions, and showed no remorse, telling three different people, 'If he ever attacks me again it will be his last time', 'Next time it will be a clean cut', and 'He escaped me this time, but the next time will be a clean one.'

After the stabbing incident, predictably relations further deteriorated. Laurence was still locking away food from his brother, only to realise that food was continually missing from the locked cupboard.

Laurence then began to lock the food into the boot of his Ford car, which he had bought second-hand in July. Shortly afterwards when a neighbour called to borrow some soap, Laurence discovered an impression of his car key in a bar of soap kept in the house. He fitted his key into the soap bar and found it fitted perfectly. Not to be outdone by his brother he bought a new lock to replace a defective one in the right-hand door of the car, and began transferring his hoard of food into the car where it now remained locked away.

'These are the conditions under which the two brothers lived. They may prompt one to answer the question: did all the fault lie on Bernard's side?' George Lawlor wrote. 'Was he a man who regarded the taking of human life as of little consequence? He had undoubtedly shown himself already as a man of violent temper. Apart altogether from the stabbing affair, he had used a sawn-off shotgun to intimidate the postman and blast the tyres off his bicycle when committing the mail robbery. On the other hand there were people in the locality who were in sympathy with him. He had served his term of imprisonment and had returned home to find his younger brother in charge and he relegated to the position of hewer of wood and drawer of water.

'It was common gossip in the neighbourhood that Laurence was very mean in refusing Bernard food and not paying him for his work on the farm — in short, that Laurence was a usurper who deserved very little sympathy and who was responsible for the sorry state of affairs in the Kirwan homestead. Whatever was the direct cause of the estrangement between those two brothers the conditions existing in the home provided a strong motive for the murder of Laurence. Thus there was no need to search for a motive here, and while absence of motive or failure to unearth one makes an investigation more difficult, the overwhelming motive in this case did not lighten the task of the investigators.'

On Thursday 20 November, Laurence Kirwan and Jack Foran drove four cattle from the farm to his cousin's house near Tullamore, so they would be within easy reach of the market the following morning in Tullamore. The cattle were sold at the fair for over £50, more or less the same as Lar had received for four cattle at the previous month's fair. When a tot was done on recent incomes to him this £100 was added to further monies earned by spraying potatoes, the sale of turf and from reaping corn. Before he left the market, Laurence bought a ten-stone sack of flour, on which he was charged a deposit of five shillings.

On the morning of the 22nd, Jack Foran was told to clean out the boiler house in the yard. Laurence said he intended cooking potatoes in it for the pigs. Later, Laurence didn't believe the boiler house was cleaned, and returned with Foran, walking the forty paces across the yard and past its hand pump and stone trough, to check. But it took only a cursory glance at the ten-foot square boiler house to realise it had already been cleaned, and a fresh fire set and ready for lighting.

Laurence spent the Saturday working around the farmhouse and used the afternoon to fix a bent mudguard.

'Larry then asked me to milk the cows as he had an appointment to keep in Tullamore,' Foran was later to tell the *Irish Independent*. 'I went for the cows and and when I returned Larry was fixing the back wheel of his bicycle in the porch. When I finished milking I went in to have my supper, and Larry began the work of separating and straining the milk in the dairy. I asked him to have his supper but he said he would not have it then, as it was getting dark and he wanted to bring the cows down,' Foran recalled.

Lar also called Jack in to help him pour the flour he had purchased earlier that day into two tea chests. Laurence remarked that he had been charged five bob on the sack and that he intended returning the sack and reclaiming his deposit that night when he went into town. He folded the empty hessian sack and tied it to his bicycle.

That afternoon Foran was asked by Bernard to go into Clara to pick up his watch which was being repaired. 'You can have my bike,' said Bernard. Foran agreed, as it was the first time Bernard had ever given him the loan of his bicycle. Bernard also gave him a two-shilling piece and asked him to buy cigarettes. Foran noticed that the coin was taken from a pouch with a zip fastener which bulged with notes. The pouch was the same one Laurence had worn since the row in August between the two brothers, Foran noted.

The twenty-two-year-old left the Kirwan house at 6.15 p.m. leaving Laurence making final adjustments to the mudguard on his bicycle. It was the last time he ever saw Lar Kirwan.

Foran didn't return to the Kirwan farmhouse until after 1 a.m., as he had gone to the local dance on his return from Clara.

Annie Flannery ran a dressmaking business in the High Street, Tullamore, and had a date with Lar that Saturday night. They had been going out together as a couple for the past two years, and met almost every Saturday and Sunday night. They had met on the previous Wednesday night also, and had parted as usual on good terms after attending a dance together at Cloghan.

'I was expecting Laurence to call.' Annie recalled: 'Between 9.30 and 10.30 p.m. I went down the town and I met Pat Horan with a few others, Smith and Dolan, and I spoke to them. Horan said he was coming up to my place, that Laurence Kirwan was coming into town and he had an appointment to meet him. He walked up the town with me as far as my own door. We all remained outside talking until about 10.45 p.m. I was expecting Laurence and was on the lookout for him but didn't see him.

'I went in home to wait. Horan went down the town with the other boys, but returned to my place in a few minutes. About 11 p.m. I remarked to Horan that Laurence mustn't be coming in. Horan stayed until about midnight expecting him. I went to bed as there was no sign of him.'

The following day Pat Horan called back to the house. He had been to the dance at Killina and met Foran who told him Laurence had gone away. Horan was a great friend of Laurence and it was the first he had heard about Laurence going away.

When Foran returned to Kirwans around 1 a.m. on Sunday morning, Bernard Kirwan was still up, and was ironing clothes. There was food on the kitchen table. Foran found it curious to see food laid out on the table. He had complained to the eldest of the Kirwans, Peter, only recently, that he had been thinking of leaving the farm as 'the grub isn't good there'. Peter had told him not to be foolish, he had a good job and should stick with it.

'Lar is gone', or 'Lar is gone on holidays' Bernard told him as he boiled up a pot of milk, Foran recalled. He wasn't too sure which Bernard had said. Bernard made cocoa, another first, Foran noticed, but passed no remark. The house was tidy and apart from the food, Bernard's hospitality, and the fact that he was wearing Lar's pull-ups and rubber boots, everything was in order. Lar's bike was not in the tiny porchway that led directly into the kitchen where it was normally parked, but Foran thought nothing of it because Lar always had a date at the weekend.

Foran slept deeply and late until 11 a.m. When he got up to go to Mass in Clara, Bernard gave him seven shillings and instructed him to buy him a bottle of whiskey. 'Keep a shilling of that for yourself and there's no need to rush back,' he said.

Jack Foran took him at his word, surprised at the shilling gift as it was the first time Bernard had ever given him money. It was 7 p.m. when he returned with three 'Baby Powers'. After washing and shaving he was gone again within the hour to a dance in Killina.

Mary Kate Lynam, whose farmhouse was across the yard and separated from them by a wall, returned from eleven o'clock Mass at Killina church at about 12.30 p.m. and her husband James was in the kitchen. 'She was in just a few minutes' said James, 'when she remarked, "There's smoke coming from out of Kirwans' boiler house. Bernie must be boiling for the pigs." I laughed at the remark because I knew that Bernie wouldn't be doing any work in the interest of his place, and especially on a Sunday.' It was the first time the boiler, which had a fifty-gallon capacity with a large furnace beneath it, had been used since the previous spring.

Foran returned at 5 a.m. on Monday morning, and was up again a few hours later to start work. Bernard told him to go to a wood approximately three miles from the house to cut scallops (twigs), which could be used for re-thatching the four-roomed cottage. Foran said there was more important work to be done on the farm, but Bernard cut his arguments short. 'Fuck you, I'm the boss, and I'm telling you to go,' he said. Lar still hadn't returned to the farm so Foran went to the wood. Bernard later denied he had sworn at Foran, and said that he often gave him orders, which the labourer followed.

Kirwans' neighbours noticed blue smoke coming from the boiler house again that day. Mary Kate Lynam said that was the last time she saw smoke coming from the boiler house — until 10 December.

When Foran returned that evening at about 4 o'clock Bernard was digging in the garden. The scallops were never collected from the wood, and neither the outhouses nor the cottage needed thatching. Foran remembered that Bernard had told him that he had been cleaning up the house and had been burning rubbish in the furnace in the boiler house.

Between 6.15 p.m. on 21 November and 4 p.m. on the 24th , Foran had only spent a total of eighteen hours in Kirwan's house and of that time he had been asleep for fifteen hours.

Again Bernard told Foran that Lar had gone on holidays. To satisfy him he showed him a chain and padlock wrapped around the wheel of his Ford car, immobilising it. Bernard subsequently broke open a link on the chain, using a pincers normally used to shoe a horse, so that he could move the car.

On the following day Bernard went to Tullamore where he ordered and was measured for a new suit, and paid a £1 deposit. The following day he paid the rates on the farm.

On Tuesday 1 December Joseph Foran, a brother of Jack, was chatting to Garda Finneran in Rahan. In their conversation he mentioned that it was ten days since Laurence Kirwan had been seen and he was supposed to be on holidays in Kildare. Peter Kirwan's shop was next door to the Garda station, and later in the day the Garda asked Peter about his brother. No, he didn't know anything about his whereabouts, he said.

However, after the statement was read over to him he refused to sign it. He made a number of comments and these too were written down, witnessed and read back to him, but he also refused to sign these additions. 'That portion of the statement "I didn't make any enquiries beyond speaking to my own people about him, I didn't report to the Guards about him missing" is correct , but I don't see why I should have made any enquiries,' he told the three Gardaí.

Lar's bicycle was missing from the porch; missing also were his good blue suit, his grey tweed overcoat and his pair of light shoes, which were black in colour.

'I was standing at my door when Bernard came along,' Annie was to tell the Gardaí. 'I went in when I saw him, but came out to talk to him. He began speaking about Larry saying he was going to send an SOS message, he appeared to be worried and he started to cry. He said "If he would only let us know where he is we wouldn't mind,"' she said. She helped him to draft the SOS which included a description. The missing man was six foot tall and built in proportion, was strong, athletic and had been in the local tug-of-war team.

That night Foran said he 'saw something terrible' in Bernard Kirwan's face and he left the farm and never returned to work there again.

The next day Bernard sent a telegram to Radio Éireann asking them to broadcast an SOS for Lar. The radio station checked with the Gardaí and broadcast the message the following day.

Two days later Bernard helped his brother Peter and some neighbours to drag the canal which ran past their house at the entrance to the yard, less than twenty yards from the house. Neither the body nor the bicycle was discovered.

'At this point in the investigation,' said George Lawlor, 'when everything pointed to the fact that Laurence had not left home on the night of the 22nd, evidence became available that he had been seen in Tullamore. His girlfriend and his male friend were however, satisfied that if he had come to town he would not have left without calling on them. In all, three persons made written statements that they saw and spoke to Laurence that night between 7 and 9 p.m.

After painstaking inquiry and talks with those persons the Gardaí were satisfied that the night they were referring to was 19 November and not when he had visited Tullamore as he normally did on Saturday nights and called on his girlfriend.

'Bernard Kirwan was aware of these mistakes as subsequent events proved and was using them for his own ends. Naturally if Laurence could have been placed in Tullamore on 22 November, Bernard was provided with a pretty good alibi. Apart from the retraction of their statements by the three persons, it was established that there were three men on the road between 8.30 p.m. and 11 p.m. whom Laurence would have passed on the way from Rahan to Tullamore, one of whom was Laurence's first cousin, and all of whom were satisfied that Laurence did not pass that night while they were there.

'These established facts forced us to one and only one conclusion, that Laurence had met an untimely end and that he had met it at the hands of Bernard, his own brother,' said George Lawlor.

The Gardaí investigation continued. On 16 December Kirwans' house was searched and a number of items were discovered, which it was known Lar would normally wear with his good blue suit. These were a pocket watch and chain, a tobacco pouch with zip fastener — which it was known in the locality Lar used as a wallet for his money, a grey scarf, a light brown cap, pipe and cycle pull-ups. They were items that he would normally wear or bring with him on a visit to his girlfriend.

Searches of the area continued, involving up to fifty Gardaí. On Christmas Eve traces of ash were found in the garden at the back of the house. Among the ashes were the burnt remnants of a pullover.

'Lar's jumper was woollen, machine-knit with a collar and a green stripe running through it,' said Annie Flannery who identified the charred remains. She had knitted him the jumper as a present. There was no other jumper like it, she said. Other pieces of well-burned clothing were also found, but could not be identified. On St Stephen's Day Gardaí drained a four-and-a-half mile-long section of the Grand Canal. Gardaí walked through the bottom of the canal from Ballcowan to Carnalour lock gates engaged in a fruitless search.

As the Gardaí spread their net wider and made inquiries in an increasingly wide radius of Lar and Bernard's home, two women independently told them that they had seen and heard a car late on the night and in the early hours of Saturday 22 November and Sunday 23rd.

Two men said they saw a car going towards Derrycooley, some distance from the Kirwans' home and they both gave the same time for this. One of them said the car had a bike tied to the back of it. About an hour later the same car returned, travelling in the opposite direction towards Rahan. However, the car was never traced. But the claim changed the direction of the searches, and bog holes were dragged in the areas around Pulloguh, Ferbane, Kilcormac and Mountbolus — all within a short distance of the Kirwan farm.

Low turf banks which had fallen in were also dug up, and Gardaí became more and more certain as time went on that Laurence Kirwan was a dead man. Gardaí also began keeping tabs on Bernard's movements — even when he was working on the bog Gardaí watched him in relays.

Sections of the canal beyond the two nearest locks to the Kirwan house were dragged, and sections of the River Brosna and the River Shannon at the bridges in Shannonbridge, Banagher and Portumna were also dragged.

'We examined the boiler and furnace and found they had both been cleaned out. Bernard first denied lighting a fire in the boiler house, then he said that he may have boiled food for the pigs either on the Sunday or Monday. Yet we have the Lynams' statement that the fire was going both days. Bernard's evasiveness when questioned on the matter was highly suspicious. Had he become more industrious? Or did his action point to something more sinister?' George Lawlor asked.

'Bernard had the reputation locally of being an expert in the slaughtering and the boning of pigs and his skill at such was appreciated and utilised in the neighbourhood. It was also established that on a former occasion when a horse died and when the difficulty of burying the carcass was discussed, he made the suggestion that if the head and legs were cut from the animal it would not take such a large hole to bury it. If we accept the theory that he used the boiler house to carry out the partial destruction of his brother's body, then he did his work well. Despite a most careful examination of the boiler house and its contents under the directions of the State Pathologist, Dr McGrath, no evidence was forthcoming to substantiate such a theory,' he wrote. On 17 January Bernard Kirwan was arrested on a charge of housebreaking, and was remanded in custody, and was convicted and sentenced to seven days imprisonment. As a consequence of breaking his convict's licence the Minister for Justice ordered that he should return to Portlaoise jail to complete his original sentence. Between the revocation of his licence and the completion of his seven days jail sentence Bernard Kirwan returned home.

On 18 February, while he was in the District Court waiting for the committal order to be signed by the District Justice, he engaged a solicitor, Mr R.J. Fetherstonhaugh, and passed him a bundle of bank notes.

Mr Fetherstonhaugh agreed to be interviewed by detectives and told them that Bernard had given him £73 in bank notes, and he had taken the numbers of the notes he received prior to lodging them in the Bank of Ireland in Mountmellick. However, he declined to say anything else or to give the Gardaí the numbers on the bank notes, as he claimed the transaction was a privileged one between a solicitor and his client.

By the time arrangements had been made with the bank to stop the issue of all ten and five pound notes by their cashiers, only one ten pound note, numbered O8VO79034, which had been lodged by Bernard Kirwan's solicitor, was still in the bank. The list of bank note numbers had been obtained when the solicitor's office was searched under warrant.

'Enquiries established that on 17 October 1941 Laurence Kirwan had sold cattle for £50 to farmer Mathew Moore, for which he was paid by cheque,' George Lawlor later said. 'He cashed the cheque at the bank in Tullamore and he endorsed it with his signature. In the bank on 17 October there was a bundle of new ten pound notes — which had never been issued until sent to the Hibernian Bank in Tullamore — which included the note 08V079034 and they were all paid out on the same day, which was a fair day in the town. It was a reasonable assumption that the ten pound note recovered from the bank was in the possession of Laurence Kirwan.

'But we obtained further evidence to prove our belief. The wallet or pouch in which Laurence had kept his money with the receipt for the flour bag was lined with a rubber material. An examination of the ten pound note showed that it bore minute flecks of a material which was foreign to the note itself.

'The receipt for the flour bag bore similar fleck marks and consequently the note and receipt were passed to the State Analyst who was able, by both a chemical and spectrum analysis, to confirm that the flecks on the note and on the receipt were of the same rubber material which originally formed the lining of the wallet. The analysis indicated that both the receipt and the note had been carried at some period in the pouch.

'Bernard refused to account for the £73 he handed his solicitor. His previous statements in the earlier stages of the investigation in which he admitted having a total of £1-4s-8d and that he had earned little or no money since his release from Portlaoise prison, were a stumbling block now; and to circumvent them he endeavoured to get people to come forward and state that they had lent him money. Fortunately the honesty and public spirit of these persons prevailed and Bernard was soon to find that his endeavours only provided the Gardaí with further evidence against him.

'By this time,' Lawlor confided to his files, 'it had been established that his spendings since Laurence's disappearance totalled approximately £33. Taking into account all the monies he had received and spent, it left him to account for £98 odd — approximately the amount of money Laurence should have possessed the day before he disappeared. And this was the state of a man's account who had no income.

'Small but important pieces of evidence began to fit into the chain of circumstantial evidence and each link was solidly welded.'

On 18 February Bernard was committed to Portlaoise jail, but was released on 7 March pending his appeal to the Circuit Court. Ten days later he celebrated St Patrick's day by going to a dance that night. He lost his waterproof coat at the dance, and approximately one month later he was seen wearing a black overcoat in Tullamore. Gardaí stopped him and asked him about the overcoat, for surveillance reports had not described him wearing a black overcoat before.

'That's an old overcoat, can't anyone see it is an old overcoat,' Kirwan said when stopped by the Gardaí. Not satisfied with the reply the Gardaí insisted on taking the coat, which, on close examination, appeared to have been dyed black.

Lar Kirwan's girlfriend, a dressmaker, had no difficulty recognising the coat immediately. It had been dyed, and she knew it by the repairs she had carried out on the sleeve of the coat for Lar. 'I noticed the stitching I did on the ends of the sleeve for Laurence some time before he disappeared. That's Laurence Kirwan's coat,' she had no hesitation in saying.

Further inquiries showed that Bernard had purchased three packets of 'Fairy' black dye from Thomas McGowan's shop in Tullamore, and a textile expert in Dublin was able to say that the coat had undoubtedly been dyed, and by an amateur. A firm of Dublin cleaners succeeded in removing the black dye from a portion of the coat and restored it to its original grey colour. When questioned again about the coat, Bernard said that he had bought it from a street trader at a fair in Tullamore. The five second-hand clothes dealers who traded at the fair and who came from all parts of the country were contacted and they all made statements saying they had not traded in or sold the coat when it was shown to them by the Gardaí.

As these enquiries continued, Peter Leonard discovered a bicycle hidden under hay in the loft of an outhouse on his farm at Ballinsragh, Tullamore, just over four miles from the home of his first cousins, Laurence and Bernard. It was 30 April, and Peter had gone to the little used loft to get hay for cattle when he made the discovery. Bernard knew the farm well, as he had stayed there when he was attending school in Tullamore.

Bernard was asked to identify the bicycle, but refused, saying he had more important things to do, such as feeding his cattle and attending to a sick horse. However, the bicycle was identified by the dealer who had sold it to Lar Kirwan and subsequently carried out repairs to it. The carrier on the back of the bicycle was empty and contained no flour sack as expected, according to the details in the statements given by both Bernard Kirwan and the labourer Jack Foran.

In the course of a further search of the Kirwans' four-roomed cottage, a large flour bag was found neatly folded in the loft. It had obviously been placed since the last search.

It was the ninth flour bag discovered in the Kirwan household since Lar had gone missing. In all, over 130 different types of bags and sacks were found on the farm. The sack found in May, over the kitchen, bore the brand 'MF and L Goodbody, Branch of Ranks (I) Ltd., Clara. For flour only, 140lbs. Bag must be returned.'

It was another link in the chain of circumstantial evidence that was winding slowly and inexorably around Bernard Kirwan. This type of bag was known in the trade as a 'Hessian retail flour bag' and had not been issued before 22 September 1941.

'Foran was positive' wrote George Lawlor, 'that prior to 22 November 1941 there was never a bag of the hessian kind on the premises, as before that, all flour had come in white cotton bags. He had helped Laurence to empty the bag into the tea chest on 22 November and remembered that the bag was different from those which had been formerly used.

'The tracing of the bag entailed quite an amount of spade work and whilst it was not possible to positively identify it, since it bore no number, we were able to produce very strong circumstantial proof that the bag found in the loft was the one which had been bought by Laurence on the day of his disappearance.

'If we reflect that this bag was, according to Foran, on the fateful evening then tied to the missing man's bicycle and was even admitted by Bernard himself to be there between 8 and 9 p.m. when he said he left the house, the fact that it was not on the bicycle when found, but still on the premises, left him with a situation which was not easily explained. If he had killed his brother and taken the bag from the bicycle and put it in the loft, he had made a fatal slip in considering that the bag was just an ordinary one. He could not possibly visualise that a flour bag could be identified as a particular one, and up to a point his reasoning was correct. But the tightening of the food regulations and the shortage of material due to the war emergency was something which he had not bargained for which, in this particular instance, made an ordinary flour bag almost positively identifiable.'

Supt Nicholas Delaney in Tullamore asked Bernard's brother Peter if he recognised the flour bag which had been found in the Kirwans' attic? But no, he hadn't ever seen it before.

On another, perhaps more delicate matter, he said that some-one had been seen digging at his parents' grave in the village cemetery. He didn't tell him it was Bernard.

John Lowry, an eighty-year-old labourer who lived in Rahan, was praying at his wife's grave when he saw Bernard in Rahan's churchland graveyard. 'He had the soil dug up and had some of the flowers sown or planted on it. He had it nearly completed. He removed the border of coping stones which outlined the grave,' the pensioner told the Gardaí.

Peter said he knew nothing about it, but he had noted that the grave had been done up recently. Someone had planted it with flowers and the top soil had been turned over. 'I can't say who done up the grave or where the flowers came from which were used. I never heard who had done it up,' he said. In response to the Garda's tentative query he said he had no objections to the authorities opening the grave.

But before any such action could be considered Joe Bracken discovered the torso in the bog. The limbs had been cut away, the spinal column was neatly dissected and the ribs had been hacked away entirely from the back bone on the right hand side and almost completely on the left.

The sack which contained the gruesome remains was shown to Jack Foran and he pointed to holes in it which, in his opinion, had been made by tools and spare parts carried in a 'Blue Seal binder twine' sack which had been attached to the binding machine but which had vanished. The tools and spare parts were found scattered around the house and yard. 'There seemed to be little doubt that Bernard had used this tool sack to carry and shroud his brother's torso,' said George Lawlor.

'Apart from the indirect evidence which was available to connect Bernard with the remains, there was the fact that he had shown an interest in the work which was being carried out at that particular turf bank. He even addressed questions at various times to different neighbours, and remarked to one of them: 'If Lar is found in a heap, the Guards will be after me.'

Bernard had been again taken into custody on 20 May 1942, since his appeal to the Circuit Court had failed. On 14 August he was charged with the murder of his brother, and was returned for trial to the Central Criminal Court.

While he was awaiting trial in Mountjoy jail, Bernard smuggled out a letter to a friend asking him to corroborate his story that they had spent the vital hours, between 8 and 11 p.m. on 22 November of the previous year, together in Tullamore.

Attempting to establish a false alibi wasn't a new trick for Bernard. He had previously tried the same thing when he was in jail on the armed robbery charge, and somehow had repossessed his letter and kept it wrapped in a collection of newspaper cuttings of sensational murders underneath his mattress.

'How he came to repossess this letter was never established,' recalled George Lawlor, 'but his keeping it set us thinking and later we were able to re-establish the truth of the old adage, that a leopard never changes his spots.'

The Gardaí, wary that he might attempt to obtain a false alibi, were alert to such an attempt by Bernard. Sure enough they intercepted a letter sent from Mountjoy by Bernard to a friend attempting to construct an alibi. It was to be produced in court as evidence against Bernard.

On 18 January 1943 Bernard pleaded 'Not Guilty' to the charge of murdering his brother as he stood in the dock at Green Street Court.

He wore a black suit and was clean shaven, he sat erect on a cushioned chair in the dock listening intently to the evidence brought forward against him over the next seventeen days. He was a handsome, goodlooking fellow who oiled his dark, wavy hair. He wore a white scarf around his neck and inside his jacket to keep the collar of his coat from getting greasy. Despite his imprisonment he looked fit, and prison warders would later recall hearing the regular thump of a ball being slammed against the wall of his cell as he played handball. On Kirwan's knee was a large pad which he used to write countless notes which were passed across the wooden barriers to his legal team.

The court was packed throughout the trial, and queues of people formed up outside in the hope of taking any seat that might become vacant.

There was no direct evidence that the torso found was part of Laurence Kirwan's body. But the State case claimed it was, based on the entire history of the case, the pointed enquiries made by Bernard to neighbours living near the spot where the torso was found, the fact that the bog land on which it was found was the property of an uncle of the Kirwans and less than a mile from their home, that it was found in a binder twine bag similar to that missing from Laurence's binding machine, and that the anatomical dissection of the torso pointed to Bernard, a skilled pig butcher.

There were seven major points on which the prosecution aimed at securing a conviction. These were that the torso was Laurence's; and the bag it was wrapped in provided further evidence of this. Bernard proved to have more money than he could have acquired lawfully; the missing flour sack turned up in the attic of the house; Laurence's coat had been dyed and was being used by Bernard — even though he had initially said it was missing; that a false alibi was broken; and money given by Bernard to his solicitor had belonged to Laurence.

In the court the prosecution made the point that while in Portlaoise jail, Bernard had assisted in the butchering and dressing of pigs and had occasionally dealt with their bodies by chopping them down the backbone in a similar manner to the discovered torso. The killer could have a knowledge of butchery, the State Pathologist also said in his autopsy report.

Mr Barra O'Briain, S.C., led the defence team for Kirwan, and objected to the State's counsel, George Murnaghan, S.C., telling the court of Kirwan's previous imprisonment. The judge, Mr Justice Martin Maguire, ruled against the objection.

The defence said that no proof had been given that the torso was that of Laurence Kirwan or that he was in fact dead. In all, three men had gone missing in the area in recent years. However, Supt Nicholas Delaney said that one of the men, missing from Edenderry since 1937, had been traced. He had joined the French Foreign Legion and was alive.

Another, against whom a decree for £200 had been given the

previous July for seducing a farmer's daughter, had also vanished. The father of the seduced girl told the court that he had seen the seducer, who was aged about fifty, at a local fair in the month prior to the trial.

Mr O'Briain put a question to his client, Bernard Kirwan, when he took the stand on the thirteenth day of the trial. 'You have been charged with slaughtering and butchering your brother. Is that accusation true or false?' 'False in every detail,' said the prisoner who was requested by both his counsel and the Judge to speak up.

Kirwan went on to pour scorn on the Gardaí, and accused them of shadowing him 'morning, noon and night'. He claimed that he had been followed to the bog by Gardaí with rifles, and was also followed to Confession. Kirwan also reluctantly revealed that he had applied to join the Gardaí in 1934 and had been turned down. At that time he had just committed armed robbery.

In a lengthy summation for the defence, Mr O'Briain S.C., said that his primary point was that the State had failed in identifying the body, and doctors had even disagreed before the bench of the court as to the sex of the discovered torso.

Mr Justice Maguire urged the jury to leave aside all feelings of 'indignation, horror and revulsion' and to approach consideration of the case with only one purpose in view — to find a just verdict.

In his charge, which was to span three days, he told the jury that there was no evidence of any missing women in the locality and both the other missing men were found to be alive. The Gardaí had been attacked by the prisoner but it seemed they had given their evidence fairly and there was no substantiation of the accused man's claims that he had been 'hounded'.

Over 500 statements had been taken by the Gardaí in the investigation and over 100 witnesses gave evidence at the trial. It took the jury of eleven, as one person had been taken seriously ill during the trial, three hours to return a verdict of 'Guilty'. Kirwan stood erect when the question was put to him, had he anything to say as to why sentence of death should not be passed on him.

He paused for a moment before replying: 'At the outset of the case I pleaded "Not Guilty". Throughout the trial I have reiterated my innocence, and that is all I have to say. For all the sins of my life I ask forgiveness of God and ask no forgiveness of man.' The Judge sentenced him to be hanged, and before being led away from the court to the cells, Kirwan said, 'I forgive my enemies.' He appealed against the sentence of the court but lost, and was hanged on 2 June 1943.

Eleven years later Bernard Kirwan's memory was to be evoked with the first staging of Brendan Behan's play, *The Quare Fellow* at the Pike Theatre Club, Dublin. The play, which examines attitudes to capital punishment, centres on a man about to be executed. Bernard Kirwan — who carried out, according to George Lawlor 'a crime that for sheer brutality not only has no parallel with any murder that ever occurred in this country but matches anything which is chronicled as having happened elsewhere' — was Behan's 'Quare Fellow'.

9.

The Named Killer

EARLY in January 1944, James Herbert Lehman, his wife Margaret and their two toddler children took furnished accommodation at number eleven Leinster Road, Rathmines, Dublin. They had arrived in Ireland the previous year after Lehman, a native of Canada and an ex-private with the Royal Canadian regiment, had been discharged from the Army as medically unfit.

Shortly after his arrival in Rathmines he had opened a shop specialising in baby foods in nearby Chelmsford Road, Ranelagh, a residential road linking Ranelagh village through the Appian way with Leeson Street.

The couple led a quiet life, according to their landlady who lived on the ground floor of the house, and Mrs Lehman occupied herself with her household duties while her husband was busy in his shop.

Their flat was tiny, with the living accommodation on the top floor, while the kitchen was on the floor below, with a shared sink on the landing. Despite having their own kitchen, cooking facilities were still poor, and on Sundays Mrs Lehman would cook their dinner in their landlady's kitchen.

However on Saturday night 18 March 1944, Margaret Lehman informed her landlady that she had a heavy cold and that she wouldn't need the facility to cook the joint the following day as they'd be eating a light meal instead.

It wasn't until almost 7 p.m. the following day that the landlady, Winnie O'Callaghan, saw her tenants the Lehmans. At approximately 7 p.m. she heard a noise upstairs and came out of her rooms to investigate. There appeared to be nothing wrong and she was about to go back when she noticed an extraordinary smell. She recognised the smell but couldn't identify it. It seemed to come from above her in the house. A few minutes later James Lehman came down from his flat to return a box he had borrowed. As usual he had taken off his jacket when he came into the house and was wearing a dressing gown over his shirt and trousers. Winnie enquired about his wife's health; there was little improvement, said James. She should see a doctor, said Winnie, and the two chatted for a few minutes, with Lehman commenting that his wife was always reluctant to visit doctors, before returning upstairs.

Within five minutes he had rushed back down again in a very agitated condition, calling on Mrs O'Callaghan to come upstairs quickly as his wife had taken very ill. 'Come quickly! My wife is terribly ill. I brought in some rum for her and she must have taken it,' he said frantically.

Margaret Lehman was extremely ill: she was lying in the bed unconscious. There was froth on her mouth. Her face was distorted, racked with pain and had a purplish colour. Her forehead was wet and clammy to the touch.

Mrs Lehman was pregnant and another neighbour was roused to call for an ambulance as Mrs O'Callaghan tried to comfort the seriously-ill woman.

Lehman was little help and ran up and down the room crying as they waited for the ambulance. As his wife was carried out of the house on a stretcher he was asked if she had been in this condition for long. 'A couple of hours,' replied Lehman. The ambulance man was surprised, saying she should have been brought to hospital before now, and Lehman said that he had tried to get a doctor in the district but couldn't find one.

On the way to the Rotunda Maternity Hospital at the top of O'Connell Street, Lehman asked the driver how was his wife? 'Bad enough,' came driver Jimmy Quirke's reply.

As the ambulance silenced its siren and pulled up at the entrance to the hospital, the doors were opened, by chance, by a sister of Margaret Lehman. Bridie Hayden, who worked in the hospital laundry, saw her sister being carried by stretcher into the hospital and promptly fainted.

Dr Cross examined Margaret Lehman and found she was dead on arrival. He decided to operate immediately in the hope of saving the child, a girl, but to no avail.

Lehman paced the corridors outside the operating theatre where his wife had been rushed, and wept and became distressed when the news was broken to him that his wife was dead. Bridie Hayden asked him what had happened. Lehman said she had been having dizzy spells.

While Lehman was at the hospital Mrs O'Callaghan again noticed the distinctive smell in Lehman's bedroom. In the kitchen on the

113

floor below there was the same smell, the aroma of bitter almonds. 'It made me gasp and almost took my breath away,' she said. That day was the first time she had ever noticed the smell in the house.

Lehman returned at about 9.30 p.m. that evening to tell her his wife was dead. 'Poor Peg, I knew she had something on her mind! Poor thing,' he said. He was upset and said that his wife had had an earlier attack, but when questioned by Winnie O'Callaghan, he said that he had not called a doctor.

Lehman also told her that his wife had been married before and her real husband had just recently turned up in Dublin. It was the first time Winnie O'Callaghan had ever heard of Margaret's background she was to say later. He also said that he thought leaving their children to Margaret's family would be 'unsuitable'.

Although Lehman had suggested suicide, the cause of death had not yet been established. Dr Raymond Cross, the Assistant Master at the Rotunda, who examined the dead woman, could find no particular reason why she should have died, and not being satisfied, he sought and was granted the Coroner's permission to carry out a post mortem examination.

Dr Dockery, the Rotunda Hospital Pathologist, carried out the examination which showed that Margaret Lehman had been quite healthy and in a normal state for a woman who had an advanced pregnancy. There was no apparent reason for her death, his report concluded. He informed the Coroner of his findings and suggested that some of the internal organs should be sent to the State Analyst. The examination of the organs was conducted the following day. At 4 p.m. that evening, the Gardaí at Fitzgibbon Street were notified of the results by the Coroner. The stomach, spleen and liver of the dead woman showed traces of hydrocyanic (prussic) acid or cyanide poisoning.

This type of poison is extremely fast-acting. The victim could literally drop dead or could linger for up to twenty minutes, as the length of time for the poison to take effect can also be affected by whether or not the victim suffers from chronic gastritis. A pink or purplish hue to the face plus the smell of bitter almonds from the mouth and stomach at a post mortem examination are known to investigators as clear indicators of cyanide poisoning.

Station Sgt Alexander Sheppherd was on duty on 20 March and went to the hospital to discuss the death of Margaret Lehman and afterwards to talk to James in Rathmines.

The doctors had not been able to ascertain the cause of death yet, and they were making inquiries about how Margaret might have died. There was a possibility she had been poisoned, said the Garda. 'Well, she got no poison here,' said Lehman.

Margaret had been in excellent health up to about ten days before her death when she suffered from a cold and had been taking tablets to rid herself of it. She had got up as usual that Sunday morning although he had asked her to stay in bed. He had been out on a number of errands and returned at about 5.30 p.m. An hour later Margaret had gone to the bedroom and put the children to bed, and at about seven o'clock he went into the darkened room and thought he heard his wife crooning to the children so he did not disturb them and went downstairs. It was about an hour later, he estimated, when he heard one of the children crying and went back into the bedroom where he found his wife lying unconscious on the floor and called for help.

Mrs Winnie O'Callaghan was interviewed separately and she volunteered a statement. She remembered an unusual smell about the house that evening, both in the bedroom, and again, where it was at its strongest, in the kitchen waste pipe. The bedroom was orderly and there was no vessel or container from which the dead woman could have taken food or drink in the room. She told the Gardaí that Lehman had also said something about 'she must have taken the rum' or 'I gave her the rum', but there was no sign of a bottle.

The following day, Tuesday, Margaret Lehman's funeral took place in Lippstown, County Kildare. James and the two children attended the funeral service, and he moved into the Hayden family home afterwards. On the Thursday of that week he returned to his home in Leinster Road with his sister-in-law Bridget to pack the family belongings. He took his wife's overcoat off the back of the bedroom door and going through its pockets he found a crucifix and a bottle. He was later to tell his landlady that he had also found a letter in the pocket of the coat which he tore up.

During his time in County Kildare with his wife's family he told them of his wife's dizzy spells, that she had tried to abort the child by taking pills given to her by a woman friend and even told them that the dead baby was black. This comment, like the one that Margaret had been previously married, was a total fiction.

Lehman ignored a message to call to Store Street Garda station in Dublin, in connection with the inquiry into his wife's death.

Meanwhile, Det. Inspector Reynolds, who had been involved with the investigation from the start, made an appointment to meet Supt Lawlor, the head of the Technical Bureau in Kilmainham to discuss the case with him that Saturday. The Analyst's report showed that Margaret Lehman had been poisoned. It was imperative that a detailed statement should be taken from Lehman as soon as possible, said Supt Lawlor. The following day Lehman was interviewed by Gardaí at Ballytore Garda station in County Kildare. This was the first time Lehman was told the outcome of the State Analyst's examination — that his wife had been poisoned. 'What! Cyanide?' was his response to the news.

Lehman gave a long and detailed statement to the Gardaí, setting out his life story, and the events of the Sunday his wife died. He had been born in Canada, he said, and concluded his education at the Montreal College of Law. Both his parents were dead, his mother being from County Wicklow; his father was a surgeon. In September 1939 as the world faced war, he had enlisted in the Royal Canadian regiment in Ontario and had been drafted to England; however, an injury to his spine prevented him from being sent to mainland Europe and he rejoined the regiment on their return from France.

During the intervening period he had met and married his wife, a domestic servant who had been employed in a NAAFI services canteen at Aldershot. They had married within a month of meeting. On 24 December 1942 he was discharged as medically unfit and was granted a pension of £11-12s-8d per month. Although he secured civilian employment in Britain and a commission in the Home Guard, he abandoned both and came to Ireland with his family on 26 August 1943, and went to County Kildare to live with his wife's family.

Lehman went on to describe his business ventures, wrote George Lawlor, and his plans to analyse coffee for impurities, using chemicals. 'He alleged' wrote George Lawlor, 'that a chemist had given him a list of chemicals to be purchased for use in these analyses, and this list included prussic, sulphuric and caustic acids. Experiments were carried out at the shop without success. His wife knew of these experiments, but she did not know if acids were used nor where they were stored. His wife had visited the shop on Friday and Saturday he said, when he was out. In this there may have been a veiled suggestion that she went there for the purpose of obtaining the acids, as he had said that she was in mortal fear of her forthcoming confinement. On two previous occasions he alleged that she had attempted miscarriages and had been violently ill as a consequence.'

Lehman told the Gardaí that he would be in Dublin by the end of the week, and would call to the detective branch, which was based in Dublin Castle, to see if they had any more queries. On Thursday 6 April, Holy Thursday, he left Ballytore with his eldest child in a hired car, for Dublin. He placed the boy in a convent, leaving the baby, a one-year-old girl, with his in-laws.

Lehman then called to his landlady Mrs O'Callaghan and asked if she had read the newspapers which featured his wife's death. 'Yes,' she replied, she had read them. 'Wouldn't you think I had done it?' he said before leaving to go to his brother-in-law who lived in Swords in North County Dublin.

But he never arrived, he simply vanished. He had also failed to pay the car hire bill for the trip from Kildare to Dublin.

Meanwhile the Gardaí had been delving deep into Lehman's background and were checking out his rambling but plausible story. Lehman was six feet two inches tall, in his mid thirties, he had retained his good looks, high brow and a neatly trimmed full moustache. When he smiled, two gold teeth flashed, and he smiled a lot as he talked and charmed audiences with his easy engaging manner.

Lehman was not the man he purported to be. A probe into his background showed he was a liar. In 1939 he joined the Canadian army and had been stationed in Aldershot where he met and married Margaret Hayden in February 1940. The following December she became ill, and when he could not get leave to be with her, he went AWOL and remained a deserter until 7 February when he gave himself up and was sentenced to ninety days detention. He subsequently injured his back on manoeuvres — an injury that was to give him a limp when he was tired — and was discharged as medically unfit. He served with the English Home Guard for a while, until he moved to his wife's family home in County Kildare in August 1943. That October he was referred to the British military pensioners' hospital in Leopardstown, Dublin for treatment of his back injury, spinal arthritis. He was admitted on 9 October and released on 3 December.

While he was in the hospital he met a nurse, Annie Caroline McCaigue from Monaghan. He spun her a tale, telling her he had recently discovered his marriage was void, as he had found out that his wife had been previously married to a man called Stokes and she had had two children by him. She had gone back to England, he said. However, when his wife had later visited him he spoke slightingly about her saying she had only come back to Ireland when he was hospitalised.

Lehman told Nurse McCaigue that he was a Canadian and his parents were Irish. He had studied medicine but switched his studies to become a barrister. He gave her the general impression that his family was extremely wealthy and that he was an ex-officer.

On his discharge from hospital Lehman lived in a small hotel with his wife and two small children, but the money started to run out quickly as Lehman wasn't working. By Christmas there was no money and they had resorted to selling their personal possessions to pay the bills. On 25 December the Christmas spirit pervaded the small hotel near Merrion Square, and the Lehmans, who were penniless, were treated to their Christmas dinner by the hotelier and his family.

In the New Year they left suddenly, owing a large bill, and moved into the flat in Leinster Road, Rathmines, leaving no forwarding address. Meanwhile Lehman had been busy, and had used his charms to extract a total of £225 from people he had met since coming to Dublin to open a baby food shop on Chelmsford Road, which he called the 'Sister Ann Baby Saloon'.

Meanwhile he had continued his liaison with the nurse, Annie McCaigue, whom he had met while hospitalised in Leopardstown at the foot of the Dublin mountains. He met her off the train that served Monaghan in Amiens Street on one occasion, and brought her to a restaurant. On another occasion they had paid a repeat visit to the movie house that they had visited while Lehman was recuperating during the final weeks of his stay in the hospital. Annie had also introduced her former patient, the man with dashing dark good looks and an easy manner, to her friends.

Lehman told her he had bought her an engagement ring, which had cost £300 — expensive, he said. 'But why?' asked Annie McCaigue. They were only friends, and she had a boyfriend in Belfast. 'I've been deceived before and I know a decent girl when I see one,' said Lehman. Annie asked Lehman for a look at the ring, but he declined, saying he would wait until she wanted to do more than just look at the ring.

Later he told her he was opening a chain of babywear shops and that she should give up her job and come to work for him. He would pay her well, and offered her £20 a month and the use of the company car — which, although she didn't know at the time, didn't exist. He also wanted her to come into the business with him, for a consideration of £25. She agreed to make the investment but continued working as a nurse.

Lehman also maintained his story about Margaret Lehman not being his wife, repeatedly saying she was living with a man called

Stokes — but failed to mention he was still living with her and not at the Dublin hotel address he had furnished.

Meanwhile, he had advertised in the newspapers and recruited three women staff. One of them, a nurse, who was taken on to advise expectant mothers, was let go shortly after opening. Miss Anna Finucane was employed at thirty shillings a week as the female manager. She had put up a total of £40 as an investment in the shop, believing Lehman's story that he was the manager of the first in a chain of American shops in Ireland. He had initially sought £50 from her, but accepted £40 after fudging his story about the directors he had persuaded to accept her investment.

Nurse McCaigue called to the shop on a number of occasions in its short life and she was grandiosely introduced as the original 'Sister Ann'. Lehman also introduced her to Anna Finucane as 'the woman I intend to marry'.

'The real boss of this place is the nurse, and we are getting married in June,' he told his two shop assistants. He also described the £300 ring he had bought for his engagement to Nurse McCaigue. This impending marriage was possible because his marriage to Margaret Lehman was bigamous, he said. Lehman said he had discovered this when her real husband turned up in Dublin, and he continually referred to his wife as 'she' or 'her', refusing to call her by name. Margaret, who was now expecting their third child, visited the shop once, and he told his staff that she was his 'ex-lady love', and later said she was the only person he had ever hated. But he failed to tell them that he was living with her.

Anna was also told that Margaret Lehman was 'unbalanced' and that their bigamous marriage had followed a drinking bout and pressure from the Canadian authorities.

Within a month of opening, the babywear shop closed, as it had been a financial disaster. However, Lehman decided to remain in business and sell coffee instead from the shop premises, renaming it 'Leigh's'.

Early in March Lehman visited Gilsenan's chemist shop on Lower Rathmines Road, and said he wanted to purchase some cyanide for an experiment on coffee. The chemist asked him if he knew it was a very dangerous poison. 'I do,' said Lehman, and then told him he had read an article in a magazine about a method of testing for impurities in coffee. The chemist agreed to order the 2.5 gram crystal which made up 150 grains of the deadly poison. A fatal dose of cyanide is between two and five grains. A few days later Lehman collected the order, but did not sign the poisons book — the register of sale of restricted poisons.

Lehman brought the poison into the shop in Chelmsford Road, where Anna Finucane saw him flaking the crystal into a powder. He had rolled out a piece of brown paper under a bottle which he was flaking the crystal into, using a scissors. It was a poison, he explained, used for testing coffee. However, Anna never saw him carry out any tests on coffee on that or any other day.

Two days later, on St Patrick's Day, Lehman came into the shop with his young son Kevin, and Anna asked him how his wife was. 'Low. Very low,' he said.

Lehman had also been keeping company with a young widow who owned a neighbouring shop. She lived with her two children in the seclusion of Belmont Avenue, Donnybrook, a wealthy suburb of the city. The widow, who still wore black, had become attached to the 38-year-old with the distinctive accent. She had asked him to go to the St Patrick's Day race meeting with her when he had called to her home earlier that week, but he told her he was unable to attend.

Two days later his wife was dead.

On the night his wife died Anna Finucane called to his flat in response to a note from Lehman, who told her his wife had died. He had previously told her she was taking 'something', and Anna asked 'Was it poison she died from?'

'I'm afraid so,' said Lehman.

'Have you any idea what she took?'

'None,' replied Lehman, who then wondered if Anna thought it was possible she had taken an overdose of aspirin.

The following morning Miss Finucane returned to his flat, helped him tidy up and, at his request, made some telephone calls for him from a public call box. One of them was a cryptic message to Nurse McCaigue. 'I am speaking for a friend of yours,' the nurse heard down the line. 'There has been a death in the family,' and instructions followed for a rendezvous. Nurse McCaigue turned up, but Lehman did not.

He also called that day to the chemist who had supplied him with poison. He told Gilsenan, the chemist, that his wife had died the night before in the Rotunda, in childbirth, and then burst into loud sobs. His wife had not been feeling too well, and he made her a cup of coffee, she took it and she seemed to be alright. He went to get more coffee and when he came back he found her unconscious. 'The little beggar was always taking something and did not want children,' he said.

The following day Garda Finneran called to the Kirwan farm, where he met Bernard, two years his brother's senior. He told the Gardaí that Lar was inside the house. But then, he hastily added, 'Well no, some one from Ballinamore said he is gone to Kildare to my aunt's.'

The Garda reported back to his district headquarters, and Supt Nicholas Delaney instructed the Gardaí in Kilcullen, Co. Kildare, to call to Kathleen Gallagher's house — but no, Laurence hadn't been visiting, she said.

The routine missing persons inquiry took a new turn when Gardaí in Tullamore learned that Lar Kirwan was due to meet his girlfriend Annie and friend Pat Horan on Saturday 22 November. Pat Horan, who knew the bitter feeling between the two brothers, told the Gardaí that he wouldn't be surprised if Bernard had put Lar 'out of the way' — unless it turned out that he had visited his aunt's house.

On Thursday 3 December local Gardaí searched the Kirwan house for Lar's shotgun and for anything that might give a clue to his disappearance, but nothing suspicious was discovered. The gun was in Peter Kirwan's house, as Bernard had said. Bernard gave a cautioned statement, in which he said that he had left his brother in the house on that Saturday night.

'I was leaving the house between 8 and 9 p.m. Laurence was doing himself up. He was wearing a greenish grey pullover and he had the looking glass on the table and I believe he was doing his hair before it when I was leaving. It appeared to me he was going some place,' Bernard Kirwan said in a statement recorded by Detectives Tom Mullen and Edward Quinlan and Sgt Michael Hunt.

He told them that he walked along the line of the canal to his brother Peter's house and left a bottle of milk there, met no one, and continued on to his sister, Mrs Conroy in Newtown. 'I am unable to say what time I entered my sister's but I was there for the Irish news at 10.10 p.m. Some time after the Irish news was over I left for home. When I arrived the light was out. I don't know what time I got home at. The front door was on the latch. I came into the kitchen, there was nobody in the house when I entered, and the turf fire was fairly good. The 'horse' was beside the fire but Laurence's clothes were gone off it.

'My brother Laurence did not give me any indication that he was going away beyond that he was dressing himself up and that it was customary for him to go away frequently. I can't remember him ever going away before for such a long period,' said Bernard.

On the Thursday, two days after the funeral, Lehman met Anna Finucane again. She had already been interviewed by the Gardaí and she asked him whether he expected any further questions to be asked.

He then asked a favour of her: that she would tell the Gardaí she knew nothing about his life, whether he was married or single or any other details.

'I can't and I won't tell lies to the Gardaí,' she said, adding, 'What about those poisons you were working on in the shop?'

'I got rid of those a long time ago, and anyway, you know nothing about them,' he replied curtly.

That evening Lehman called to Nurse McCaigue's lodgings. He told her that Margaret was dead and that her death was due to heart trouble. 'A post mortem examination has been held and nothing was found. Isn't it plain it must have been the heart?' he asked her. But the nurse had had enough of his lies. She did not believe it was a bigamous marriage. She had heard that his wife Margaret Lehman had died on the way to hospital, she told him bluntly. She wanted nothing more to do with him. She had also learned that she was supposed to be the real owner of the coffee shop, and that Lehman's claims to own another shop in Camden Street nearer the city centre were false.

The following week, Anna Finucane received a letter from him postmarked 29 March, Carlow. 'Please close the shop or do whatever you should like or think best. I am terribly sorry. Will call at your residence when I get back, sincerely, Jim,' it read. It was her last communication from Lehman. When he hadn't returned by the following Monday, 3 April, she went to the shop which had already lost significantly, and sold off the remaining stock and fixtures, salvaging some of her £40 investment.

On Friday 7th it was realised that Lehman was missing, and the hunt was on. His children were being cared for, so the Gardaí knew they were searching for a lone man away from his usual haunts and in wartime Ireland the major cities and border towns were crowded with unfamiliar faces and provided an easy hiding place for someone on the run.

On Saturday 8 April, the day after, James McCaigue with an address in Belfast, booked into the Oriel hotel in Monaghan town. He left on the 10th for Belfast and had returned again on the 12th. He appeared to be a refined, intelligent man, who was clean shaven and wore spectacles.

121

He told the manageress of the hotel, Miss Kathleen Sherry, that he was an American airman, single, and that he had relations of the same name in Castleblayney, Co Monaghan. He also showed her a ring and a wristwatch a widow had given him as a lucky token to keep him safe every time he went on a mission.

He told her he had to go to Belfast and would return on the Friday, but he returned two days earlier, saying he had got an extension of his sick leave. He didn't sign the register, and asked her to do so in his stead, as he was in a hurry to take a bath. McCaigue also told her he had forgotten his identity papers, and when she asked how he had crossed the border, he had laughed, saying the officials knew him too well to object.

A friend of the manageress was told by McCaigue that he was in the Canadian Army. He brought her out, and gave her small gifts. A schoolteacher he met at lunch on Sunday 9th was also shown the lucky mascots, the watch and the ring. McCaigue gave the ring to the teacher, Margaret Kelly from County Tyrone, after he had regaled her with his war exploits and had taken her to a dance. He had told her he was born outside Monaghan town.

Two customs officers, and a taxi driver from whom he sought a loan of money, were all given different stories about his background. The taxi driver, Charlie Scott from Belfast who had refused to give him the loan, had joked with the hard-drinking McCaigue that he had a fortune in gold fillings in his mouth.

In a number of the bars in the town, however, he had introduced himself in his usual easy manner as Captain Lehman, an airman with the Canadian Air Force who had variously been a rear gunner and a bomber pilot. He was now 'grounded' because of his age, and he feared, he told a rapt audience, that he would never be allowed to fly again.

It was not long before he was about to get his wings clipped, as he tried the impossible — to maintain a dual identity in a small town.

On Tuesday 11 April a description of Lehman, the thirty-eight year old charmer, had been prepared, and the Garda authorities backed the decision to have it published in all the national newspapers to alert the public. It appeared the following day. By Thursday 13th, a plainclothes detective had been despatched to keep tabs on a suspicious character, answering to the description of the wanted man, James Lehman.

'The following morning McCaigue was quite cool, calm and collected when, with one one shilling and two pence in his pocket he called the manageress and ordered that his breakfast be taken to his bedroom,' wrote Supt George Lawlor.

But before it arrived two Gardaí knocked at the door, and entered. McCaigue was still in bed. 'What's your name' they asked him.

'James McCaigue. I am an American airman, and I am now grounded,' was his reply as he sat up straight in bed in his pyjamas.

Det Sgt James Cahill asked him for his identity card, and McCaigue said all his papers were in Belfast. Sgt Thomas Keating showed McCaigue a photograph of James Lehman published in the *Irish Independent* with the statement requesting information printed below it. 'Do you know that man?' asked the Sergeant.

'I never saw the man,' said McCaigue after a long pause.

McCaigue dressed and was brought to the Garda station where his clothes and suitcase were searched while he was served breakfast in a cell in the two-storey Garda barracks that looked like a Victorian school.

In the Garda superintendent's office, McCaigue, who was clearly identified as Lehman, denied that he had ever been married or had any children. He had never given any girl a ring, and had stayed in hotels since he had come to Ireland. He also denied that he had ever been in Dublin, although when his pockets were turned out Gardaí found two tram tickets for destinations in the capital. Only a small amount of cash was found in McCaigue's possession, but the two distinctive gold fillings which had been in his teeth were discovered in the pockets of his jacket — most likely on their way to the pawnbrokers, Gardaí surmised.

Lehman *alias* McCaigue had gone to Belfast on 12 April to enlist in the Royal Air Force, in an attempt to take on a new identity and life abroad. He called himself James Joseph Feely, of the Oriel Monaghan — the name of the man signed into the Oriel Hotel register, just in front of his McCaigue alias. He said he was born in London, had come to Ireland with his sister in 1938 and had bought a farm, but was a cook. Because he had no papers, the recruiting officer decided to defer his application. Gardaí discovered that all the presents he had given to women in Monaghan town were items that had belonged to his wife, buried less than three weeks previously.

Lehman was taken to Dublin and charged with the murder of his wife. The defence case was that his wife had committed suicide, it was up to the prosecution to prove murder.

The courthouse was crowded for each of the nine days of the trial. Women, in particular, filled the benches of the Green Street courthouse, queuing outside to catch a glimpse of the handsome devil charged with murdering his wife.

One potential juror, who said that he had a conscientious objection to capital punishment, was excused from jury duty. Another, who told the bench that he had been suffering from nose bleeds, was also excused.

Dressed in a smart, well-cut suit, the accused man told the court 'I am James Herbert Lehman,' and pleaded 'Not guilty' when the charge was read out to him.

Lehman was the first witness for the defence, and when asked if he had given his wife poison, he replied 'No, Sir.' His counsel Mr C. Casey, S.C., said that Lehman was devoted to his wife and children, and that he had no motive to kill her as he would lose £4 a week from his pension by her death. Lehman, if he had committed murder, had made mistakes which would make a schoolboy blush, he said. Firstly he had picked a poison which was easily discovered, and had supposedly gone to the one chemist who knew him, and had then brought the poison crystal to his own premises to flake it into a powder in front of a witness, after telling her it was a deadly poison.

There were two explanations for Lehman's behaviour in Monaghan, that he was trying to flee the scene of the crime or that he had a disordered mind. Could anyone say his action was consistent with sanity, his counsel asked.

Lehman would tell the truth now, and reveal a secret he had kept until now, said Mr Casey. Both he and his wife were drug addicts. They took morphine, he said.

Lehman, called to the witness box to give evidence on the fifth day of the trial, said that he was an orphan, born in 1905 near Montreal, Canada and adopted by a Dutch family called Hianes. From 1921–25 he studied law in Philadelphia. He had married in 1933 and had divorced three years later because 'of religious difficulties over the child and because my wife was mental,' he said. Lehman was later to admit to Mr Justice Maguire that in fact he was born in 1899.

He had joined the US army and later, in 1939, he joined the Canadian army in Ontario and they listed him as William Martin; later he took the name Lehman. He met Margaret Hayden in Aldershot, married and returned to her home in Ireland. In 1943, a year ago, they started taking morphine and both had persistently taken the drug since then, he said.

He claimed that he had received a letter from his wife when he was in hospital in Leopardstown saying she was previously married and sought to be released voluntarily. He said his wife would take whiskey with aspirins to satisfy her craving, and threatened to take her life unless he got her morphine. He eventually found an American medical officer named Drewitt who came to their rooms and gave her two injections. In response to questioning from prosecuting counsel, George Murnaghan, he said he could not describe the American doctor who had given his wife injections, nor could he remember the names or describe either the students or the pub where he claimed to have met them when he discussed carrying out tests with acids on coffee to test for its purity.

'What experience, if any, had you as a chemist?' Mr Murnaghan asked him.

'None,' came the reply.

'Or as a doctor?' asked Murnaghan.

'None,' came the reply again.

'And how did you think you were going to get any result from the experiment?' pressed the prosecution counsel.

'I was only going by the advice of certain medical students,' said Lehman. The only detail he could recall, to locate or describe the pubs was that the seating was done out in red upholstery.

Lehman told his own counsel that he had taken the poison home to his flat, where his wife helped him with the experiments on coffee.

Dr Patrick O'Connor who had a string of qualifications including Professor of Pathology at the Royal College of Surgeons, and extern examiner at the National University, dismissed the coffee tests Lehman described to the court as 'of no value'.

Lehman had told Margaret he was using a deadly poison, and kept it stored on the top shelf of the linen closet. In her suicide note, which he had destroyed to save shaming their children, aged one and three, she said she had decided to take the poison as she could no longer live as a drug addict.

This addiction was not something he told the doctors at the hospital about when he was admitted on the 19th, nor had he told her family about the addiction, he admitted under cross examination.

He said that he had been away all afternoon on the day his wife died, visiting a young widow who lived nearby. The widow, despite visiting him in jail 83 times since his arrest and appearance in court, later contradicted him, saying he had visited her the previous day.

Lehman denied that he had ever told Miss Finucane that his wife had died from poisoning, denied that he had ever asked her to telephone Miss McCaigue and said he had phoned his lawyer, and also denied that he had spoken about poison when Sgt Shepperd called to the flat to interview him.

Lehman said that his wife's death had so upset him that he took four morphine tablets and some codeine after her death, and he could remember nothing until some time around the middle of July. This statement was called into question by Mrs O'Callaghan's evidence that he had flourished a newspaper at her on 7 April and demanded 'Would you not think I had done it?'

Lehman admitted under cross examination that he had 'forgotten' to tell Sgt Sheppherd, when he called, that there was cyanide in the flat. He had also omitted to mention that there was cyanide in the flat — in the linen closet according to his own statement to the court — to either Mrs O'Callaghan or to Nurse McCaigue.

Lehman's testimony in the witness box was the first time anyone had ever heard that the couple were morphine addicts or that deadly cyanide had been stored in the house, said the prosecution. However, what was certain was that Lehman left the house and returned shortly afterwards on the afternoon his wife died. Was that visit perhaps to fetch the poison, counsel asked the jury?

Dr Harry Lee Parker said that he had examined Lehman and found him to be a psychopath, very unstable and a pathological liar. But he was not insane, and was capable of full responsibility for his actions. Lehman had told him about his memory loss, and this could be attributed to learning that his wife had killed herself. A man might possibly lose his memory for a time as a result of such a discovery, he said.

The defence also made the point that the amount of cyanide used to kill Mrs Lehman had not been specified. They claimed there was ample opportunity for her to take the poison, and wash and replace the vessel from which she drank it before being found crumpled up in the bedroom.

The case of the 'Mad Monk' Grigori Rasputin, who, although poisoned with heavily doctored wine and chocolate cakes, suffered no ill effects, was cited to back up this claim. However, doctors called for the prosecution said that either Rasputin had not been poisoned with cyanide at all or else he had supernatural powers!

In his charge to the jury, Judge Martin Maguire said that Lehman was not charged with lying, or with obtaining money from young women. 'You are not here for the purposes of sympathy but to investigate a crime,' he said.

The case depended on circumstantial evidence, and the nature of the poison was that it worked instantly. No poison had been found in the room, nor had there been any sign of a drinking vessel in the room. The assumption of suicide was based on the letter, according to the accused, which had been shown to nobody and found by nobody, said the Judge. On 25 October 1944 Lehman was found guilty of the murder of his wife, and was sentenced to be executed on Wednesday, 15 November. When asked if he had anything to say, he replied , 'I have nothing to say.'

Lehman appealed the case and a retrial was ordered. He was found guilty a second time, and was executed on 19 March 1945 which was, by coincidence, the anniversary of his wife's murder.

Lehman wrote his life story in a child's lined exercise book while he awaited Pierrepoint, the executioner, in Mountjoy jail. But even in his final days his pencilled scribble showed he was still inventing stories. He was a fully trained efficiency expert, he wrote. And as if someone might some day doubt it, despite the evidence of his commercial failure, he wrote, 'I have been trained in commerce. I know business. I am an efficiency expert and that is correct.' His diary ended with the words, 'I am innocent of it all.' Then with nothing more to do except wait for the hangman, he began reading a French novel, Ferdinand Celine's 'Voyage au bout de la nuit' — (Voyage to the end of the night).

During the Gardaí investigation Lehman's fingerprints were taken and copies were sent to the FBI, Scotland Yard and the police in Montreal, Canada. 'The FBI were able to report back that Lehman had ten convictions in the USA,' wrote George Lawlor. 'They included robbery, grand larceny, false pretences, fraud and other offences. He had been convicted under the aliases Arthur Edwin, Arthur James, James E. Richards, and James E. James. 'He had deserted from the US Army, for which he had also enlisted and was wanted in Canada for three offences of fraud, escape and breaking parole. In England too he had been convicted, and received a six months' sentence for false pretences under the name James Herbert Lehman.'

He concluded : 'As far as could be ascertained his true name was George James.'

10.

The Howth Murder

'HOW often has the intensity of emotion betrayed a man — or a woman — into making that one false step that can never be recalled?' asked Supt George Lawlor after a particularly vicious killing. 'How tragic can it be when that one false step has at the same time taken away the life of one loved deeply, perhaps too well? Those who live ordinary humdrum lives, untouched by the depths of such tragic emotions and feelings, may find it hard to understand their terrible strength and the more terrible consequences of the failure to control them.' The following case goes some way to perhaps giving an understanding of that depth of emotion.

Brackenhurst, which overlooks Howth Harbour, gives a clear view of the harbour. Along the coast, Clontarf stretches out to Dublin docks and on to Dun Laoghaire in the distance, with the Sugarloaf mountain providing a dramatic backdrop to the capital. Near the summit of Howth Head, Brackenhurst, with its large pasture fields and overgrown spots dotted with furze and white-thorn bushes was a favourite spot for lovers during the summer months. 'The summer of 1948 was no exception,' wrote George Lawlor, 'but on 27 May there was enacted a tragedy that was to make Brackenhurst, for a time, a rendezvous of morbid sensation seekers.'

On the morning of 28 May, farm labourer James McKenna, who lived in a terraced house in Howth, went to inspect cattle which were on the lands at Brackenhurst. He saw something 'like a bundle' lying in the field, and, suspicious, he called to his employer, farm owner Joseph Rickard. The two men went to the field, but couldn't see the body from the road. Once in the field they found the body lying on its side in one of a number of hollows popular with courting couples. Rickard told McKenna to stay at the spot and he went for the Gardaí at Howth. They had found the body of a woman, lying

128

on her right side in the depression, partly hidden by two bushes. The woman looked as if she was asleep — except there was blood on her mouth and under her nostrils where it had congealed after bleeding.

The Technical Bureau team, called to the scene later and led by George Lawlor, swung into an immediate routine, and in this case the first priority was to identify the woman. The body was photographed exactly where it was discovered before the State Pathologist, Dr John McGrath, had it moved to the city morgue beside Store Street Garda station, to carry out a post mortem examination.

There was nothing on the woman's body to identify her. But a search of the area around the body quickly turned up two newspapers, a *Daily Express* and an *Evening Herald*, published the previous day, which were found spread out on the ground in the hollow. They were both torn and crumpled, and appeared to have been used to sit on, as a protection against the cold damp grass. A few feet away in the grass two good quality fountain pens were found, one a Parker and the other a Waterman. The Waterman was particularly distinctive, for the clip on its cap to secure it to a jacket or shirt pocket was missing. Twelve burnt-out matchsticks were also discovered on the grassy area near the spot where the dead woman lay.

A handbag which had been hidden under a nearby furze bush was also uncovered in the search. It was open and its contents had been rifled. On the ground beside the bag were a lipstick, a mirrored powder compact, a lace handkerchief, three headache tablets and other odds and ends, but most importantly of all, a letter. The top of the envelope was neatly torn, and it was addressed to Mrs K. Boyne, with the business address, Prescotts, Drumcondra. The letter, addressed to 'My dearest darling Kay' was a love letter, and was signed 'John'.

As Gardaí travelled into the city to check on the dead woman's identity, the post mortem commenced. Dr McGrath had visited the scene of the killing, and found the body with the left leg crossed over the right while the woman's left hand was tucked well inside her overcoat. There were bloodstains on the back of the collar and the right sleeve of the stone-coloured overcoat. A section of grass near the body was flattened, but there were no obvious signs of struggle in the area.

There were the obvious signs of a number of 'very violent' blows to the woman's head. He estimated 'three substantial blows' and at least one of them had smashed her dentures. One section of these was found knocked from her mouth onto the grass nearby. The bones on both sides of the woman's face had been smashed into tiny fragments. She could have been kicked in the head as she lay on the ground, although at least one deep wound to the left side of her face would have had to be inflicted with a blunt object — but he ruled out the possibility of a shoe causing so much damage.

Dr McGrath estimated that the woman had died within an hour or two of midnight the previous evening. The body had also been dragged by the legs across the grass, but the lack of substantial earth or grass marking would suggest, for a short distance only. The lungs were congested, and he concluded that the wounds to the face and head had been inflicted while the woman was alive. She had been strangled into an unconscious or dying condition and the blows were then inflicted thus hastening her death. Her death was due to shock and asphyxia caused by manual strangulation.

The Gardaí quickly established her identity as Kay Boyne, a thirty-eight-year old widow who lived with her brother-in-law at Geraldine Street. She had married in 1936, and had two sons aged ten and eight years who had been placed in an orphanage when her husband died in 1946. She worked as a clerk with Prescotts the cleaners in Drumcondra.

A further check showed that at 1 p.m., later on the same day as she had been discovered on the open hillside, she had been reported missing by her brother-in-law at Mountjoy Garda station, beside the prison on Dublin's North Circular Road. She had told him she was going to the pictures the previous evening and had left home at 7.30 p.m., but she never returned.

Supt Lawlor's team of investigators' task was to fill in the missing hours and find her killer. One of the first people to come under suspicion was the dead woman's boyfriend, John Fanning, a twenty-eight-year old chemist's assistant.

He lived at home with his father in Shandon Park, Phibsboro, and was serving his time with the chemists firm of Hayes, Conyngham in George's Street. Fanning was switched from one branch chemist to another, and met Kathleen Boyne regularly when he was on temporary transfer to Drumcondra on the north side of the city. They had been going out for eighteen months at the time of her death, despite the fact that he had again been moved, this time to the Ballsbridge branch.

Fanning was well known to her family, had attended card parties at her brother-in-law's home in Crumlin and was a regular caller to Geraldine Street. On the evening Kay was killed he had been at the house having tea with Kay and her two boys who were out from the orphanage on a visit for the afternoon. Fanning left the house in the afternoon. Kay later brought her sons back to the orphanage, and was seen for the last time alive by her niece Mary Flanagan as she closed the front door behind them.

The following day Mary rang Fanning at the chemist's shop in Ballsbridge. Had he met Kay or left her home the previous evening, she wanted to know. 'To tell you the truth, I did not,' Fanning told her. His speech was excited then and she couldn't understand what he was saying. 'She met some friends in a car at the bus stop and got a lift home,' he told her. But he wasn't sure of their name, it was Howley or Howlett or something like that, he said. The car was packed and there was only room for one and he told her to take the lift and he would get home by the bus.

'She's missing. There must have been an accident,' he said as Mary Flanagan tried to butt into his rambling speech. 'Why did I let her go in the car? Good God, good God,' he kept repeating. Fanning continued talking, making little sense, but Mary remembered he told her, 'They were all jarred,' referring to the crowd in the car.

Fanning slammed the phone back into the receiver cradle, startling another apprentice in the shop, Kathleen Noonan. He turned away from the phone and walked a few steps to the prescription counter and put his head between his hands, saying 'Oh, God' over and over again. His hands were shaking.

'Did you get bad news?' asked Kathleen with concern in her voice. Fanning was terribly upset, and told her he had 'a lady friend' and she had not gone home last night, and her bed hadn't been slept in.

'Is she your girlfriend?' asked the curious Kathleen.

'She's my fiancée,' he replied.

'Well then, when did you last see her?' asked Kathleen.

'That's the point,' he said. 'I was with her last night. We were to have gone to the pictures, but we went to Howth instead.'

Fanning said they went to Howth by train and went for a drink together. They met friends of his fiancée's, who were 'a horsey type who were jarring heavily'. He didn't pay much attention to them, he said, and when they were leaving they offered Kay a lift. It was only a small car and there was only one small seat free, so he urged his fiancée to take the lift and he'd go home by bus.

Fanning smoked incessantly as they talked, saying he was 'desperately worried. I always get worried, I worried ever since the car went over the pier at Skerries,' he said referring to an earlier accident. 'But if the worst comes to the worst thank God, I'm working in a chemist's shop,' he said.

'Why?' asked Kathleen.

'I can always fix myself up a little dose,' he said.

Kathleen was shocked at the suggestion of suicide and told him not to be silly, to put the idea out of his head, and bustled about trying to comfort him. Fanning sat chain smoking, and when she commented on it, he said he was so worried he'd already smoked forty cigarettes. He ate little for lunch, but his mood improved. He thanked Kathleen for her kindness, and told her not to mind him being gruff as he was upset, then he left the shop to go to George's Street to collect his wages.

That evening at about 7.30 p.m., Fanning called to Flanagan's house in Geraldine Street, where Kathleen Boyne lived. 'This is awful about Kathleen,' said Fanning shaking hands with a worried Jim Flanagan, Kathleen's brother-in-law, who answered the door to him.

'I don't know what happened her,' said Jim. 'A Garda's just arrived. He said they'd found her handbag, then you knocked, come on in,' and Flanagan led the way back into the house.

Inspector Hennon, from Howth Garda station was waiting for them. He was investigating the woman's disappearance, and he needed statements from them both as they had to try and trace the woman's last movements.

Jim Flanagan sat down, and, looking at Fanning, noticed he had gone very pale and swayed unsteadily as if about to faint.

'Oh, God why did I let her go in the car?' asked Fanning. The inspector told them he needed statements from both of them, as they had to trace the dead woman's last movements.

'I met Kay last night outside the Carlton cinema, in O'Connell Street at 7.45,' said Fanning. They had taken the 8 o'clock bus to Howth and went into the lounge of the Royal Hotel there and had a few drinks together. They left the hotel at about ten o'clock and walked up past the chapel and turned left. Fanning said he was smoking as they walked along the road talking. They walked on until they reached a broken stone wall where they turned left. They had stopped along the way, and sat on the grass margin for a few minutes before continuing. They were back at the bus stop at ten past eleven, said Fanning.

As they stood waiting for the bus a car came along. He thought it was an Austin, he wasn't sure, but it pulled up beside them. The people inside had recognised Mrs Boyne and addressed her familiarly as 'Kay'. There were seven people in the car, four men and three women and they were 'jarred', but had room for one person if they wanted a lift back into town, said Fanning. Kay took the lift.

Fanning's voice cracked as he spoke and he was 'excited', recalled Jim Flanagan. Fanning said he stood at the bus stop for a while and decided he'd go for a drink, before returning home. He went into the nearest pub, Eugene Cassidy's, where he had a few pints, and by the time he came out the last bus and train had gone. He started walking home, but was lucky enough to get a lift after walking about half way back into town.

The inspector asked him if he'd mind going to Howth and pointing out the last place he'd seen Kathleen. Certainly not, said Fanning, but he wanted to get in touch with his own home first as he hadn't been home yet since leaving work. They detoured by Shandon Park, and fifteen minutes later were heading out along the coast road by Clontarf for Howth.

Fanning sat in the back of the squad car with the inspector, while a plainclothes sergeant drove the car. Three times on the way to Howth Fanning put his hands to his head, and asked aloud, 'Oh God, why did I let her go with them? What could have happened to her?' The inspector wrote down what he said.

Their first call was to the Garda station for an update on the post mortem. The inspector went behind the counter and left Fanning sitting in the public area by the hall. In a quiet voice, so they couldn't be overheard, the duty sergeant told him the result of the post mortem examination — that the girl had been murdered. She had been strangled and had received a severe beating. 'Oh God, this is terrible. Terrible,' moaned Fanning when the inspector told him that Kay Boyne was dead.

Fanning was told he was one of the last people to have seen Mrs Boyne alive and he was cautioned. Fanning said he knew nothing of how the woman had met her death, and he agreed to point out the places to the inspector where he had brought Kay the previous evening. The sun glinted off the sea in Dublin Bay, but it had lost its heat and there was a chill in the long evening air as Fanning pointed out the broken stone wall at the junction of the Rocky and Nashville roads.

'I asked him where did he and Mrs Boyne go when they reached the junction the previous evening,' said Inspector Hennon.

'Kay and I always turn to the left here and return to the bus stop,' said Fanning.

'But what way did you turn last night?' persisted Hennon. Fanning didn't answer. He looked up the Rocky Road. 'Were you ever up that road?' asked the Inspector.

'We were only up a little bit,' came the hesitant reply.

'How far is only a little bit?' asked Inspector Hennon. Fanning didn't reply, instead he walked up part of the road, looking at the grass verge. 'We sat down somewhere here last night,' he said. He walked on another few yards, still examining the grass verges, 'Kay and I sat here last night,' he said pointing to a spot, which the inspector noted down with Fanning's comments, in his small pocket notebook.

They returned to the car and drove back towards Howth, where Fanning pointed out the bus stop and Cassidy's pub where he said he'd had drink the night before. The detective sergeant parked the car and the three men went into the bar of the pub. None of the barmen remembered serving Fanning the previous evening. Eugene Cassidy, who had called out the barmen to help the Gardaí investigate Fanning's claim, was standing behind the counter.

'Haven't you a dark-haired barman here?' asked Fanning.

'No, indeed we do not,' replied the pub owner. The only dark-haired barman employed by Cassidy's had left over four months previously. There had been four customers in the pub between eleven and midnight said Tom Cassidy, the son of the owner, and he knew them all to see.

Fanning was brought back to the station, and was told he was being detained in connection with the murder inquiry and was asked if he was prepared to make a statement detailing where he went and what he did the night before.

It was a long statement, written on the lined and cream-coloured foolscap pages provided by government stationers.

He had first met Mrs Boyne in November 1946, he said. Since then he had met her twice a week, and although nothing had ever been formalised, and he had never bought her a ring, it was understood they were to get married when he qualified.

He had met Kay the previous evening and they had taken the bus to Howth. They had a couple of drinks in the Royal Hotel and later walked up the hill, entered a field and he spread out some newspapers on the ground which they sat on. They stayed there for about fifteen minutes, and then got up to go back down the hill. They had to climb through a barbed wire fence to get on to the road and Kay snagged her coat on a strand of wire. 'My coat is ruined,' she had said looking at the tear.

'I'll buy you another,' Fanning said.

His statement continued: 'She replied "I can get plenty to buy for me." I said, "You are vexed." I put my arm around her but she broke away. After the row we walked down the lane. We did not talk much. When we came to where we parted I said "OK. Enjoy yourself."'

Fanning said he walked down the hill until he reached the bus terminus. The last time he saw her was at about 11 p.m. that Thursday night as she stood at the gate at Nashville Park. He discovered that the last train had gone, and thumbed a lift from a passing motorist.

Before being ushered into a cell Fanning's pockets were emptied as he was searched. In the outside breast pocket of his sports coat were two GNR bus tickets. On the turn-up of the left leg of his trousers were two small bloodstains, and there were two more small bloodstains on the other leg of his flannel trousers.

Fanning was asked where they came from, but refused to say anything about them until his solicitor was present. He was also asked to pull up his trousers, and the Gardaí saw a scratch on each leg. There was a scratch one inch long on his left wrist.

'If I am being detained I do not wish to say anything until I see my solicitor. In my job I have to deal with a lot of chemicals,' he said before entering the cell in Howth Garda station.

He was charged that evening with the murder of Kay Boyne and was transferred to Mountjoy jail to await trail.

An interesting feature of the case, which was to be put forward by the defence, now emerged: Fanning had a rare physical abnormality which was discovered when he underwent a routine medical check on admission to the jail. The medical officer at the jail, Dr T. Murphy, discovered that Fanning's heart and liver were transposed, his heart was where his liver should have been and vice versa. This was due to a congenital defect and was liable to affect the victim's mental capabilities, said the doctor's report. Fanning was badly developed physically — weak, round-shouldered and he had a 'fish-mouthed' expression which was 'usually associated with stupidity'.

The medical report also noted that there were five scratches on Fanning's left shoulder which could have been made by a sharp object like a pin, or alternatively a woman's fingernails. On his left breast there was another scratch two inches long which was surrounded by a bruise about the size of a half-crown. All the bruises and cuts appeared to be of recent origin. There were also scratches on his legs which could have been caused by briars.

As Fanning awaited trial the Gardaí delved deeper into his background and his relationship with the dead woman; they also continued their collection and collation of evidence in the case under Supt Lawlor, for final presentation as a Book of Evidence.

One of the witnesses to the couple's night out on the 27th, tracked down by Supt Lawlor's investigation team, was the bus conductor, John Delaney , who had been working on the Eden Quay to Howth bus route. He had issued 31 eight-penny tickets to Howth on the run on the 27th, and was able to identify two tickets found in Fanning's pockets.

Another witness, Michael Mitchell, was the white-jacketed bar waiter in the Royal Howth Hotel that evening, and he told Supt Lawlor that he had served Fanning and a woman at about 9 p.m. in the hotel lounge. They ordered four rounds of drinks and 'seemed to have very little to say to each other', he said. The man had been wearing a sports jacket and was carrying an off-white showerproof coat on his arm. He also carried a copy of the *Evening Herald.* A woman living in the village of Howth was also in the hotel lounge that evening having a drink with her husband. The hotel was always busy during the spring and summer months and she had got to know Kay Boyne by sight. She described Kay as wearing a cream or stone-coloured coat and looking rather pale, and gave a description that fitted John Fanning, specifically saying he was dark and of a slight build.

Mrs Annie Mathews, who lived on the Rocky Road, also saw the couple that evening. It was about 10.20 p.m. when she saw them coming up the road, near the pathway that led into the Bracken-hurst field. It was twilight at the time and they were walking slowly; she didn't pay them much attention as it as not unusual to see couples on the road since the field was a well-known spot tor lovers. That was the last sighting George Lawlor could find of the dead woman Kay Boyne. Later that evening however, John Fanning was seen by a number of people, alone.

Cathal Meehan, who lived in the village by the East Pier, was able to identify Fanning — recognising his looks and describing his clothes — as the man he saw running towards the railway station at about 11.45 on the night of 27 May.

It was just before midnight when Fanning burst into the station, breathlessly asking if the last train to the city had gone. It had, it was gone six minutes, said railway porter Patrick O'Connor who also subsequently identified Fanning.

Fanning had just left the station when a car travelling towards the city appeared. He flagged it down and asked the driver, Tom Dunne from Fairview on the city's northside, if he'd give him a lift as he'd missed the train. Sure, said Dunne. Both he and his passenger Alice Currivan from Oxmantown Road chatted to him long enough during the forty-minute drive to recognise and identify him again. It was twenty minutes to one when they dropped him off at Doyle's Corner.

As the search for witnesses continued, the hunt for a possible weapon used to beat the dead woman continued also. It was to last for two days as a team of fourteen Gardaí systematically examined the field where the body was found on their hands and knees. When the field had been searched the net was cast wider and two days were spent unsuccessfully trying to find a weapon. But the Garda search of the murder site did turn up other valuable evidence — two fountain pens, a Parker and a Waterman. The Parker had apparently been borrowed from Fanning's employers, but the second pen was his own and was identifiable because it had no clip.

Twelve burnt-out matchsticks were also found in the field — an indication that Fanning had searched the area looking for something before leaving — most likely the pens which slipped from his pocket during the killing and which were traceable back to him, suspected George Lawlor.

A search of Fanning's house on 29 May by Supt Lawlor's team turned up vital pieces of evidence, inextricably linking Fanning to the death of Kay Boyne. Her handbag had been emptied out on the ground near her dead body. Elsie Hunter, an assistant in Prescotts where Kay worked, knew she always used a Mentmore fountain pen to write with, and that she always carried it around in her bag. That pen was found by a detective wrapped in a piece of material in the breast pocket of a jacket hanging in John Fanning's bedroom at his home. The detective sergeant also found a light showerproof coat with a red stain on the right-hand side near the label. There were red marks at the end of the left sleeve and there were green marks all along the right side of the coat.

Supt Lawlor's attention to detail and his insistence that all leads should be chased to their end brought out further evidence. In the chemist's shop after the murder Fanning had told the young Kathleen Noonan about his worries about his fiancée. She had told him about how she had borrowed a Parker fountain pen from another assistant in the shop, and now she couldn't find it and the

137

likely trouble her carelessness would cause. He too swapped a confidence, telling her, 'I lost my own pen last night too. I did not miss it until I was going to address an envelope. It had no clip and would fall out of my pocket if I stooped.' Kathleen Noonan was able to identify the Parker pen found at the scene of the murder as the one she had borrowed from a colleague and thought she had misplaced. She also recognised the handbag found near the dead body as belonging to Kay Boyne, a present from Fanning.

'In a search of his home,' Supt Lawlor wrote, 'fourteen letters were found signed 'Kay' and it was clear from their contents that he was infatuated with the deceased woman but that she was endeavouring to break off the courtship and had decided to finish relations with him. Probably with that end in view she had met him on the night of 27 May.'

The strained relationship noted by the waiter in the hotel between the two on the night of the murder, was well-known to John Fanning's aunt Mary, who lived on the city's North Circular Road. She had met Mrs Boyne on one occasion, and knew that John had had a number of rows with her. He was often depressed after a row and would telephone her seeking reassurances and comfort, she recalled.

At about 2 o'clock on the afternoon after the murder she got a phone call from John. He said that he was 'always in trouble or worrying,' and when she asked what was wrong with him, he said Kay had not been home the previous night. Mary Fanning tried to cheer him up, telling him not to worry. She'd turn up and would soon be home. Then he told her they had had another row and parted, going home separately.

The love letter found beside the dead woman's body bore testimony to John Fanning's intense feelings. In it he refers to a change in her feelings for him and his desire to continue their relationship. It had been written just one month before her death:

> My dearest darling Kay,
> I have gone through hell for the past few weeks, and only for your sympathy and kindness, I do not know what I would have done. A whole lifetime of service to you would not even repay you. But, my darling, please do not give me up, but let me prove my love for you, and I swear to you that you will never regret the waiting. At the moment I feel crushed and desolate and humbled and have no one to turn to in a cold and dreary world for comfort but you, my own sweetest little Queen.

138

My destiny is in your hands — a life of love and happiness with you or a life broken and crushed with anguish without you. I know you are probably fed up with me, but please darling give me a chance, and I will make up for everything. God knows how I have tried to love and serve you, and how I have adored you, and will go on loving and adoring and worshipping you always,

John.

Kay had replied to the letter saying simply she didn't want to respond to such a 'long epistle'. Fanning had just failed his examinations again, and she said she'd have to give him up in favour of someone richer.

The trial of John Fanning for murder opened on Monday 18 October 1948 in Green Street courthouse. It was to last for a week, and a total of 47 prosecution witnesses were to be called. Fanning pleaded not guilty to the charge.

No person saw the actual murder, so the prosecution case had to depend on circumstantial evidence, said Counsel for the State, Mr Charles F. Casey, S.C.

He outlined Kay's family circumstances and her eighteen-month-old relationship with Fanning. Letters they had written to each other would show the state which their affections had reached. 'John Fanning was very much in love with Kathleen Boyne,' said Mr Casey.

The dead woman had received five blows to her head, two of them were strong enough to break bones in her face. There was evidence that the accused man was excited the next day and smoked incessantly. 'You will have to ask yourselves how they separated,' he said, addressing the jury. 'Was it in innocent fashion or did they part, as the State would urge, he going his way having murdered her?'

Sir John Esmonde, S.C. for the defence, said that if Fanning 'had murdered Mrs Boyne in the language, idiom and sense that murder is understood in these courts, then it was a most senseless and absurd crime. That is something that may have struck you from the beginning of this case,' he said to the jury.

If Fanning intended to bring Kay Boyne to the field, a place used by courting couples, and murder her, he had picked a ridiculous location. Within a hundred yards of the spot where the body was found there were families living, although admittedly there were six depressions in the field, he said. He suggested there would be a lot of traffic in the field as darkness fell and courting couples visited the area. There was no motive for the killing, the place was absurd, the time was absurd and no weapon had been found, he said.

The letters Fanning wrote to Kay Boyne showed he was wildly in love with her. Just 48 hours before her death he had written to her. He was so 'demented with love,' said Sir John, that his first thought of the day was for her. In that last letter he addressed her as 'My dearest darling Kay'. He had gone to a play with his father, he wrote, but had missed her so much that he had taken a drink as a stimulant because he missed the stimulation of his own 'wee widow'. Five months earlier he had written her another letter, saying she was the only thing he had to live for — 'Please my darling, when I am away, think kindly of me. You are my first and last love for always, you and the kids, that is all I want.'

The case was a human conundrum, there was no revolver, hammer, and no bottle of poison. If Fanning had malice aforethought he had had the whole of Hayes, Conyngham and Robinson's chemists' shelves at his disposal,' claimed Sir John.

Even if the jury had removed all reasonable doubt from their minds that Fanning had killed Kay Boyne, they must still have the doubt whether he was a murderer within the definition of murder as known to the law. They might have already come to the conclusion that the accused had killed Mrs Boyne, but, he said, they could not come to the conclusion that it was done with malice aforethought. 'Didn't all the evidence point to the fact that either the man was mad or else he never intended to kill Kay Boyne or do her harm? One explanation was that if the accused man did in fact commit the crime he was insane at the particular time,' Sir John told the jury.

Fanning entered a plea of 'Not Guilty' at the trial but opted to give evidence. He related how he had made an appointment to meet the dead woman outside the Carlton cinema on Dublin's O'Connell Street, and detailed their trip to Howth, how they had a few drinks at the local hotel, left and went to the field at Brackenhurst. Then with dramatic unexpectedness he told for the first time that a 'tiff' had developed and that 'something snapped in his brain,' Supt Lawlor recalled.

On the Thursday , the third day of the trial, Fanning swore to tell the whole truth before the court in Green Street. There was silence in the crowded public gallery as he spoke, and the occasional mutter and whisper failed to distract his attention as he stood pale-faced in the dock, remembering and recounting the events of that evening. Twice he broke down sobbing, but continued without interruption by either his own counsel or the judge.

'I asked Kathleen where we should go that night and she said: "We will go to our usual spot",' said Fanning. 'We went up along by the Catholic church. We entered a field by a gap in the wire fence. We had to walk in single file. I think I was first. It was very bright at the time. We went to the right-hand side of the field to a kind of hollow. We had been there many times before. We sat down for a while chatting and smoking cigarettes.

'We were sitting on some newspapers and then we started courting for about a quarter of an hour. We then had a slight row. It was a kind of tiff. She wanted to get up and go back home. We were both sitting on the ground. I wanted to make friends, and I wanted to kiss her goodnight, but she refused. She got up and I was sitting on the ground. She was half way down the hollow.

'I got up and we were both standing. I put my arms around her and tried to kiss her, and both of us fell on the ground on the slope. After that, something snapped in my brain. The next thing I had my hands around her throat. I kept on squeezing and I could not take my hands away. I had to kind of drag them away and then she fell limp. When I had my hands around her neck I had not the slightest intention of doing her the slightest harm. I did not know what I was doing.

'I remember feeling her heart. That was after I dragged my hands away. As far as I can remember life was extinct. I remember trying to lift the body. I was not able to lift it. It fell from my hands onto the ground. I dragged her by the hand away from the hollow down towards the fence. I dragged her partly towards the road. I was in a kind of frenzy or something, because I remember kicking the body several times. I remember turning over the body where it was partly concealed in the bushes.

'Then I staggered away from the spot. I was going towards the gate and trying to light a cigarette. I put my hands in my breast pocket and I missed a pen which I had taken a loan of, belonging to Mr Casserley. Then I lit a match and saw her bag. I scattered the bag around. It must have been open. I flung everything away from it. I did not know what I was doing at the time. I flung the bag away from me. It was when I picked up the bag I found the pen which I put in my pocket. Then I went to get out towards the entrance and I have only a faint hazy recollection of how I got down to the road from the field,' Fanning concluded.

In response to his own counsel Fanning said that he came to his senses again when he got out onto the main road. 'And at any time that evening had you any intention of doing any harm to her?' asked Sir John. 'Not the slightest. I loved her too much,' replied Fanning.

Under cross examination by Mr Casey, Fanning said that they had had 'hundreds of rows', but their informal engagement, which dated back to the previous August, had never been broken.

Another letter from Fanning was produced, dated five months before the killing, which was an apology. Fanning begged Kay's forgiveness for his rude behaviour at a dance on 13 December. 'It was all about a row we had at a dance. It was a very ordinary row. She was very touchy at times and she often said it was better for us to part. That used to upset me, but it would be fixed up two or three days after. That has happened umpteen times,' explained Fanning.

Mr Casey then asked him about the row in Brackenurst field. 'It was more or less a slight row,' said Fanning. 'She said she was going on holidays and would have a good time. I said I hoped she would and that I would get someone else while she was away. Then she said if that was the case we had better call the whole thing off. It happened many times before like that — that if we said something, all of a sudden she would get huffed.'

'She said she wanted to get up and go away?' asked Mr Casey.

'She said that if that was the case we had better go home. I asked her would she kiss me goodnight, and she said "No",' said Fanning.

Kay had walked half way down the slope at this stage, and Fanning ran up behind her, grabbed her and tried to kiss her. She pushed him away, resisting, and they both fell to the ground. 'She fell under you?' asked Mr Casey. 'Partly I think,' replied Fanning. 'I don't know what happened after that.'

The State Pathologist said that the transposition of Fanning's heart and liver should have no effect on his mental state. The prison doctor confirmed this view.

As Fanning stood down from the witness box, the defence announced it was calling two medical experts. The first was a radiologist from the Mater who told the court that Fanning's heart was on the right-hand side and his liver on the left. The condition was so rare that there was no data available about it, he said. Dr John Hannon from Ballybunion, Co. Kerry, who knew Fanning since he was a child, described him as poorly and underdeveloped

142

physically. There was nothing wrong with either transposed organ, the condition was a congenital abnormality and this was always associated with a high incidence of mental deficiency, said the doctor. Asked by the defence counsel for a medical opinion, Dr Hannon said that having heard the evidence presented, it was his opinion that Fanning was insane at the time.

Dealing with the defence of insanity in his charge to the jury the following day, Mr Justice Davitt said that the fact must be proved by medical experts. If the jury failed to make up their mind as to whether he was insane or not, then the defence failed because the onus was on the accused to establish his insanity. The charge was murder but the jury was entitled to find manslaughter if the evidence justified it. Murder became manslaughter when the act was committed through lack of self-control due to severe provocation, but in this case there was not one jot or tittle of evidence of provocation.

Neither premeditation nor motive was an essential ingredient for a verdict of murder. Provided the intent to kill or seriously injure preceded the fatal act, it did not matter at all how long or how short the interval by which it was preceded. 'You have of course to judge his intention' said Mr Justice Davitt, 'and, in estimating what his intention was, to take into account his relations of feeling towards the woman. I think you will come to the conclusion he was very much in love with her. Probably up to the time when this terrible tragedy occurred. If his letters are to be taken at their face value he was almost obsessed with her. There was no doubt he gave her presents, he visited her children, and in every way acted, as he said himself, as if they intended to marry.

'Regarding the facts of this case in the light most favourable to the accused, what do you find? Here is a man who, for the purposes of this part of the case, must be sane. Having no discoverable reason, without provocation, without justification, without excuse, he strangles this unfortunate woman into insensibility — a dying condition — feels her heart to see if she is alive, and, coming to the conclusion she is dead, drags her by the hand some distance and then kicks her face in, inflicting injuries which alone would have been sufficient to cause death, apart from the strangulation. He swears to you he never had any intention of harming her.

'If you believe the accused that he never intended to harm her then you must acquit him. In all seriousness, I must say to you that I find it utterly impossible that any reasonable jury could accept that evidence or give any effect to it whatsoever,' said Mr Justice Davitt.

It took the jury exactly one hundred minutes to consider their verdict. They returned to pronounce Fanning guilty of murder but with a strong recommendation for mercy.

Asked if he had anything to say why sentence of death should not be passed on him, Fanning trembled as he grasped the rail of the dock, his knuckles whitening. 'I have nothing to say,' he said in a clear, loud whisper.

Mr Justice Davitt said that he was in complete agreement with the verdict, saying it was the only one possible. He then donned the black cap and sentenced Fanning to death, fixing 10 November — seventeen days time — as the date for execution. A visibly shocked Fanning hurried from the dock and could be heard running down the stairs to the cells. However, Fanning was to escape hangman Pierrepoint's rope. He was granted a reprieve and his sentence was commuted to a life sentence.

'This case,' said Supt Lawlor, 'in at least one element is similar to the murder of Hannah Doherty at Malin Head, Co. Donegal. Premeditation in both cases was difficult to sustain, because the murders appeared to have been committed on a sudden impulse. There was no evidence in either case that the accused men had made preparations. In the Doherty case the large stones to hand on the hilltop were used to inflict death, while in the Fanning case the evidence went to show that the accused's account of his actions was true. No weapon was found at or near the scene of the crime. They differ completely however, when one comes to consider the motives which inspired the deeds. Doherty had an overwhelming motive, while Fanning's was difficult to comprehend.

'Undoubtedly the law does not require proof of motive in the prosecution of a crime, and murder is murder no matter how one may look upon it. Yet there are cases in which one feels that a line of demarcation might be drawn. Apparently the jury thought so in the Fanning case when they returned a strong recommendation to mercy, which was duly acted on by the State.'

11.

The Tenement Murder

IT was 8 p.m. on Monday 23 August 1948, when the phone rang in George Lawlor's house. 'I picked up the receiver to hear the voice of Harry Nangle the duty officer at Garda Headquarters. He was always the bearer of news of a serious crime. He was brief and to the point, as he usually is on such occasions. There had been a suspected murder at number five Upper Abbey Street, Dublin. The dead body of a man who had been struck on the head had been found lying in a back room on the ground floor, he told me,' George Lawlor wrote.

The murder had been reported to the Bridewell station near the Four Courts, by a Mrs Peggy Gambon, who lived in the Abbey Street flat with her husband. She couldn't see the dead man and didn't know him, but her husband William Gambon was missing.

'I collected a photographer, a mapper and a fingerprint expert and arrived at the scene shortly before 9 p.m.,' said George Lawlor picking up the chain of events. 'As we drove from Capel Street into Upper Abbey Street we had no difficulty in locating the premises; it was marked by the 'C' District squad car parked at the pavement outside. The house was a shabby three-storey tenement, the ground floor was a lock-up dairy shop, and a side door gave access to the dwellings above it and to the back of the dairy.

'A member of the uniformed force who blocked this entrance was apparently carrying out his instructions to the letter. We heard him tell the half-dozen reporters who had gathered around that his duty consisted in keeping out unauthorised persons and that he had no information to offer as to what was happening in the house. We entered a long dark hall which led past the dairy to the room behind it. Outside the room were two uniformed members from Store Street Garda station who were awaiting our arrival.

'The room was filthy, the furniture old and ready for the junk shop or the dump and the atmosphere was depressing. A round

145

table occupied the centre of the room. On it were the remains of a meal, an evening newspaper dated 21 August 1948 and an old towel. Two windows overlooked the yard at the back of the room. Their curtains were drawn and between them there was a rickety dressing table of sorts. In the right-hand corner was a wooden bed covered with a bedspread.

'On first sight the bed appeared to be empty, as the bedclothes were level and not raised as one would expect to see in an occupied bed. On drawing back the counterpane the dead body of a man was revealed, lying on its back with the head inclined slightly to the right. It was sunk down in the bed and the head was almost completely off the pillow. On the forehead, just above the eye, there was a deep wound. There were two smaller cuts clearly visible at the side of the head.

'The man was dead and had been for some time. The lower portion of the pillow and the sheet beneath it were drenched with blood. Small flecks of blood dotted the wall, the bedspread and the upper part of the pillow. It looked as if the unfortunate man had been done to death by being struck with a heavy weapon whilst he lay in the bed in a reclining position — in all probability whilst he was sleeping. There was no sign that a struggle had taken place,' recalled George Lawlor.

A new suit of clothes was thrown across a chair in the room, and at the foot of the bed there was a labelled suitcase. The label read: John Long, 31 Tara street, Dublin. In the case were a few items of cheap men's clothing, an English post office savings book, which bore the name John Long, 90 Chivers, Westcoth, Aylesbury, England. The account book showed that it had been closed on 18 August 1948, with the withdrawal of £55. Sergeants John Heffron and John Dunlea of Store Street Garda station had earlier gone to the flat in Abbey Street after two women called in to the nearby Bridewell station. They had found that the room was locked with a padlock and hasp. Sgt Dunlea forced the door, and his colleague picked up the broken lock and retained it for examination. They found the blinds on the two windows of the south wall were drawn and a piece of dirty curtain about a foot high was stretched across the base of the window panes. On the bed in the corner of the room the two sergeants saw a bundled bloody white sheet which covered the face of a dead man. The bedclothes were saturated with blood, which had soaked through the bed and dripped onto the bare wooden floorboards beneath it.

146

A copy of the final edition of the *Evening Herald*, dated 21 October, and the *Daily Herald*, dated 21 August, lay on a table in the room. A man's two-piece, blue, pin-striped suit was lying across the back of an armchair, a blue spotted tie lay on the floor under the chair, and an empty black cloth wallet also lay on the floor near it.

A suitcase in the room contained some clothing, a number of Easter and Christmas cards from William Gambon addressed to John Long, a travel permit and a number of photographs including one with a scrawling handwritten caption on the back of it, identifying the subject as William Gambon.

The State Pathologist was called in and arrangements were made to have a post mortem the next morning.

The *Irish Press* of the following day, carried the story:

'Mr Andrew Kavanagh, who lives in the room above the one in which the body was found, stated last night that the room had been occupied for the past few months, by Mr and Mrs Gambon.

'After experts from the Technical Bureau Kilmainham, led by Supt George Lawlor, had made a thorough investigation of the room in which the body was found, the door was sealed, and Gardaí were left on duty outside. Today Mr John McGrath, State Pathologist, will hold a post mortem examination,' said the report.

Sgt Mick Wall, the official photographer attached to the Garda headquarters staff, took four photographs of the miserably furnished room, which measured 18 feet 7 inches long by 11 feet and 7 inches wide. He was no stranger to such scenes as he had photographed most of the victims of serious crimes in the past fifteen years, since he headed up the newly established Garda photographic unit, and had grown to be a longtime friend, advisor and confidant of George Lawlor.

He returned the following morning with the State Pathologist and took two more photographs of the dead man lying in bed. Dr McGrath then carried out his initial examination of the dead body, which was afterwards moved to the city morgue, where Sgt Wall took two more photographs of the corpse as it lay stretched out on a ceramic slab.

In the tiny flat Dr McGrath turned back the bedspread and two grey blankets to fully examine the dead man. 'I saw ten tiny spots of blood evidently caused by flying drops of blood on the wallpaper behind the head of the bed. Some similar tiny spots of blood were present in the wood of the head of the bed and on the pillow. The pillow and clothes immediately beneath the head were soaked with blood. When the bed-clothes were removed, the body was lying on

147

its back, but slightly more on the right side in a depression in the middle of the bed. The body was clothed in a blue shirt which came down to the waist and covered the left hand. The right hand lay over the groin. On lifting up the shirt an old waistcoat could be seen on the body next to the skin. The cloth of the waistcoat was roughly slit vertically on the left side.

'The head was sunken into a depression in the pillow and it was bent slightly to the right with the chin upwards. The appearance of the bloodstains indicated that the head had been in the same position approximately at the time the blows had been inflicted and it had not since been removed. Rigor mortis was universally present in the body. The various articles of furniture in the room were not particularly disturbed and there was no indication that a struggle had taken place. A flat perforated iron bar lay on the floor near a wash table at the head of the bed. After this preliminary examination I then made arrangements to have the body moved to the city morgue,' Dr McGrath wrote in his report.

There were a total of fourteen blood spots on the wallpaper, one blood spot on a curtain near the head of the bed, and tiny flecks of blood on the wooden head of the bed at about pillow level. Dr McGrath also examined the two blankets, a pillow, one sheet and the bedspread which were soaked with blood. The dead man had bled so profusely that even the mattress had been saturated.

In his post mortem notes, he wrote that the body was that of a well-developed man, weighing about 10½ stone, standing 5 feet 8 inches. There were no recent injuries to the body or arms. The man's right middle finger was missing, but this had been surgically removed some time previously.

There were four wounds to the head, the two largest were 2.5 inches long, one from the middle of the left eyebrow to the middle of the forehead; the other on the left side of the head just above the ear. The skull had cracked inwards in a fracture running the length of the face. There was also extensive brain haemorrhaging.

The other organs were normal, and the stomach was empty except for a small amount of watery fluid. From the examination, Dr McGrath concluded death was due to cerebral haemorrhage and shock caused by four severe blows on the head.

John Long told people that he came from Co. Wicklow. However, he was born in 1909 in the Rotunda Hospital to a single mother living in Dublin's city centre behind O'Connell Street. He was a non-drinker, described by one man as 'simple'.

John Long was an inmate of St Kevin's Institute for a number of years. When he left the hospital in 1939 he went to work in England as a labourer. He followed work wherever it became available, and had been living in Westcott, near Aylesbury, Buckinghamshire, before his death, where his weekly pay packet averaged £6-12s-0d. While he worked there, he lost a finger in an accident and was paid a weekly compensation allowance of eighteen shillings.

He returned to Dublin between jobs, where he lived in hostels or in lodging houses. In May 1942 the rector at St Michael and St Paul's Church, Rev. Robert Kerr, first met Long while he was living in Church Street, near the Four Courts. The rector gave him small sums of money on a regular basis because Long was not working at the time. Long stayed in Dublin for a few months, then went to England where he found work and sent back cash to the clergyman. In total he sent back £44, which he subsequently drew on when he returned in 1943, only to go back to England again.

Michael Butler, who worked alongside John Long in the Ministry of Works building site in Buckinghamshire, and shared a hut which served for living accommodation with him, identified the dead man from photographs. 'He was a quiet, harmless, inoffensive hard working man,' said Butler.

During his time in St Kevin's, Long made friends with a Dublin man, William Gambon, who was being treated for a knee injury sustained while working on a farm in Co. Kilkenny. Gambon entered St Kevin's on 20 December 1936 and left on 30 April 1943. He was born in 1920 and his parents soon moved to Liverpool seeking work; his father deserted his mother while he was still a child, and he never heard from him since then. His mother later re-married. Gambon was put into the institute for boys in Artane, north Dublin, with his three brothers, while his sister was sent to a home in Goldenbridge, which she subsequently left and went to England where she married.

Gambon had little education, was able to read but wrote with difficulty while his arithmetic was basic. He said he wanted to become an office clerk at one stage, but acknowledged he didn't have the necessary educational standard. He was also prone to adding a little colour to his dull life and told his future mother-in-law that his limp was caused by a lion which had mauled him when he worked in a circus in England. He also told Mrs Annie Jones, his mother-in-law, that because of this accident, he received a weekly pension. He told her it was for 50 shillings a week, but adjusted this downwards later to 25 shillings.

149

Annie Jones hardly knew Gambon before he married her daughter, Margaret — who was known locally as Peggy — in April 1948. He had been living in the Morning Star hostel in North Brunswick Street before the marriage. The Joneses didn't approve of the marriage. Aida, in an elder sister's attitude, mirrored that of her family, 'I hardly ever spoke to him. We were not on good terms,' she said. The Joneses and their three daughters and two sons lived at 26 North Brunswick Street near the hostel, and the two eldest daughters were married when Peggy met William.

'William had a lame leg. He said he was expecting a legacy belonging to some relation of his, in September. He mentioned this before he was married,' Annie Jones told the Gardaí.

'After they were married I helped my daughter, and William had a small pension every week. After they were married they spent a few days staying with a cousin Annie Young in Kilkiernan Road, Cabra, then I got a room for them to live in at Abbey Street. I bought the furniture that was in that room. I visited my daughter there only twice after they were married. The first time was when they would have been about three weeks married. William wasn't there on that occasion. He wasn't working at the time. I visited him again about two months after, when I asked him to go to the Labour Exchange to apply for assistance but he said he wouldn't. I don't think there was anything else ever said about work,' said Annie.

Gambon paid the rent of 6 shillings a week for the room, every Tuesday, without fail. After the couple married, Annie would send a basket of food to them almost every day. Shortly afterwards Gambon sent back word to stop; no more food parcels, he said.

On Thursday 18 August, Peggy and William Gambon called to see Annie Young at her home where they were infrequent visitors. Peggy said that William was going to Wicklow on Saturday and that she was afraid to stay in their own room by herself, and could she stay the night in Cabra? Annie Young said, yes, although this prompted Gambon to say maybe he wouldn't be going after all. He didn't talk about the pending trip to Wicklow or his friends. On Saturday evening at about 7 p.m. Margaret Gambon arrived at her cousins with a few overnight items packed into a small bag.

Gambon had told his wife he was expecting a friend from England about 21 or 22 August. Peggy alone shared the secret of her idle husband's regular income. She knew he had been receiving sums of money varying from 10 shillings to 30 shillings each week from his friend over a number of years. That Saturday he told her that his friend was arriving into Dun Laoghaire that evening on the mail boat, and that he would be going to meet him before they went on to Wicklow. Gambon told her he'd call for her the following day.

Money was a constant topic of conversation with Gambon, so much so that people remarked on it. Annie Young's husband, John, had only met Gambon in the summer of that year. 'He told me at one time he was expecting a legacy of about £400. He said something about his brother getting the money and that the brother was deceased and that he himself was getting it. He was to get the money in September.' That conversation took place about the second week of August.

Gambon had also told Annie that he would soon be able to buy a house. He was due to get a legacy, but didn't say who was to leave it to him, or how much it would be. He told her in July that he expected to get it in August or September.

Gambon never told anyone other than his wife that there was no weekly injury compensation money. His 'pension' was in fact money sent to him every week by his old hospital friend John Long from England. The sterling cash, which was legal tender in Ireland and interchangeable at the time, was sent by registered post every week.

James Whelan, a postman, had delivered registered post every Monday to William Gambon at the Morning Star Hostel from mid summer in the previous year, when he was first assigned to that round. Gambon would sign for the letter on each delivery. Another postman, Rory Hanna, was also able to produce receipts to show that Gambon received regular mail from Aylesbury. A social worker at the hostel, Joe Keegan, knew Gambon since the latter end of 1942, and saw him get weekly registered post from England.

Peggy, who was giving up her home for the night to accommodate a man she didn't know, was told very little about John Long. Gambon had left his past behind him, and sometimes replaced it with an imagined more glamorous life. In the case of his old friend, he consigned their relationship to silence.

Later Gambon was to explain. 'I met John Long about four or five years ago in Dublin and we got to be friends,' he said. 'I understand he was a native of Wicklow but I knew nothing about his friends or associates in the city. He did not appear to be a man who would have many friends as he was very bad-tempered and it was very hard for anyone to make friends with him.

'About twelve or eighteen months after I met him he decided to go to England, and since then he has returned to Dublin on two or three occasions. When he went to England he corresponded with me and when he returned to Dublin on holidays I used to meet him at the boat. He wrote to me about ten days ago saying he was coming over for a holiday, and said he hoped I would meet him at the boat as usual.

'In letters to one another we had written of the difficulties of getting accommodation here, and I had told him in a letter which I sent him that I would manage to fix him up for one night, but that in order to do so I would have to send my wife to friends, but that I felt I should do something for him as he had helped me out many times himself. When I told him that in the letter he answered it and said he was grateful and would make it worth my while. But he said he did not like the idea of putting myself and my wife to inconvenience.'

Margaret Gambon left their one-roomed flat at 1.30 p.m. that Saturday afternoon.

The following morning at about 10.30 a.m., Peggy Gambon and her friend's daughter Elizabeth left the house in Cabra to go to Mass.

In the city centre, William Gambon was settling down to breakfast in the 'New Eva' café in Capel Street with James Nolan, a man he had spent two years with in St Kevin's Institute, and later knew from the Morning Star Hostel.

Nolan had left the hostel four years earlier, was now married with two children and he bumped into Gambon on the corner of Abbey Street and Capel Street at about 10 a.m. 'I asked him how he was getting on,' Nolan related. 'He just nodded his head in reply. He asked where would we get breakfast. I told him I had my wife and children with me. I told him to wait for a minute while I had a word with her. He gave me a one pound note. It was an ordinary English note, he took the note from a wallet which had other notes in it, I couldn't say how much. He told me to fix my wife up, and told me to keep the money. I got change and gave my wife all the money except two shillings which I kept for cigarettes.' He sent his wife and two children home and brought Gambon to a nearby café.

'Gambon ordered breakfast for both of us. I asked him during breakfast how John Long was getting on and he did not give me any answer. He heard what I had said, when I asked him, but he spoke about something else. He asked me if I knew any place where he would get a lock. He wanted it for the door of his room, then he asked me how I was fixed for clothes. He offered to get me a suit. I told him that his size would not fit me, but he said he had one large enough for me but too big for him. He said he'd got it off a friend, and he arranged to meet me at the General Post Office in O'Connell Street on Tuesday evening after 5 p.m.

The two men parted after Nolan had gone to a bicycle shop and purchased a two shilling lock for his friend.

It was just after 11 a.m. when Gambon reached Annie Young's house to call for his wife, but he had missed her. He said he had called earlier, at about 6 a.m., but didn't like to knock them up when he saw no sign of life.

'I asked him how he had got on in Wicklow,' said Annie, 'and he replied "As a matter of fact, I didn't go to Wicklow." I didn't ask him why he didn't go and he didn't tell me. He said that he had met his friends on the Saturday night and they all got drunk. I said to him "You don't drink." He said "No." He also said that they got very drunk and one of them got that violent that he had to use force. He also said that he was worrying that they had broken up the furniture, as it was not his. The bed was all broken, and he didn't know where Peggy was going to sleep that night. He suggested that she should stay with me a few days until he had bought a new bed and furniture.' Gambon appeared edgy, and stayed for about an hour before leaving.

He then returned to Abbey Street where he fixed the hasp and padlock to the outside door of the flat.

His wife called to the flat twice that day. She found it double-locked and, with no reply to her shouts and hammering at the door, she left.

William returned to Cabra about 5.30 that evening. He had two half-pound boxes of chocolates, one for his wife and the other for Annie Young. It was another hour before Peggy returned, as she had been to Bray on the train to visit friends. Peggy had tea, and as she was about to leave the house at about 8 p.m. with Annie, Gambon joined them, although he had said a number of times that he had to meet friends that evening.

Gambon had told Peggy he had had a dispute with a friend in the flat the previous night, and that because of the names his friend had called her, he had given him a 'dig'. He said he had called to nearby Jervis Street Hospital, and they had told him his friend should be left quietly, and because of this advice she couldn't go home for a few days. He reached into his jacket pocket at this stage and gave her £13 in English notes.

They went to Cafolla's ice-cream café in O'Connell Street, where they had ice-creams in fluted glasses which Gambon paid for. They didn't delay for more than about fifteen minutes and then walked to the Fun Palace on Eden Quay where they played the slot machines. Annie later said that she had suggested going for an ice cream, but Gambon had wanted to play the slots; it was the first time she had seen him gambling, she said.

All three returned to Cabra that evening. The following morning Gambon brought his wife and Annie a cup of tea in bed. He left the house shortly afterwards at about 9 a.m. Peggy left the house at about 10 a.m., having arranged to meet Gambon at the flat. When she arrived, the door was still padlocked and he wasn't there. She called back again in the early afternoon but the door was firmly sealed.

At about 5.00 p.m. that evening Annie Young opened the door to Peggy. Annie had found a letter in the hall postmarked Dublin and addressed to Mrs Peggy Gambon, c/o Mrs Annie Young, 129 Kilkiernan Road, Cabra West, which she handed to her. Peggy ripped open the envelope and started to read; as her eyes made their way down the first page she went pale, and looked upset. Annie took the letter from her and read it.

Peggy decided that she wanted to show her mother the contents of the letter, and so she marched off with Annie to Brunswick Street. Her mother wasn't in, but her sister Aida was, and after listening to her sister's story she too read the letter. Its contents shocked her. A determined Aida carefully folded the letter and put it into her pocket, took her sister by the arm, and led her out the front door.

The two women then went to the flat in Abbey street. The door of the room remained padlocked, and they couldn't force it. So they went around the back to the yard, where they found a full dustbin which they dragged over and positioned under the window so Aida could scramble from its lid onto the window sill. She was able to force open the window a few inches, but not enough to get in. The curtains were pulled tightly across.

'It was dark,' Aida related. 'I could see the bed in the corner. There was a body in the bed. I could see the lower part of it. There was a strange odour in the room. After I had looked in the room my sister and I went to the Gardaí.'

It was 6.40 p.m. that evening when the two women walked through the main door of the Bridewell, the city's largest holding centre, and gave the letter to the Gardaí. It read:

Dear Peg,
I am leaving you for a while. I must get out of the country within the next few days. That man who I hit with the

154

iron bar died last night and that, darling, is murder, and if I stay in Dublin I will be caut [*sic*] for it and hung or life in jail. I will try and get to America. If I get there I will send for you someday, or maybe you will have nothing to do with a murderer.

I have ruined your life, darling, you who I love more than anything else in the world. My only chance now would be if I could bury the body which is locked in the room. He had no friends. I would give the world and everything in it to undo what I have done and you and I would be happy. Forgive me darling if you can. Well if he kept a clean tung [*sic*] he would be alive today and you and I would be happy. Forgive me darling if you can. If you keep it quiet for a few days I would be grateful. You go up and pay the landlady, say I lost the rent book. I can't write anymore at the moment. I am going around in a sort of maze. I can't seem to get that awful thing I have done out of my head. And it is not myself that I am thinking of. It is the desgrace [*sic*] and ruin I have brought to you and your people.

Goodbye darling and if we ever meet again remember I love you. It will break my heart as well as yours.

William

Peggy Gambon was brought to Store Street Garda station where she voluntarily made a lengthy statement about her husband and his recent movements.

Gardaí went to the house in Abbey Street where they broke down the door of the flat to discover the body. The local superintendent had rung the Technical Bureau and alerted George Lawlor. An immediate watch was put on all ports, and the police in Belfast, Liverpool and Holyhead were also contacted and given a description of the wanted man. Detectives were also sent to Busaras and every railway station in the city in case Gambon made a last minute dash to the country in order to lie low.

The Garda investigation conference that evening also decided to issue a description of Gambon through the media, in an effort to trace him quickly. The Assistant Commissioner was contacted and he cleared the request.

The following morning the newspapers carried this appeal: 'The police are anxious to interview William Gambon, who is aged about 28 years, 5'6", thin build, thin faced, sun-burned complexion, dark hair, wavy in front. His left leg is stiff at the knee, and he had a small mole on the right-hand side of the jaw, near the neck. He was dressed in a light fawn tweed suit, brown sandals, white shirt and collar, brown and cream paisley tie. He wore no head-dress, and speaks with a Dublin accent. So far as police know he has no occupation.'

At 8.40 a.m. the following morning, a man wearing a new water-proof coat, a trilby hat, grey trousers and jacket walked up the granite steps into Store Street Garda station, at the side of the bus station.

'He walked to the office counter and placed a copy of the morning's *Irish Press* on it. He then pointed to the top right-hand corner of the front page,' said Sgt John Murray who was on duty at the desk.

'I said to him, "Are you Gambon?" He replied "Yes." I then said "Are you giving yourself up?" and he replied , "Yes I am, there is nothing else for it."'

He was put into a cell, asked if he had had breakfast, and then interviewed by investigating detectives Ryan and Lawlor. 'He didn't appear very upset, but I noticed that when he was sitting down he was trembling,' said Sgt Murray.

When he was searched, Gambon had keys to the padlock which was broken off the door to his flat, a packet of notepaper and some envelopes, loose change, a fountain pen, a letter from the dead man to Gambon posted in England, and a total of 39 one-pound sterling banknotes.

When Gambon was formally charged with murder that afternoon, he answered, 'You said something about malice aforethought. I did not do it deliberately. I did not intend to kill the man at all.'

The trial was to be brief, opening just two months later. Gambon pleaded 'Not Guilty' to the charge. He told the Central Criminal Court that he had met Long when he disembarked from the mail-boat at 6.30 p.m. on the Saturday evening as planned. He had brought him back to the flat where he prepared a meal for him, and they sat chatting.

'I told him that my wife was going to have a baby and that my financial position wasn't any too good,' he said. 'He said he would give me a loan if I wanted it. I told him I did not like borrowing money off anybody.' He continued that he played patience with a pack of cards, and advised Long to get into bed if he wanted to, as he must be tired after the journey.

'While we were talking,' he went on, 'he suggested that we play a game of cards, and said that, as his stomach was a bit upset after

156

the boat, he was not sure he could sleep. We started playing pontoon at one shilling a time. I had £5 which he had given me for the use of the room. After a while we began to play for higher stakes. He was beginning to lose.

'The game finished sometime in the morning. He was then broke as I had taken sixty pounds from him. He then started getting cranky saying he did not think it was a very fair game, that he had worked very hard to get the money and he thought I should give it back to him. I told him I would give him back half of it, that I wasn't cheating and had no intention of doing so. He refused half of the money and wanted the whole of it.

'The rest of it is a bit hazy. He started calling me all classes of names and threatened to get up and kick the guts out of me. I told him to cool off and not be like a child. He started to get more excited after this and made a movement as if to get out of the bed and he stated that it was a trick on the part of me and my wife to coax him to come to the room to get his money out of him.

'He was using filthy language all the time. Then he started saying filthy things about my wife, and I got mad altogether. I made a dig at him in the bed and missed him. I struck the head rail of the bed with my hand. Then he tried to get a grip on me by the coat. It was then I saw a bar on the wash-stand which I used to use for holding up the window as there was no pulley on it. I took the bar in my hand and pushed him away from me with the bar back in the bed. After that everything went blank, but I am sure I hit him with the bar as I saw blood and the bar in my hand. When I saw the blood, he was lying down on the bed. I was out on the street when I came to my senses and it wasn't until I got to the Cabra Road that I realised what I had done. Then I wanted to go back, but I was afraid I might find I had killed him.' He hadn't given himself up sooner because he was not sure of what he was doing or what had happened, Gambon said. His counsel, Mr Bell, told the jury that their defence was manslaughter. There was no doubt that Gambon hit Long, and that there was certain provocation in the argument that took place before the fight, and there was evidence that brought the case within the definition of manslaughter. If there was a planned murder why was the wallet left behind as an indicator that Long had money, and what about the other evidence such as the post office savings account withdrawal showing Long had taken all his money to Ireland with him from England? Was there ever a murder more absurdly planned, he asked the jury.

157

'I did not at any stage intend to kill John Long. I regarded him as the best friend I ever had,' said Gambon.

Cross-examined by Mr R.F. McLoughlin, S.C., he said that he was expecting to get about £300 from a legacy, in August or September. Gambon said that when he got married he had said he received a weekly pension of twenty-five shillings, but he considered the money he was getting from Long as a type of pension.

'Between Long and your friends, how much money did you get every week on average?' asked Mr McLoughlin, who had called him an idler.

'Between £2 and £3 a week,' Gambon replied.

'On Monday you knew you were spending money which you had won from a dead man?' questioned Mr McLoughlin.

'I didn't know he was dead,' came the response.

'Didn't you lock him in the room?'

'Yes,' said Gambon.

Mr Justice Davitt then put a question from the bench, 'If Long was not dead he would be lying very badly wounded and in need of assistance?'

'Yes,' admitted Gambon.

The Judge also questioned the State Pathologist when he gave his evidence. 'Is it your opinion of this affair,' he asked, 'that even when the first blow was struck, Long's head was on the pillow?'

'Yes,' replied Dr McGrath.

'And, is it your opinion that it was in the normal sleeping position when the first blow was struck?' he then asked.

'Yes, the head was turned sideways,' said Dr McGrath.

The blows could have been inflicted with an iron bar found in the room measuring approximately 19 inches in length and two inches in diameter. Dr McGrath said the bar had no bloodstains on it. 'The bar could have readily caused the wounds if used with considerable force. On close examination I found that the bar had the appearance of having been heated towards the end. If there had been bloodstains on the portion that had been heated, they would have been obliterated,' he said.

In cross examination Gambon said he 'just threw down the bar and left it there. I didn't interfere with it.'

Summing up for the jury, Mr Justice Davitt said that among the conclusions which they might come to were that Gambon had inflicted the blows while Long lay in bed, that he had taken the money from a secret pocket on the inside of Long's waistcoat, and that he had arranged for his wife to be out of the flat and then had endeavoured to keep the killing a secret for as long as possible by double-locking the door.

If these conclusions were the only useful ones that could be drawn from the facts, then the accused man would be guilty of a particularly callous and brutal murder for a sordid motive — the robbing of a man who, according to himself, was his best friend.

The jury also had to consider carefully whether they could come to any other conclusion that would be consistent with a less serious crime. Gambon himself said they had a quarrel, and that he hit Long with an iron bar.

It took the jury just sixty-five minutes to consider and deliver their vedict, of 'Guilty'.

Gambon said he had 'nothing to say' when asked if there was any reason why sentence of death should not be passed on him. Mr Justice Davitt said he was in complete agreement with the verdict; there could be no other verdict, he said. Leave to appeal was refused. An appeal to the government was also turned down.

Four years later George Lawlor was to set down his own assessment of the case that had become known as the Abbey Street murder. After the post mortem examination, Dr McGrath reported that the deceased died of the injuries to his head, and specifically stated that he had received four distinct blows. An examination of the house revealed that there were blood splashes on the window behind the curtains, which indicated that Long was killed, probably in daylight, before the curtains were drawn.

Earlier enquiries revealed that Gambon had spread a rumour that he was expecting a legacy. Was Gambon preparing an explanation for any sudden affluence on his part? Was he actually planning the murder of Long at this time? He certainly lied in his statement to the police with his account of how Long met his death. More than one blow was delivered and the weapon used was an iron bar. Clearly the motive was robbery.

'The case, though a simple one from an investigator's point of view, presents much food for thought,' George Lawlor wrote.

'It seems extraordinary that a man who was not in what one could describe as fairly good circumstances, could be so charitable as to share the little he had with a fellow creature, and, what is more difficult to understand, to share it so consistently. It was, at the very least, charity to a degree which would be ordinarily described as a foolishness, or was it blackmail? Apparently Gambon became so accustomed to receiving his weekly allowance that he had begun to consider it as a pension or perhaps as a right. He even married on it.

'Was Long's visit to Dublin for the sole purpose of calling a halt to all this, and had he so informed Gambon? The story in many respects is reminiscent of the Hans Christian Anderson fable, *The man who killed the goose who laid the golden eggs*.

'Whatever the motive, there is no doubt from all the circumstances of the case that Gambon committed a cold-blooded and calculated murder for which he paid the extreme penalty.'

At 8.05 a.m. on Wednesday 24 November, three weeks after his sentence was passed, a notice signed by the Prison Governor of Mountjoy Prison, was posted at the entrance door, certifying that the sentence of the court had been duly executed.

12.

The Cup of Poison

THE Coxes were a prosperous Protestant family who farmed a 126-acre farm in Roskeen, Mountmellick, County Laois. In 1949 the head of the household was Mrs Jemima Cox, a widow for the past ten years who had two children, Frances aged thirty and her elder brother Richard.

But it was hard-working Frances who kept the farm in profit as she worked alongside her thirty-four-year old brother. Frances was the dominant person in the household. She was capable of taking on and completing any job as well as if not better than any man, and had a flair for work on tractors, reapers and binders. So much so that the Coxes never hired help to work on the farm. Frances was effectively the farm manager, and it was said by her neighbours that she did most of the work on the farm. Their social life was almost non-existent; Frances had almost stopped going to local dances since her father's death. Her brother Richard rarely went to a dance, and he had no interest in sports or other local entertainments.

'To all their neighbours, and their very intimate friends, they appeared to be a respectable, happy and contented family, hard-working and industrious,' wrote George Lawlor, who at this time was chief of the Technical Bureau.

Thursday 26 May was a fine late spring day and Richard Cox spent the morning sowing turnips in a field near their thatched whitewashed farmhouse. At 2 p.m. he returned to the farmhouse, and sat down to a lunch of steak, sausages and a large pot of tea, with his mother and sister. He had a few small jobs to do in the afternoon around the house, and it was about 5 p.m. when they sat down again for their evening tea. The day had remained fine and as they sat at the tea table Richard announced he was going to cycle over to the Kellys, their closest friends. He pulled on his new boots, just pausing long enough to drink a glass of orange squash his sister gave him before leaving. Putting his left foot on one pedal he punted the bike up the yard with his right foot before swinging it over the bar to mount the bike.

As he pedalled towards the Kellys' house in Killeagh, Richard Cox suddenly felt extremely ill. His head felt as if it was about to burst and his stomach was nauseous. The sudden attack was so severe that he fell off the bike at Ashtree hill unable to continue, and had to lie down in a field. He recovered enough to stagger to the gate post, and sat down as the temporary postman, Patrick Coulton, who was cycling home saw him and stopped. Cox told him he was ill and there was 'lightning in his head'. Coulton saw he was trembling and there were beads of sweat forming on his face. He looked frightened and complained of a series of pains and cramps. Coulton helped him to his feet and said he'd bring him to a neighbour's house. Cox walked stiffly and leaned heavily on the friendly postman's arm.

They had walked just beyond the gate back onto the road when Richard Cox, and said that 'his feet were sort of going to sleep or something' and asked Coulton to help him take off his new knee-high rubber boots, which he thought might have been tied too tightly and might be to blame. Ten minutes later he said he felt better, and put his boots back on but he still had to be helped to walk down the road. Cox coughed heavily, and spat blood about six or seven times as they walked, Coulton estimated. On the way they met the local blacksmith, George Plunkett, who stopped to ask if they needed any help. Cox told him he had just taken 'an awful turn'.

It was about 7.30 p.m. when he reached Kelly's house. Patrick had met him at the nearby bridge and they walked back to the house together, Kelly noticing his friend's stiff gait.

Patrick's mother, Mary, thought Cox was in a terrible state when he came into the kitchen complaining of having had a 'bad turn'. He was flushed and trembling. His hands shook so much he spilled a cup of tea she gave him, over himself. He told them that he had taken a drink of orange squash, which tasted bitter, before he left his home.

It was about 11 p.m. when he went home, drank some more tea and went to bed at about midnight. He didn't sleep well that night he told his mother and sister in the morning and took a light breakfast of tea and bread before cycling to the bog.

William Weston met Cox on the bog at about 11 a.m. that morning, and as they chatted Cox told him about the strange attack he'd suffered the previous day. He said he was inclined to blame his new boots for restricting the circulation of blood. The two men knew each other, as Weston would sometimes put cattle to graze on Cox's land. He was on friendly terms with Frances whom he often met on his visits to the farm, and lived on a six-acre farm with his mother at Naclane.

Richard spent the remainder of the day on the bog, returning home at about 7 p.m. Frances had cooked rashers for her brother but he said he couldn't face them, and instead ate a slice of soda bread and drank tea.

After their supper Frances left to check on a cow that had been brought in from the fields, and Richard did his few household chores, including bringing in turf for the fire, before going up to his bedroom at about 11 p.m.

Thirty minutes later Richard called out to his mother; the pains had come back and they were even worse than the previous night. His mother came into his room and after she saw how bad he was she roused Frances from her bed and despatched her to their neighbour, Jim Fox, who called out the local doctor James Keena. Frances was crying when she called to Fox's house and she went on from there to raise three other neighbours who also called to the house to offer assistance.

Mrs Cox met the doctor at the front door. Richard was complaining of pains in his legs, she said, as she led him up the narrow stairs to the attic bedroom with its tiny gable window. Richard was stretched out over the two beds in the room, still clothed, and was sweating profusely. The doctor asked him what was wrong as he loosened his clothes to examine him. Richard's heartbeat was erratic, his limbs were tender and he winced with pain when the doctor probed him, his muscles were rigid and his reflex reactions were slow. His temperature was just over 100 degrees. It was the first time Dr Keena had ever treated Richard, who told him about the previous evening's attack.

'I considered that his life was certainly in danger,' said Doctor Keena. He gave the Coxes his opinion, and instructed them to give him only a mixture of milk and water to drink, saying that he was not to eat solid foods of any kind. His mother told him that Richard was inclined to avoid meat believing it was bad for him and normally ate a diet based on milk and eggs. Dr Keena had noticed that Richard didn't appear to be very robust, and diagnosed neuritis and heart trouble. In the parlour downstairs he wrote out a prescription for tablets and a liniment, which he gave to Frances. She told him Richard suffered fits about every two months and that occasionally he lost power over himself.

Richard spent an uneasy night after the doctor left, and the following day was confined to bed. On the Saturday afternoon, he got out of bed wearing his shirt and moved into a bedroom downstairs. He said he preferred it as there was more air in it. Frances and his mother had been giving him drinks of milk and water, and it was Frances who went to the chemist's that morning to get Richard's prescription filled.

At about 3.30 that afternoon Frances again left the house to go to a nearby shop, Conroy's, to buy bread. She returned later than expected, as she had taken shelter briefly from the heavy rain. On her return she learned that Richard had suffered another serious attack. Richard had been calling for her and was anxious for her return, her mother said. The symptoms were the same as for the previous attacks, cramps in the legs and arms and pains in the stomach with sweating fits which came and went spasmodically. After the attacks he felt depressed.

Richard slept well that Saturday night and on the following day was feeling much better. He took more drinks in the morning and at about 3.30 p.m., Jim Fox called in to see how he was feeling.

Richard was asleep when he called, but he woke as Fox chatted to his mother and sister, and he was then brought into the ground floor bedroom where Richard was sitting propped up in bed. The two men chatted, and Mrs Cox told her son that he should take a powder as it might prevent him from taking a 'turn'; the last attack had happened about the same time 24 hours earlier.

Frances was in the bedroom and commented that the powder tasted awful, a bit like bread soda, she said, and asked Jim Fox to taste it. She smeared a little on his hand, and he licked it off, grimaced and agreed with her. As the powdered drink was being prepared, Fox noticed Frances with a bottle or a small jar in her hand.

Richard drank from the cup he was presented with, and commented on its bitter taste. The women left the room and Fox continued chatting. About ten minutes later Richard suffered another attack but it passed quickly, and Jim left to give the sick man a chance to rest. As Jim told the women what had happened, Richard called out to him again, 'Jim, Jim,' and in response to his call Fox returned to the bedroom. The attack was worse, he sweated profusely, his limbs jerked, and his face became contorted with the pain.

Frances Cox described the scene. 'He said the ould cramp was back in his stomach and legs again. The perspiration started to fall off him. He kept at that and Jim Fox kept wiping if off him and holding him up in the bed. In ten or fifteen minutes he died.' Dr Keena, who had treated him for heart trouble, was called, and he gave a death certificate, which recorded Richard Cox's death as due to natural causes.

The news of the death of Richard Cox spread around the locality rapidly, and alerted suspicions just as quickly.

The traditional wake was held, and arrangements were made to have the funeral and burial on the Tuesday after Mass. That morning the lid of the coffin was sealed in the house by the undertakers, and was carried out into the yard and placed in the hearse as his weeping mother and relatives stood watching. A small group of detectives from Portlaoise arrived just as the hearse was about to pull out of the farmyard. It was stopped, and the Coxes were hustled into the house for a short meeting with the Gardaí. It was agreed that the funeral be delayed until that evening — and in the meantime a post mortem was held.

The Gardaí had been immediately suspicious of Richard Cox's death — his symptoms suggested he had died of poisoning, and they were aware of another factor which wasn't to be revealed to the public until much later.

The post mortem was conducted by the State Pathologist, Dr John McGrath, with the assistance of Dr Keena, who had attended the dead man at the weekend. They removed a number of organs from the body, and these were sent by car in a sealed bucket of preservative, to the State Analyst's Department.

Almost three weeks were to pass before Hubert Earle's report from the analyst's office was to confirm the symptoms and suspicions of the Gardaí and the State Pathologist. The dead man had been poisoned. Traces of strychnine, in excess of a fatal dose, had been found in his organs. The chemist's report supported the symptoms of strychnine poisoning which Richard Cox had exhibited before his death. It also indicated that a dose of the deadly white powdered poison had been given to Richard Cox before each 'turn' he suffered before his death. Dr McGrath estimated that Richard had been given between one-and-a-half and two grains of the poison.

One of the characteristics of strychnine is that it has a peculiar and very bitter taste. Sometimes this can be masked long enough if it is mixed with either food or drink, so that the recipient is not given enough time even to spit it out. Within fifteen minutes of the dose being administered, the muscles catch, the chest feels tight, and suddenly the body stiffens, and then is gripped in a series of convulsions. The convulsions continue until the poison's exhausted victim dies.*

The Gardaí, confronted thus with the suspicious death of Richard Cox and the likelihood that the man had been poisoned, launched a full-scale investigation.

'It was established early on in the investigation that only four people had been present in the room when Richard Cox had died; the dead man, his mother, his sister and Jim Fox, the neighbour and an intimate friend of the Cox family,' wrote George Lawlor. 'Yet all three gave conflicting accounts of the terrible tragedy. None of them could state who actually gave the unfortunate man his last drink or the circumstances surrounding it.

'I well recall travelling with Chief Supt McManus from Galway to Dublin on 1 June 1949. I had been engaged with him over the previous forty-eight hours in the investigation of a series of frauds at Galway greyhound racing track. I had only time for a hurried lunch before proceeding to Portlaoise, where after a consultation with Chief Supt Mooney and Supt J.J. Sullivan, I went to Roskeen. In the early hours of the following morning I spoke to Jim Fox in a police car outside his own home.

'He told me,' continued Supt Lawlor, 'that he had seen Frances Cox in the bedroom on that Sunday afternoon with a container which had some white powder in it. He believed she had given it to her brother fifteen minutes before the fatal seizure. However, the following day, when I was taking a statement from him in writing, he said he had been thinking over the affair and that he now believed it was Mrs Cox who had administered the powder.' The statement he gave was similar to evidence he was to give subsequently in court.

Jim Fox said that when he visited Richard his mother stood at the head of the bed, and Frances stood at the foot. They talked to Richard, and the mother said something about giving him a powder to make his bowels move, as it might help him avoid another attack. 'I am unable to say which of them gave him the powder. Francie had the powder in a jar or a bottle — a small bottle. I hadn't seen it with her when she entered the room, it was only when she came back from the head of the bed that I noticed it,' he said. Fifteen minutes later Richard Cox was dead.

'In conjunction with the taking of statements and the questioning of persons who might have been of assistance in unravelling the mystery of the death of Richard Cox, the house and its precincts were carefully searched on 31 May, but nothing of importance was revealed,' said Supt Lawlor, who was heading up the investigation. 'In the examination of a premises it often happens that nothing incriminating is found, and the searchers are inclined to consider that their labour has been in vain. But, as was clearly demonstrated in this case, a search which throws up nothing and where conditions are carefully and accurately noted can be at times more important than the finding of some clue which can easily be explained away at some later stage.'

Every room in the house was searched. Cupboards and drawers were turned out, Gardaí checked under chairs, mats, beds and rugs, behind pictures, and even looked up in the sooty wide-breasted inglenook chimney. The rubbish tip and outhouses were also gone through. But despite the time-consuming search, no poison was found on the farm. Meanwhile, a Garda had been despatched to all the chemists in the area and had checked the poisons register which every chemist had to maintain, recording the name and address of each purchaser of poison.

Denis McCarthy, a chemist and director of the Offaly Pharmacy in Tullamore, kept his records in a large bound ledger. The listings dated back years, and showed that between 24 and 29 February 1936, thirteen years previously, the father of the dead man had bought thirty grains of strychnine. Similarly revealing records were found in the Medical Hall, Mountmellick. Chemist's assistant Walter Walsh was able to point out a sale of thirty grains of strychnine to Frances Cox in December 1947. The strychnine was bought to poison dogs, said the record. Neighbours of the Coxes were able to verify that they had been complaining about dogs which had been worrying their sheep. A number of dead dogs were subsequently found on lands near the Coxes' farm.

When confronted with the evidence by the Gardaí, Frances admitted she had bought the strychnine. She told Det. Sgt James Galvin, who was stationed in Portlaoise that the poison purchased by her father was kept in a tin in the cart house adjoining the dwelling.

As they walked to the shed to get the poison she told him that she had decided to give her brother a purgative powder on the Sunday afternoon, but he wouldn't take one so she threw it behind the fire. What kind of powder was it, asked the Sergeant. 'Oh, bread soda,' she said. Later that Sunday she had wondered if Richard had poisoned himself, she told the detective. Her father had had strychnine which he had bought years ago to poison dogs, she said, and she remembered how he had told her, for a joke, to taste some of it when she asked how much it would take to kill a person. However, although Frances said the tin was kept in the rafters in the shed, when they searched the shed they could not find the tin. The last time the strychnine had been used from the tin was a few years previously, but then she added hastily, 'I mean, I saw the tin box, in which the bottle of strychnine was, about three years ago. I never saw the bottle, I didn't look for it when I wanted to poison the dogs.'

The following day, Wednesday, the house was searched a second time. Frances was also asked to produce the suit of clothes worn by the dead man on Friday 27th. She handed over a nondescript dark brown suit — trousers, jacket and waistcoat — which were immediately examined and found to contain nothing. The bedroom off the kitchen was then searched a second time and a few paper packets were discovered in a press near the bed used by the dead man, but their contents were harmless.

Among the other rooms that were searched a second time was a lumber room off Richard's own bedroom upstairs under the eaves. Garda Daniel Synott had heard about Richard's odd ways from his sister before he joined the team of searchers upstairs. 'Richard used to be very depressed at times, he could have taken something,' she said.

In the lumber room Garda Synott found a small bottle lying on top of a pile of clothing. It was clearly visible to anyone walking into the room, and strong black type on a red label warned, 'Strychnine'.

Det. Garda Maguire, attached to Portlaoise station, was also searching the lumber room. He had already met Frances when the Gardaí first asked to see the dead man's clothes. He had searched the pockets of the jacket, trousers and waistcoat and found nothing the previous day. He was also certain that the poison bottle had not been in the lumber room when he had carried out his examination of the dead man's clothes.

Det.Garda Maguire called Frances Cox into the room, and asked her if she had been in the room the previous day. She had, she said. She'd been watering the flower. The Garda turned around to look at the pot plant, and pushed his fingers into its soil. It hadn't been watered for a long time, and was badly in need of watering. He told her so. 'Oh, that's right. I forgot to water it. It was in to open the window, I came,' she said. The window in the lumber room was open as they spoke.

Frances was shown the small glass bottle marked poison. 'I never saw it before,' she said. Garda Synnott wrote down her comments. 'I know nothing about it. That is definite and genuine. If I bought it, I would have to sign for it. It is beside his clothes anyway,' she said.

The significant point about this find was that the bottle had not been present in the room the previous day when it was searched, noted Supt Lawlor.

As part of their training, members of the Technical Bureau spent many agonising hours on their knees learning how to search properly. Part of their training included supervising searches. One test they had to go through was to search a roughly overgrown section of land attached to their offices near Heuston station. This was a minute search conducted on hands and knees. The following day the same area had to be searched again — and the eagle-eyed detective had to say what object had been placed there overnight — was it a matchstick or a button or perhaps a hairpin? The searches of the Coxes' home had presented a puzzle: if the bottle wasn't there the previous day somebody had obviously placed it there to be found by the Gardaí — but with what purpose? That purpose was to become clear over the next few days.

Two days later the Gardaí returned to take possession of the suit worn by Richard Cox before his death. Det. Sgt Galvin met Frances Cox and she hurried out to the barn where her brother's clothes and bedding had been put when he was laid out. She returned with just the trousers and the jacket of the brown suit he had been wearing before his death, and a second suit. She couldn't find the waistcoat of the suit he was wearing before his death, she said. He asked her to look again, which she did, but said she had failed to find it.

As he was about to leave, Frances called him. 'I've been thinking things over, about the time Richard died,' she told him. She then went on to say that she went out to milk the cows some time before 3 o'clock on the Sunday afternoon Richard died. When she returned she heard some sort of noise from Richard's room, as if he had been scrambling around, and when she checked in on him he was asleep — or pretending to be asleep. Frances said that she thought Richard had been out of his bed, and when he heard her coming back into the house he had rushed back to bed and pretended to be asleep.

On the following Sunday afternoon, Supt Lawlor with Det. Sgt Galvin and a number of other detectives visited Cox's house. As

169

they walked up to the house, they were overtaken by Frances on her bike. She stopped to tell Det. Sgt Galvin that she had found Richard's waistcoat, and told him she had it ready for him if he was calling to the house.

Mrs Jemima Cox was then interviewed by Supt Lawlor and was asked to detail what happened the previous Sunday. She told him that her son had drunk a number of cups of milk and water throughout the day. Frances had provided some of the drinks, but not the majority. Frances had also given him the pills prescribed by the doctor which she had collected from the Medical Hall, in Mountmellick, but she couldn't remember which of them had rubbed the liniment on him.

Richard hadn't asked for anything to eat that Sunday, and in fact had insisted on only drinking milk and water. Mrs Cox had seen no powder of any sort in the bedroom, and neither she nor Frances had given him any powders. She was also emphatic that Frances had at no stage a bottle or jar of powder in her hands in the bedroom while Jim Fox was in the room either before or during Richard's death. Apart from the medicine there was no bread soda kept in the downstairs bedroom, but there was a large jar of it in the kitchen.

Richard had been in the downstairs bedroom for most of the Saturday and all day Sunday. He hadn't left the room, and she would have known if he had, she told the Gardaí. He had come down the stairs in his shirt and wore no other clothes. None of his clothes were in the downstairs bedroom, she said emphatically.

To the more obvious question, was Richard likely to have taken poison himself, his mother replied no. He was not the sort to take such a drastic measure and she could see no reason why he might.

Richard and Frances got on very well together, said their mother. Richard was physically weaker, he had a weak heart and complained occasionally of stomach problems. As a child he tended to rely on Frances and would not go to school without her, and took her side in arguments against anyone else.

Frances, in the meantime, had produced Richard's waistcoat. She had found it between the back of a press and the wall of his room. Asked where exactly, she brought the detectives into Richard's room and showed them a cupboard on the left-hand side of Richard's bed. 'I suppose Mrs Dunne stuffed it there when she was tidying,' she said.

Mrs Bridget Dunne, who lived nearby, had helped to wash and lay out Richard's body. The detectives called to her home too, and asked her about the day Richard had died. There had been no men's clothes of any kind in the downstairs bedroom Richard had moved to and which was subsequently used to lay him out. She knew the Gardaí had been looking for Richard's waistcoat. 'Francie asked me to tell the Gardaí if they asked about it, to say I put it in the press in the wake room,' she told the detectives.

Frances was re-interviewed by the Gardaí that day. In her first statement about Richard's death, given earlier that week, she said: 'I gave him an occasional drink of milk and water. He said that he would like to make his bowels move, but when I offered him bread soda, he said , 'No, give me a cup of milk and water,' and I did so. It was about 3.30 p.m. at this time and he died at about 4 p.m.,' she said.

That Sunday Supt Lawlor took a second and more detailed statement from Frances Cox. 'There were only three or four drinks prepared by me for Richard,' she told him. 'The drinks were got ready in a cup. Mammy used put half a cup of milk into it, and I would add the hot water. I would just pour the water into the milk and Mammy would take it to him. He was looking for something to make his bowels move before he took the last drink. He asked both of us. Jim Fox was present in the room at the time. I went to the cupboard and got a spoonful of bread soda and brought it up to the room. At this time he was sipping the cup of milk and water. I didn't give him the spoonful of bread soda. He had the cup in his hands and was drinking the contents. I actually went over to him with the spoonful of bread soda and he said "I won't take it." I had the remainder of the bread soda in a jam jar in the cupboard. I had a cup in my hand as well as the spoonful of bread soda and I put the spoonful of bread soda into the cup and left it there. He was still sipping the milk and water at the time. Jim Fox put his finger down into the cup of bread soda and took up some and swallowed it. He said, "That wouldn't be much use to shift anyone's bowels." With that Richard started to take the turn as he was still sipping the milk and water. Jim Fox took the drink out of his hands and he left it on the table — a little card table — it is still there. I brought out the other cup and left it on the table. That is all the cups that were in the room at the time except a cup which was on the little table and had been there all day. It was there for him to take a drink out of it if he wanted to. Mammy had brought it in and left it there. The pills were over on the dressing table and the rub which the doctor had prescribed was with them. There were no other bottles in the room. My mother had no bottle in her hand. I had no bottle in my hand. At no time on Sunday either before Jim Fox was there, or during the time he was there, had I a bottle in my hand, I am sure of that,' she said.

But despite her story, Supt Lawlor still had strong doubts about her version of events, particularly her story about the strychnine bottle.

'I decided to test her veracity,' he said. 'Det. Garda Denis McGuire, from Portlaoise had just entered the sitting-room where I had been engaged taking the statement. I knew he had possession of the small strychnine bottle as I had directed him earlier to put some questions to Jim Fox about it. I asked him for the bottle and in Frances Cox's presence I examined it for fingerprints, and left it on the table; next I took her hands and examined her fingerprints, at the same time nodding to those around me, undoubtedly leaving her under the impression that her fingerprints were on the bottle. She took a keen interest in the proceedings but said nothing,' Supt Lawlor recalled later.

On the following day, two detective Gardaí, Sgt Galvin and Garda McGuire, were at the Cox house. Frances struck up a conversation with them and, for the first time, said that she had seen the strychnine bottle before the Gardaí had found it in the lumber room where Richard's clothes lay in a pile. She was asked to make a written statement, and she readily agreed.

'On Saturday 28 May, before my brother Richard died,' her statement read, 'I was tidying up the room upstairs where Richard was sick. It was about twelve noon and before Richard came downstairs I saw the same bottle that I had seen out in the tin in the cart house two months before. I picked it up and threw it into the lumber room.

'I passed no remark about it to Richard. I did not see the strychnine bottle again until Wednesday last. I was up in the lumber room either yesterday or the day before. I found a baby Power's bottle with a small drop of stuff like milk in it. I got it into my head that Richard may have had the bottle full of milk and could have something in the milk in the nature of poison. I just got this idea into my head,' she said in the statement. She also said that on the night Richard died when she went to get Jim Fox to help, she asked him if he thought Richard had taken anything?

In conclusion, she asked that the waistcoat should be examined. Frances was also brought outside to show the Gardaí where she had thrown the tin which she had found near the stairs by Richard's room. Det. Garda Maguire went outside with her, and she showed

172

him the tip where she had thrown the tin. 'There's the lid of it,' she said pointing. But Det. Garda Maguire had searched the small rubbish tip a few days previously — and there was no such lid of a tin on the dump then as she claimed should have been.

It was on 30 June that the State Analyst reported the finding of strychnine in the various organs of the deceased man and the estimated amounts. He had also examined Richard Cox's waistcoat. The top left-hand pocket contained traces of a white powder which on examination were found to be strychnine.

'It was now quite clear that Frances Cox was endeavouring to suggest suicide on the part of her brother. She was indeed a clever woman,' wrote George Lawlor. 'After Sunday 5 June she was apparently worried by the thought that the bottle bore her fingerprints and she had to unearth some explanation. Consequently, on 6 June, she told the detectives that she had picked the bottle up in Richard's room and thrown it into the lumber room. This provided Richard with the means and opportunity, but she did not bargain for Richard's request to be taken downstairs. She had to invent something new. Strychnine must be placed in his room or it must be made to appear that it was readily available to him. Hence, the small amount in Richard's waistcoat.

'However,' Supt Lawlor went on, 'we were able to establish that when he came downstairs on the Saturday he was wearing only his shirt. But she solved this problem to her own satisfaction by getting Mrs Dunne to say that she had found the waistcoat when she was cleaning the room, but didn't reckon on Mrs Dunne telling the truth, which was that she had neither found it nor placed it in the room.

'In another instance also in endeavouring to press home the case she was making for Richard's suicide she overstepped herself. On Monday evening 6 June, Frances called to Mrs Conroy's shop nearby. In the course of the conversation, she said to Mrs Conroy. 'They have me heart scalded. They were up with me again today. They took away a waistcoat and they had found strychnine in the pocket and that should convince them Richard took it himself.' It was to take another 24 days before the State Analyst could confirm precisely that the tiny traces of white powder found lining the waistcoat pocket were strychnine.

'An account of another conversation which Mrs Conroy and Frances had at an earlier date, on Saturday 28th, the day before Richard died, gives an idea of the working of Frances's mind. At about 3.30 that afternoon, Frances called at the shop for bread. When Mrs Conroy asked her how Richard was, she replied that he was only 'middling' and that when she was coming away he was taking the same 'turn' as he had the previous evening. It was definitely established that Richard had taken the 'turn' during Frances's absence, and, concluded the Superintendent, 'she could not have otherwise known about it until she was told about it by her mother on her return from Conroys.'

Frances Cox was charged with the murder of her brother, Richard, and the trial opened on 15 November 1949.

She pleaded 'Not Guilty' to a murder that Mr Sean Hooper, S.C., prosecuting on behalf of the State, described as 'particularly malicious, malevolent and utterly callous'.

'In this case the motive was somewhat obscure,' wrote George Lawlor. 'One motive put forward at the trial was the intended marriage of Frances to a neighbouring farmer, and as both held different religions it was suggested that Richard would not have agreed to the marriage, and that only by his death could the marriage take place. While there was rather conflicting evidence as to the date of the proposed marriage, it was clear that Frances Cox and the farmer had been keeping company with such an end in view.'

The farmer, William Weston, lived nearby on his tiny farm with his mother. He told the Green Street murder trial that the question of marriage had come up with them in November of the previous year, but they had not got engaged. He would not agree to a marriage unless she 'turned' or changed her religion, and she agreed to do so. They went to Fr Burbage, the parish priest in Mountmellick, and classes for Frances's religious instruction were arranged and she attended them for a short time. His mother was quite happy that they should live on their farm, but no final date had been set for the marriage which was initially intended for May, he said. He subsequently became convinced that they would not and could not marry.

Mrs Jemima Cox said that she would 'much prefer her daughter to marry a Protestant.'

Under cross examination by Sir John Esmonde for the defence, Supt Lawlor said that he was trying to test the veracity of Frances Cox's statements when he examined her hands and the bottle of poison.

'Would I be right in saying that you were endeavouring to lay a trap for her?' asked Sir John.

'I was endeavouring to get the truth of the crime I was investigating,' he replied. He also discounted suggestions that Frances Cox was 'an ignorant, simple country girl'.

Supt Lawlor's ruse was to be raised again in a later court case. However, an appeal against the admissibility of statements made after the ruse was subsequently heard and lost. 'I am not aware of any other judicial decision in an Irish case on the admissibility of evidence of a statement obtained by means of an artifice or a trick,' he wrote in 1952. 'In this case the fact that the accused woman was left under the impression that her fingerprints were on a small strychnine bottle found in the lumber room, resulted in her making an admission that among other things she had handled the bottle. If she had not handled it why should she make such an admission, which she at no later stage tried to deny? The real purpose of the artifice, ruse or trick — call it what one may — was to test her veracity and it had the desired effect, eliciting the truth without doing her an injustice.'

Frances Cox was to spend over four hours in the witness box of the fifth day of her six-day trial. She appeared calm and spoke clearly, and was a striking sight in the witness box wearing a black well-cut overcoat, a blue scarf and a wide brimmed black hat.

The wedding plans had been kept a close secret from Richard Cox and his mother. Frances told the court that she thought they would both be displeased at the plan, and she denied that she had ever attended any religious instruction classes in the local convent.

Frances denied that she had spoken to Mrs Conroy about a turn her brother had taken while she was out of the house — and supposedly could know nothing about unless she had engineered it. She also denied that she had asked Mrs Dunne to tell a lie. 'I passed some remark to her that the waistcoat was missing and that I had got it outside in a bundle of clothes from the corpse bed, and that it may have got mislaid,' said Frances.

In response to the blunt question 'Did you kill your brother?' posed by her counsel, she replied simply, 'No.'

'Would you tell us why you went out to the cart shed to look for a can in which strychnine was kept about two months before your brother's death?' asked the prosecuting counsel.

'I went out to see if what was in it still remained in it,' she said. 'And what insight into the strychnine did you want two months before your brother's death?' asked Mr Hooper.

'I am not sure it was two months, it could have been two years,' she replied.

'And how did you get it into your head that your brother might have taken something?' asked Mr Hooper.

'He took so suddenly bad,' she replied.

Mr Hooper kept up the pressure, asking why she thought he might have committed suicide.

'I wasn't really of that opinion, it just crossed my mind,' came the final reply on the topic.

Similarly on other issues she refused to admit she had lied, but left the jury in little doubt about the veracity of her statements.

In a fierce barrage of questions, which drew an answer out of the accused woman, bit by bit, she said that she hadn't or couldn't remember telling Dr Keena that her brother had epilepsy. 'You know that Dr Keena has sworn that you did say it. Are you prepared to contradict him?' asked Mr Hooper.

'It would not be up to me to contradict a doctor,' replied Frances.

'Do you realise it is of some importance to you whether this happened?' he asked, drawing the response, 'Yes, I don't actually remember saying it, although I could have said it, but I don't remember saying it.'

'If you did say it, was it true?' asked Mr Hooper trying another tack.

'I never saw it happen,' said Frances.

'Then if you did say it, it wasn't true and could not be true?' he questioned.

'I don't remember saying it and I never saw it happen,' she said.

Frances admitted she had failed to tell the Gardaí about finding the strychnine bottle in her brother's bedroom and how she had thrown it into the lumber room. It was the only strychnine in the house and she was the only one who knew where it was, she said under cross examination.

'If this was suicide, your brother would have to go upstairs out of the bedroom beside the kitchen, find the strychnine where you had thrown it into the lumber room, take it, and then go back to bed again before the attack. Isn't that obvious?' asked Mr Hooper.

'Yes,' replied Frances.

On Monday 21 November, there was a crowd of approximately 1,000 people outside Green Street courthouse, queuing to get in to hear the verdict. Witnesses had difficulty forcing their way through and when they got inside they found that the public gallery was already packed out.

The prosecution, in their summing up, asked who was likely to submit themselves to the 'excruciating, tearing and writhing agony' of trying to kill oneself four times over a weekend, with poison? Once they ruled out suicide, Frances Cox fitted into the picture.

Not only had she the opportunity but she also had the important opportunity to wash the poison cup afterwards.

On the question of her distress and her anxiety to get the medicine, that was a safe step for her to take, said Counsel. After all, neither the liniment nor tablets would have any effect on someone suffering from strychnine poisoning, and according to Dr McGrath, death had followed within ten minutes of the strychnine being administered.

There had been an arrangement that Frances Cox would get married which had both spiritual and material consequences. She was going to have to move from a farm of over 120 acres to one of just six, and live under another woman's roof. That carried implications which were not likely to be ignored by anyone with experience of rural communities, and could prove to be the key to the crime, said the prosecution.

They also asked the jury, if Frances Cox's story about the poison bottle were true, why then when she had seen her brother writhing in agony had she said nothing about finding the strychnine?

The explanation of Frances's decision not to tell the Gardaí about the strychnine bottle was simple, her defence claimed. She was suffering from mental strain after long questioning by the Gardaí and it was hardly surprising that she had decided to say nothing.

The defence also made the point that any motive prompted by an engagement was totally exploded by the fact that the liaison had ceased long before Richard's death.

Even if the jury believed Richard Cox had suffered strychnine poisoning throughout that weekend there was no evidence that Frances Cox had administered the poison or that Richard had not his own supply of it.

The circumstantial evidence before them was consistent with the guilt of many others besides the accused, said the defence counsel.

Mr Justice Dixon in his summing up before the crowded courtroom was brief. The jury could have no difficulty accepting that death was caused by strychnine poisoning if they accepted the evidence of Dr McGrath, and they had no evidence to the contrary. If they discounted the possibility of accident or suicide, the State must satisfy them that the accused woman had administered the poison. It would also seem that Dr Keena had not been given the full medical history of the case he was treating because of the reluctance of the people involved to divulge all the details, said the judge.

The jury left the court at 6 p.m., and in eighty-five minutes they returned with a verdict of 'Guilty'. Frances Cox stood silently when asked if she had anything to say before sentence was passed on her. The sentence was death by hanging, and Wednesday 14 December was fixed as the date of execution. Her mother, Jemima, who had sat in the well of the court, didn't look up at her. As she was led from the dock, Frances sobbed into a handkerchief, her sobs audible from the cells below the court.

Within a couple of weeks the Court of Criminal Appeal dismissed an appeal, and fixed 5 January as the date of execution. However, three days before Christmas day the President commuted her sentence to life imprisonment and she escaped the gallows.

During her trial the court was only told that Frances Cox was arrested in Dublin. There was no further reference to the incident. In fact, the incident masked another strand to the story. Nine days before Richard Cox died the Gardaí were searching the Cox household at Roskeen on the basis of 'received information'. Hidden in the house was the dead body of a newly-born infant. Frances was charged with concealing the birth of the illegitimate child and was given bail.

Her trial was set for July 1949, and on the 22nd she appeared in Green Street court. She pleaded guilty to the charge of concealment and was placed on probation. As she left the Dublin Court, she was arrested by Supt J.J. O'Sullivan from Portlaoise and charged with the murder of her brother. She replied, 'I have nothing to say. I had neither hand, act nor part in it.'

Frances was to tell the Gardaí that she had been pregnant on two other occasions before the birth of the baby, and in both cases had kept the fact a secret from her immediate family and the neighbours.

'One motive suggested [for Richard's murder] is that Frances was about to be arrested and charged with the murder of her illegitimate child. It was not known, nor could it ever be established whether Richard was, or was not aware of this,' wrote the Technical Bureau chief. 'Her mother was not, and everything pointed to the fact that neither was Richard. He was always considered a quiet, inoffensive type of man, but if he learned the disgrace brought on the family by his sister, he might have been different. In either instance the circumstances were sufficient to deprive Frances of any right or interest in the farm,' he said.

'It is difficult if not impossible to differentiate between the different types of homicidal killing,' wrote George Lawlor at the conclusion of the case. 'Murder is murder under any guise. Since Cain slew his brother Abel and earned the curse of the Lord it had been considered as a terrible crime, but in murder by poisoning we have it in its meanest, most callous and despicable form. It is the most secret kind of killing, undoubtedly premeditated, and although the evidence to connect the guilty one must almost of necessity be circumstantial, it is rare that the poisoner cheats the gallows.

'Murder by poisoning has certain characteristics which make it the most dangerous method of killing by the murderer. It is a personal affair in the sense that it cannot be foisted onto a fly-by-night stranger. In other words it is an inside crime, committed by somebody well-known to the victim, whether a relation or otherwise.

'When the cause of Richard Cox's death had been established, it was not necessary to consider any suspect outside the household and this fact put his sister, Frances, in the awkward position of having to establish suicide, in order to divert suspicion from herself. In doing so, ruthless, clever and determined as she was, she only succeeded in forging an unbreakable chain of circumstantial evidence against herself,' wrote Supt Lawlor closing his casebook on the murder.

13.

The Murder of Rose Hand

ROSE Hand, of Birr Street, Kilcormac, was sixteen years of age when she was 'foully done to death', reported the *Westmeath Offaly Independent* in May 1950. It was a case that should always remind Gardaí of the importance of probing carefully all cases of death attended with suspicious circumstances, wrote Supt Lawlor.

Rose had been raised in a tiny village with her eight brothers and sisters, and attended the local convent school. She completed a secretarial course the year before her death in Birr Technical school, and subsequently beat fifteen applicants called for interview for a post as a shorthand typist with Bord na Mona at their Boora Camp works in Offaly. She began work on 16 December 1949 and left home every morning at 8 a.m. to cycle across the bog to the plant eight-and-a-half miles away, arriving there promptly for 9 a.m. The Bord na Mona plant was only three miles away across the bog as the crow flies but the bumpy bad road wound around the furze-covered bog in a casual meander. It was a fine spin on a summer morning with the Slieve Bloom mountains a purple haze in the distance, but on a winter's night it was a lonely dark and dangerous road. On the morning of 12 May Rose Hand left her home as usual, punctually at 8 a.m., but failed to report for work. By 6 o'clock that evening, Rose had not returned home, her parents were concerned, and her father Fred, a builder's labourer, and his brother Joe, left Kilcormac to check with her work supervisor. At the Boora Camp they discovered that Rose had failed to report for work that morning, but no alarm had been raised as it was assumed she was ill and was on a day's sick leave.

Her father was now very worried. Rose had never had a day off work since she started, she was conscientious about putting in a full attendance for her five-and-a-half day week so something must have happened to her. Fred Hand called in to a number of houses on his way back to Kilcormac to ask if anyone had seen his daughter. But no one had seen the girl either in the morning or later in the day. Disappointed, he returned home to see whether Rose had returned in his absence, but was met at the gate by his equally dismayed wife. Fred then went to the Garda station in Kilcormac where he reported Rose missing to Sergeant John Skehan who resided in the attached living quarters.

Although it was 11 p.m. and a dark night, the sergeant organised a search party of locals from houses in the village. Some were roused from their beds and they set out along the route Rose Hand normally took to work. They searched until almost 3 a.m., but to no avail.

At first light the following morning, a Saturday, another search was organised, with teams made up of dozens of volunteers from the village, co-ordinated by Sgt Skehan.

The search went on throughout the day. The parish priest, Fr O'Connor, had been consoling Rose's family. That evening, as Sergeant Skehan was considering calling off the search, the priest called. As the Sergeant was drawing up plans to allocate search areas to different groups, the priest suggested they try the area around Lumcloon, a boggy area bounded by countless gorsebushes that Rose would have had to pass on her way to work.

There was light and plenty of time, so Sgt Skehan said he would lead an extra search party made up of the priest and two altar servers, one of them being Daniel, a younger brother of Rose Hand. The Lumcloon area was near a large whitethorn bush, known as the Beggar's Bush, which ran straight along the roadside, and the road ran through bog covered in heather and furze.

After climbing over a wattle fence, the priest said he'd got a feeling of uneasiness, as there was a depression in the drain, as if it had been trampled on. He saw two sets of small bones, one the length of his finger, and one the size of the back of his hand, in the ditch. He thought they were rabbits' bones. The priest continued his search along the ditch, until he had to climb out of it to avoid a furze bush.

About ten minutes into the search the priest shouted out, calling to the Sergeant to come quickly. Sgt Skehan found the priest standing over a black framed woman's bike lying on its side. The bicycle could not have been seen from the road, and would be obscured from any casual search of the area.

Daniel Hand recognised the bicycle, it belonged to his sister 'Rosie', he told the men. There was smeared blood on one of the handlebar grips, and there were a few tiny drops of blood on the frame of the heavy bicycle. As he looked around the bicycle the Sergeant saw a piece of bone on the ground, he stooped and picked it up. He wasn't to know at the time, but forensic science examination subsequently showed that it was a small section of skull bone.

The four hunted in the thick gorse bushes around the bicycle, until a few minutes later the priest again called out, 'Sergeant, sergeant, here is the body.' As the sergeant rounded a gorse bush he saw the priest kneeling by the body, and heard him say, 'Oh, God bless us.'

Rosie Hand was dead, and had been for some time. The sight was horrific. Young Daniel wailed out in shock that it was his sister. He recognised her clothes. Her head had been partly blown away by a gunshot, part of her skull rested yards away from her body. Thirteen-year-old Daniel and the other youth, Joseph Molloy, were extremely upset at the horrible sight and they ran away crying. Sergeant Skehan called to them to wait back at the road-side by the car.

The body was lying on its back only five paces from the roadside, and beyond a hedge cutting off the view from the road, approximately half way between her home and work.

Sgt Skehan, who had known Rosie since she was a baby, remained at the scene and despatched Fr O'Connor back to Kilcormac Garda station to report the sad news. The search was immediately called off and Supt McCabe from Birr, the District headquarters, was informed and he in turn called in the Technical Bureau. It was 7.30 p.m. that evening when Supt Edward McCabe from Birr and Sgt Sloan from Ferbane arrived at the scene.

The Superintendent noted the position of the body and looked around the scene himself. He picked up a bloodstained shotgun cartridge wad which was in a wet boggy drain near the body. It was estimated that the dead girl would have arrived at Lumcloon at about 8.20 a.m. the previous morning, having cycled almost four miles from her home.

All houses on the route were checked by Gardaí in an attempt to trace people who might have seen Rosie Hand on the morning she was killed. The route between the works and Rosie's home was not densely populated, and it wasn't long before the Gardaí turned up something suspicious. Bernard Guinan from nearby Lumcloon hadn't seen Rosie, but at about 8.45 a.m. on the Friday he was passing the spot where her body was later found. Shortly before he came to that spot he saw a bicycle on the side of the road lying against a bush. He also saw a man he knew as twenty-seven-year-old

Patrick Heffernan, a night watchman, come out of the furze on the side of the roadway and walk towards the bicycle. Heffernan's face had red blotches on it and he was dressed in his working clothes.

As he walked closer, Heffernan lifted his hand in a wave, and said 'Hello', and Guinan returned the salute. As he got closer he could see that the marks on his face were scratches that he might have got from the furze, said Guinan.

Guinan saw Heffernan outside his own house the following morning and asked if he'd heard any news about Rosie. Heffernan said no he hadn't, and that he was very sorry about it as she was a distant cousin of his. As the hunt for the killer of the teenager continued, more inquiries were made about Heffernan, a single man who worked as a night watchman employed in the Brosna drainage scheme. He lived in a council cottage on a link road between the main Tullamore to Cloghan road and the Kilcormac to Ferbane road, with his father and sister. He cycled on the same road as Rosie, and would have met her on occasion as they cycled in the same direction — he on his way home after night work and she on her way to Boora Camp. Most days he carried a shotgun and was a good shot, often taking home a rabbit for the evening meal.

Supt McCabe called to the Heffernan home to interview him, but he had already gone. He had left for work at about 7 p.m. to cycle the three-and-a-half miles to his post as nightwatchman, said his father, Michael, who worked as a labourer on the same drainage scheme. The Gardaí asked to see Patrick's shotgun, and then took possession of it, a box of cartridges and Heffernan's clothes.

After they were put into the boot of the Garda car, Supt McCabe set out for Barnaboy Bridge, about half a mile away from Kilcormac village with his driver Sergeant Flaherty and Sergeant Sloan. When the three Gardaí arrived it was after 11 p.m. and Heffernan was sitting in the nightwatchman's hut. Heffernan said he hadn't seen Rosie Hand the previous morning. He had left work at about 8.15 a.m. and had arrived home at 9.15 a.m. Heffernan said he'd stopped briefly on the way home to fire a shot at a rabbit in Grogan's field, but had missed. He only had one cartridge with him. He hadn't brought his shotgun with him that night because he was going to Mass on the way home the following morning, he said. He was dressed in a blue pin-striped suit, which he said was his 'Sunday best' suit.

Heffernan was trembling so much as he answered the superintendent's questions that one of the sergeants asked him if he were cold. 'No,' he replied and denied that he was shaking.

Heffernan was asked if he would put his information in a statement for the investigation team. He agreed readily. As the superintendent searched him before putting him into the Garda car, Heffernan turned to Sgt Sloan whom he knew and asked, 'Won't you speak for me?'

At Kilcormac Garda station he was put into the sergeant's room, while the clothes Michael Heffernan had given the Gardaí were examined. On the dungarees and an old coat, tiny flecks of blood, barely visible to the human eye, were discovered. Heffernan was again asked if had seen Rosie Hand on the Friday morning. No, he insisted, and continued to insist until the bloodstained clothes were dumped on the desk in front of him. He burst into tears, sobbing aloud.

'I did not do her any harm, I did not rape her, will you try to help me?' Heffernan sobbed to Detective Garda Joseph McNamara who had arrived from Birr with the Superintendent. He wanted to say something, he said, but wouldn't say it or make a statement until Sgt Sloan was present. Heffernan was still seated at the table sobbing into his arms when the sergeant arrived. It was 3 a.m. before the statement was completed, signed and witnessed.

'I knew Rose Hand,' the statement read. 'On the Friday morning I caught up with her at Lumcloon. She was cycling in front of me and I overtook her.

'As I came up to her, the gun, which I had in my hand resting on the handlebars, went off and struck her round the head and face. She fell off the bicycle on the left-hand side of the road. She fell with her head towards the ditch and her feet towards the road.

'I got a shock and staggered off my bicycle as best I could and went over to where she lay. I picked her up and went through the hedge into the field and left her in the furze. I left her bicycle across the hedge too.

'I went home. She was bleeding from the head when I took her into the furze. I didn't know whether she was dead or alive. I told no one about the shooting. I didn't know what to do.'

The statement took about thirty minutes to write down. Heffernan spoke calmly and was at ease throughout what to other people would be an ordeal. He drank tea and ate bread and butter which was brought into the room as the statement was being made. The statement pointed to a terrible accident, a mistake, but certainly no murder. There was no reason to send Heffernan to the gallows.

When Supt George Lawlor arrived later, Heffernan's statement had been typed up and he was given a copy of it. 'After reading it I remarked to those present that it looked as if we would get home early. I was very soon to be disillusioned,' George Lawlor recalled.

According to Heffernan's statement it was an accident, a tragedy, but there had been no intent and therefore no murder. But a detailed investigation of the scene of the shooting and the post mortem were to combine to discredit and give the lie to Heffernan's account of the shooting.

Dr John McGrath, the State Pathologist, examined both the body and the scene. There were scattered bloodstains on the leaves and twigs in a hedge along the roadside, which would have been caused by flying or falling drops of blood. In a ditch beyond the hedge he saw pieces of bone and brain matter and blood. Further back from the road lay the dead body of the girl. Her coat was open and her clothing was in disarray and some of it was bloodstained. There were mud stains on the girl's stocking, coat and frock, the report said.

There were a total of nine pellet marks on the back of the girl's right shoulder. The main portion of the charge had hit her somewhere below the right ear. The lowest pellet was found eight inches below her right shoulder, there was one pellet mark on her right wrist and, based on his observation of the line of pellet marks, the Pathologist formed the opinion that she had been shot from behind, 'somewhat from below and from the right towards the left.'

The skull was extensively fractured on the right side, and her upper and lower jaws were fragmented from the blast of a shotgun. There were some recent scrapes on the girl's upper lip and the lower part of her nose, and a slight mark on her left cheek. There were two bruises on the inner side of the right shin, and more on her hands, which appeared to have been caused shortly before death.

Death was due to shock and haemorrhage caused by gunshot wounds to the head. The girl had been shot while in an upright position, the post mortem report showed.

Dr McGrath had also carried out a minute examination of the roadway and the grass margin that ran along its sides where Rosie had been found. But as he could find no bloodstains on the grass or roadway, he concluded that she had not been shot there.

The scene was photographed by a Garda photographer, while another Garda took measurements to draw up a scaled plan of the area, marking on this map where the shotgun cartridge, the bicycle and the body had been found.

The scene was 3.5 miles from Kilcormac village, and the road there was 11.5 feet in width with a grass margin 7.5 feet wide, sloping sharply from the road's edge to the bottom of the hedge. The hedge was made up mainly of whitethorn with a little black birch and dead twigs. At its lowest it was 2 feet 2 inches in height. On the inside of the hedge lay a dyke with a drop of approximately 3.5 feet from the base of the hedge to the dyke. The dyke consisted of liquid turf mould with an occasional tuft of reeds.

In the dyke Supt McCabe picked up a cartridge wad, and beside it lay a piece of jaw bone, blood and brain matter. The liquid turf mould bore an unmistakable trail of eight partially filled footprints. A short distance to the right of the dyke, on the grass, several small patches of blood were visible, while in the field directly in line with the cartridge wad, and 25 feet from the hedge, lay a hair slide.

From the dyke where the cartridge was found and in a diagonal line to the left of it, there were clear signs that the body had been dragged a distance of 36 feet and concealed in the furzes, hiding it completely from view from the roadside. The clothing could have been disarranged in the removal of the body from the dyke to the furze. A pair of knickers was found partly concealed in a bush over eight feet away.

The dead girl's bicycle lay in a clump of furze to the right of the body. It was 45 feet from the body and 26 feet from the road. 'The position of the undergarment naturally raised grave suspicion in the minds of the investigators but the Pathologist's examination and the subsequent post mortem examination proved that such suspicions of rape were groundless, though they did not exclude the possibility of an attempt having been made,' wrote the Technical Bureau chief.

Aerial photographs of the scene were taken from a small plane. However, they were not a success, and were not used in the court, which subsequently relied on detailed maps. If they had been called into evidence it would have been only the second time that photos would have been used in a murder trial.

The most important discovery of all, George Lawlor later recalled, was that which arose from an exhaustive and thorough examination of the scene on the road side of the hedge, the grass margin and the outside of the lower portion of the hedge directly at the point where the shotgun wad, brain matter and blood were found in the dyke. There were no signs of blood, brain matter or, in fact, anything to denote that a shooting or struggle had taken place, on the roadside or within three hundred feet in either direction of the roadway. The hedge at this point was unbroken. At the bottom of the hedge were dead twigs and some of them had been broken as if a small body had brushed through it, but there were no bloodstains here.

Directly on top of the hedge, which measured approximately 2.5 feet in width at this part, there were numerous blood spots on the leaves and branches. They had apparently dropped from the top down through the hedge — a distance of about two feet. Heffernan's account of the shooting didn't measure up to the facts, concluded George Lawlor. 'From the absence of blood or brain matter on the road grass margin and even on the outside and bottom of the hedge on the roadside, it was difficult to understand how Rose Hand could have been shot as described by Heffernan in his statement.

'The findings suggested that the dead woman had been shot in the head at a point very close to the hedge itself and that the body had tumbled over into the dyke. The deceased's bicycle was undamaged and there were no pellet marks visible although the right-hand rubber grip and the handlebars bore slight bloodstains. These were later described by Dr John McGrath as smears of human blood. A few tiny blood spots were found on the plated surface of the bar of the front brake. The smears of blood indicated that some person had handled the bicycle with bloodstained hands and the spots of blood on the brake were suggestive of flying spots or flecks of blood. Fingerprints could not be found on the bicycle.

'The absence of all signs on the bicycle, road and grass margin gave the lie to Heffernan's statement, but there was more evidence forthcoming to establish that this was not an accident, but a deliberate killing by a debased-minded creature. The major portion of the unfortunate girl's head had been blown away and twenty-nine gunshot pellets were located in the right shoulder and back.' George Lawlor estimated that the shot which killed the girl was discharged approximately twenty feet from her.

All the pathology and forensic evidence pointed to a number of facts — that Rose Hand had been shot standing up, and from behind. There were no marks on the back of the bike, so she couldn't have been shot riding it. Also there were no blood marks on the roadway and margin, further substantiating that point. Part of her skull was found inside the hedge, along with the wad from a discharged shotgun cartridge, all indicating that she had been shot as she stood close to the hedge and ditch separating the road from the adjoining bog land and that her body had then been dragged and carried further from the road into the furze.

On Sunday 14th, Heffernan was charged with the murder of Rose Hand at a special sitting of the District Court convened in Kilcormac Garda station. He was remanded to Mountjoy jail, and was brought there handcuffed to a Garda in an official car. The following day hundreds of people lined the roadway as Rose Hand's body was brought to the local church and buried.

Heffernan was dressed casually in a brown sports coat, brown trousers and an open-necked green shirt when his trial opened on 6 November 1950 in Green Street courthouse. He pleaded 'Not Guilty' in a firm clear voice when the charge was put to him, and sat with his hands clasped throughout the trial.

'It was a gruesome and ghastly story,' said prosecuting counsel, Mr R.J. McLoughlin, S.C., on the opening day of the trial.

The concentration of the shot and the closeness of its spread indicated that the range of fire was from 13 to 23 feet, which would put the man who fired the gun at the centre of the road, while the girl was near the edge.

'What was he doing there and what did he intend doing when he had the gun pointed in the direction of the girl?' he asked. That was something the jury would have to consider. There was also no escaping the fact that the girl's body was not fully clothed when her body was discovered.

'But, the prosecution didn't say that there was anything in the nature of a physical assault before she was shot,' the defence emphasised.

One of the first people to speak to Patrick Heffernan after Rose Hand went missing was her uncle, Joe Hand. On the return journey from Boora Camp where he had called to check on whether his niece had gone to work, he saw Heffernan at Barnaboy Bridge. He bade him goodnight, and thought he answered as he sailed past, furiously pedalling his battered bike. He continued on to the Garda station with his brother Fred, the girl's father, where they reported her missing. Joe Hand then returned to the bridge and asked Heffernan if he had seen any sign of the girl. No, he replied. 'I asked him was he ever along with Rosie in the mornings, and he said "no" but that she was either ahead or behind him.' Heffernan was wearing his good clothes that night, not his usual working clothes.

A friend of Rosie, Bridie Carroll, told the court that she had seen the dead girl on the Friday morning. They had been to the pictures together in Kilcormac Hall on the previous night. At the back of the hall, Heffernan was standing, 'doing terrible looking at Rose when the lights went on,' she said.

On the day of the shooting, James Daly, a labourer, was cycling home to Kilcormac at about 7.10 p.m. He could see the handlebars of a bicycle on the grass verge, and saw Heffernan emerging through a gap in the fencing near where the body was eventually discovered. He carried his single-barrelled shotgun in his hand. Heffernan mounted his bicycle and headed off, he looked back three times but didn't slow down. Daly eventually caught up with him, and they chatted. Heffernan told him he had taken some medicine and had just had time to jump off his bicycle and rush into the furze, being short taken. Heffernan told him as they cycled that earlier that morning he had seen a man, a stranger, with a gun on the other side of the road hidden behind a bush.

'Clearly' said George Lawlor, 'his intention was to create the impression that a strange man had shot Rose Hand. Why had Heffernan returned to the scene? Was he looking for the empty cartridge case which lay nearby? Or was it to conceal the body or bicycle more thoroughly? In any case there seems to be some truth in the old adage that a murderer always returns to the scene of his crime. Be that as it may, he knew Rose Hand's body lay there with its head almost blown away. Yet emerging from that scene at 6.50 p.m. he could engage in a conversation with his neighbour without betraying any nervousness. His actions up to this time were to conceal his handiwork which, if accidental, he had no reason to do.'

There was further evidence of Heffernan's nerve. On the Saturday morning, Mrs Allie Dolan from Lumcloon chatted to Heffernan as she leaned over her front gate. He asked her if she'd got a scare when the Gardaí called the previous night. Heffernan told her he hadn't seen Rosie Hand that day as he'd been home early from work. She said maybe she'd gone away in a motor car to get another job or to get married. Heffernan said he wouldn't think so, 'She wasn't gone in the head anyway,' he said.

That afternoon he met Patrick Camon, a farmer from Cloghan. They talked about the missing girl. Camon asked if he'd heard anything new, Heffernan said no, and agreed with him when he suggested that maybe she'd gone to England or ran off to get married.

Another man from the locality, Joey Cleary from Barnaboy, met Heffernan on the Saturday evening in his brother's farmyard, where Heffernan joked 'Good man Paddy — you done it.'

A charge hand on the drainage scheme, John Horan, also met Heffernan that Saturday. Heffernan had stopped to chat to a group of people; when one of them remarked they would all be questioned he said, 'Why should I do anything to her when she is my second cousin?'

When Martin Rigney asked Heffernan if it was true about 'that terrible thing' he replied it must be, judging by the number of 'shiny peaks' in the area, referring to the Gardaí.

Rigney speculated, 'Who on earth would do the like of that, kill a girl?' and Heffernan replied 'What about the boys who come in here?' nodding towards Kilcormac. 'Why would they do it?' asked Rigney. 'Over that job in Boora. Some of them thought they would get it and they didn't get it,' said Heffernan.

The only sign of strain shown by Heffernan was noticed by his sister Kathleen. On his return from work at about nine o'clock on the Saturday morning he had sat quietly by the fire, lost in his thoughts and biting his nails. It was the first time she had ever noticed him biting his nails.

Detective Sergeant P.J. Murphy, from the ballistics section of the Technical Bureau, had examined the seized shotgun which was licensed to Heffernan, he told the Central Criminal Court. He loaded the gun with a cartridge, then knocked the gun stock and then the barrel of the gun against the floor to see whether it would go off accidentally. He also tried to fire the gun by applying pressure to the back of the hammer, but nothing happened. He then cocked it and applied pressure in the same way and stamped the stock of the gun against the floor with force, but he still failed to make the gun discharge. He carried out a range of other tests, eventually measuring the pressure that had to be exerted on the trigger at 3.75 pounds — a safe pressure, he said. Sgt Murphy had also been given the cartridge case found at the scene of the shooting, and after firing a number of test cartridges from the gun, he compared them under a microscope. The distinctive barrelling marks on each of the cartridge shells matched precisely the marks on the cartridge case found at the scene of the killing, linking the gun to the scene.

Standing in the witness box, Heffernan said that the first time he had ever met Rose Hand was when he cycled up behind her and asked her was she a 'Hand'. She said she was, they were second cousins, but he never associated with her, he said.

On the way home on the morning of 12 May he was cycling with the gun resting on the handlebars of his bicycle. He noticed a woman cycling in front of him and he made an effort to pass her out at a point where the surface was not good and there were a lot of holes and gravel on the road.

'When I was coming up to the person on the bike I pulled over on my right side. I got into some kind of difficulties on the road. I don't know whether it was a stone or a bump that gave the bicycle a jerk, and the gun happened to go off,' he told the court.

'I saw the girl fall. I scrambled over to her and picked her up. I saw her bleeding from the head. I said, "Are you dead, Rosie?" That was the first time I knew who it was,' said Heffernan.

When he was asked why he took the body into the bog, he replied 'I lost control of myself and I did not know what to do.' He said that he was 'feeling nervous' and had 'begun to worry anyway' as people asked him if he had seen Rosie Hand.

After Heffernan had testified in his own defence, Edmund White, manager of Hely's gun department in Dublin's Dame Street, was called to give his opinion of the shotgun. He handled an estimated 1,700 to 2,000 guns and rifles in a year, and described the gun as a single-barrelled 12-bore, commonly known as a farmer's gun. It was in an extremely bad condition, the action was loose, the fore-end catch was missing, the stock was homemade and the bore end was held open with a rubber band. The rebound mechanism was almost worn away, and by pulling the hammer back about half-way or less and letting it slip forward it would discharge a cartridge. Having seen Heffernan sit on a bike in the courtroom to demonstrate how he said he carried the gun, Edmund White said he believed the gun could have gone off accidentally.

Mr Justice Dixon, summing up, said there was no motive suggested, proved, or attempted and this was not a necessary requirement. What was crucial however, was the position of the girl at the time she was shot. If she was within a yard or so of the hedge it was hardly credible that she was on her bicycle at the time, and it certainly was not credible that she was on the bicycle in the manner described by Heffernan — in the centre of the road. Heffernan relied on the bloodstains found on the front of the bicycle as confirmation of his story. It was a matter for the jury to consider whether the cartridge wad, a piece of skull bone, brain matter and the girl's hair slide found in the drain could have occupied the positions which they did, simply by the body being dropped, as Heffernan said, over the hedge. When the jury retired they took the gun and the bicycle with them to help them reach a decision. That decision came back approximately ninety minutes later. It was a verdict of 'Guilty', and Mr Justice Dixon fixed 6 December as the execution date. Heffernan had nothing to say, when asked, but turned pale and swayed in the dock where he stood as sentence was passed. On Sunday 12 November as the trial progressed, however, the jury had mingled with and spoken to members of the public while taking refreshments in a hotel. Because of this, Heffernan was granted a retrial in March 1951. He was convicted a second time, and appealed his conviction. The appeal was dismissed, but on 15 May he was granted a reprieve and served a jail sentence instead of hanging.

14.

The Turkey Puzzle

THE Flynns were considered a wealthy family. They had a large farm near Beaufort, Co. Kerry; it had good tillage for oats and hay, it kept cattle and turkeys and produced 30 tons of apples and 100 tons of potatoes a year.

The two-storeyed house was tiled and situated in a well-kept garden set back off the road behind an impressive entrance wall. The four-bedroomed house was close to the orchard, extensive outhouses, grain stores, and the fresh water well was just thirty feet from the scullery door. Thady and Hannah Flynn were married for twenty years and had three fine children, two girls and a boy. Thady was a Peace Commissioner, a pillar of the community, and by November 1942 had discovered a new interest in the Church and was rarely seen without a prayer book.

Hannah's eldest brother, John Joy, had returned from America after an accident with a fortune. He lived with them, but had died about eight years previously leaving over £2,000 to Hannah and the children, which provided for clothing and a top-class education.

Fifteen-year-old Marie Flynn was the first home from school on the evening of Monday 16 November. Her mother normally had her dinner ready for her and she was surprised to find no one in the house and no dinner prepared. The back kitchen had been washed out, but there was nobody about the house. She went from room to room, and found her mother's bedclothes still in disarray. She also found her mother's bicycle in its usual place in the house, the trap in the yard and her mother's good clothes still in the wardrobe, so she knew she hadn't gone to Killarney. Fearing something had happened to her, she started to cry and went looking for her father in the fields.

John Joe, the baby of the family aged fourteen, also came home to an empty house. As he wandered about the garden he sensed something was wrong. Instead of the usual two ropes with a bucket attached to a windlass, he saw there were four ropes going down the well. As he stretched in over the well to look down, the workman Donal Leen came in from the potato fields and joined him, at about five o'clock.

Marie had found her father in the meantime and they walked back to the house. 'Where's Mammy?' she asked. 'I don't know,' said Thady, saying that she hadn't called him in for his dinner that day.

Leen meanwhile was heaving on one of the ropes and eventually dragged it to the lip of the well where both he and John Joe were surprised to see a live turkey perching on the rim of a bottomless old bucket. Under the fat turkey was what looked suspiciously familiar, part of Hannah Flynn's black overall. Leen threw the bucket back down and tried to sink it but couldn't. Neither could he see the foot of the well, as it was about 22 feet down and too dark.

'We're after getting a turkey in the well, and there's something else in it,' Leen told his employer as he came into the garden. Thady tried to sink the bucket but could feel it bouncing off something, 'It won't sink,' he remarked.

As Leen and John Joe took hold of the rope, Thady suddenly became upset. 'Oh, she's there, oh, she's there,' he gasped and realisation dawned on both twenty-four-year-old Leen and John Joe. 'Go and get help, she's in there — go and get Dan Butler,' cried Thady. They returned with Dan and Mrs Catherine Burke, a nurse, who were their two nearest neighbours. A ladder was dragged over to the well and inserted into it. Another neighbour, Paddy Casey, a farm labourer, climbed down into the well which was lined with stones and decreased in diameter with depth. At its base it was two feet in diameter, at its mouth thirty inches.

'There's a body here,' he shouted up, to the heads that peered down into the gloom. He had seen a leg protruding above the water level.

The Garda and the local priest were immediately sent for as Casey climbed back up the ladder. As the group waited and worried, Thady Flynn led them in a decade of the rosary.

Mrs Burke insisted that a rope should be tied around her waist and then clutching a second rope she climbed into the well and went down to the very bottom.

The local Sergeant Denis McDonnell had arrived at the scene, and he shone his torch down the well, which had been surrounded by flickering candles, to help Nurse Burke tie the second rope around the protruding leg. That done she climbed back up again and the body was hauled to the surface. It was the badly cut and battered body of fifty-three-year-old Hannah Thady. The corpse was brought into the house and laid out on the kitchen table. Thady Flynn took no part in this operation.

'This is terrible,' Flynn told the Sergeant. He pointed to a bucket and some pot hooks tied to the ropes, and said, 'She must have used those trying to get the turkey out of the well.' Flynn said that he hadn't thought much about her absence at lunchtime as his wife often went away without telling him. There had been a timber covering over the well up to about six months ago, but Flynn had removed it and erected the windlass saying the well needed constant airing. His wife had complained at the time that her turkeys were in danger of falling into the well. He had taken one out of the well about three weeks earlier, and a second one a short time before that, he told the Sergeant.

The body was moved upstairs to the main bedroom and local women began the work of laying out the corpse for the wake and ensuing funeral.

The inquest was held the following day. Thady Flynn said that he had been happily married for twenty years, and there had never been a bad word between them. On the day of the accident he had been in the potato field with Leen while his wife was at home. She looked after the turkeys, which were a useful cash crop at Christmas time. Thady said he had remained in the field. He had not left except to go to seventy-year-old Paddy Butler's, a neighbour, to borrow a shovel. He didn't go to his own house when he went to Butlers and was away only a few minutes. He was surprised his wife hadn't called them into lunch, he said.

Two doctors also gave evidence at the brief inquest. They said that death was due to a fractured neck , and that the head injuries on the dead woman were consistent with a fall down the well.

The funeral was held the following day. Even as the woman was being buried the gossip started. At the house as the wake continued, Mrs Ellen Doyle, a sister of the dead woman, was heard to ask a number of people: 'Who put my sister in the well? She must have been put in? Who put her in?' A voice in the crowded living room hissed: 'For the sake of the children, say no more,' as Thady Flynn tried to hush her, saying soothingly, 'Mrs Doyle, Mrs Doyle!' It was the first time Ellen had visited the house in six years.

Four days later Supt Patrick Harte, based in Killarney, was to open a file on the death of Mrs Hannah Flynn, after some inquiries into the rumours had borne fruit. That afternoon, of the 20th, the Technical Bureau were on their way to Kerry, at his request, as was the State Pathologist, Dr John McGrath, with an order to exhume the dead woman's body from its grave in Kilbonane churchyard.

The post mortem examination held the following day gave weight to the rumours. There were a large number of bruises on the body, but most serious of all the injuries was a severe fracture of the skull about eight inches long. The skull bone had been laid bare by the blow which stripped the skin from her head. That type of injury needed a 'severe impact' Dr McGrath said. There were a total of six other heavy blows to the head, none as severe as the biggest one. The woman was alive when she entered into the well, but only just long enough to take a breath or two. Death was due to shock and asphyxia following injuries to the head which had caused fracture of the skull and haemmorhage, his report concluded. The most experienced Pathologist in the country, he explained that he very much doubted that the fracture of the head was caused by contact with the bottom of the well or by bouncing off the stone walls on the way down. However, it was most likely that she had gone into the well head first. The injuries to Mrs Flynn's head could only have been caused by a blunt instrument, not a knife or an axe. He also ruled out the possibility that she might have suffered a heart attack and fallen into the well. Impossible, he said, she had a healthy heart and there was no sign of scarring of the heart tissue.

Four days earlier the rumours circulating about Thady Flynn had prompted Superintendent Harte to reconsider the findings of the inquest, which had been held in conformity to law, to certify the dead woman's identity and both how and where she died.

Tongues wagged that relations between Thady and his wife were not as good as Flynn made out and that even in his advancing years he had struck up a number of liaisons with women that didn't sit comfortably with either his wife or his new image as a religious zealot.

Supt Harte decided to question Donal Leen a second time. Leen changed his story quickly. The details significantly altered what he had told both the inquest and the Gardaí.

As Supt Lawlor was to record in his file on the case, 'Leen volunteered important information to the effect that Thady Flynn had been absent from the potato field for about half an hour to three quarters of an hour, and not ten minutes as he had said in an earlier statement to the inquest.

'He had also said that during his employer's absence he had heard a scream like that of a woman and the cry of a turkey as if it were being caught.

'Questioned regarding the clothes worn by Thady Flynn on the morning of 16 November, he said that he had started the day wearing his dungarees but when he returned with the shovel from Butlers he had changed his clothes. He also remembered that the floor in the kitchen appeared as if it had been recently washed out.' Supt Lawlor noted in his file.

Mrs Flynn was in good spirits that morning as both he and Thady left to work in one of the potato fields near the house. Thady told him he was going to Butlers to get a shovel, and he estimated that it was about ten minutes later that he heard a scream, which he thought was Hannah Flynn's. After that he heard the screech of a turkey as if it had just been caught. Both noises came from the direction of Flynn's house. After about forty-five minutes Flynn returned out of breath, but with the shovel and wearing different clothes.

Usually they were called for their lunch at about 1 p.m., but that day they were not called. It was about 2.30 p.m. when Flynn said they would have to prepare their meal themselves, and he sent Leen on to the house while he returned the shovel. Normally when Mrs Flynn left the house she would leave the lunch on the table for the working men, but the table was bare. Leen saw her bicycle in the back lean-to kitchen where he noticed that the floor had been washed out. He opened the back door to look out in to the garden, and saw no one there but he did notice that the stone flags outside the back door had also been washed and were still wet. When Thady returned he asked if anyone was in, and when told no, said Hannah wasn't at Butlers either. Leen rekindled the fire and filled the kettle with water to make coffee.

That evening he had been at the house when young John Joe discovered his mother's body in the well.

The following morning Leen noticed bloodstains on the walls of the back kitchen. In the turf shed to the west and back of the house he found a piece of linoleum bearing bloodstains, and a piece of a ploughshare which also had bloodstains on it. On the following two days he noticed somebody had been trying to scratch the dried blood spatters off the walls of the back kitchen.

'Leen's statement naturally put a different complexion on the untimely death of Mrs Flynn and necessitated a further approach to Thady Flynn on the matter,' wrote Supt Lawlor.

On Thursday 19th at twenty minutes to five Supt Harte arrived at Flynn's house with a number of Gardaí. Thady Flynn welcomed them into the house, invited them to look around and was most affable. 'Thank God, you are going to clear up this matter. You will be doing me a great turn and you know it,' he told them.

He was asked to produce the clothing he wore on the day his wife died, and he produced a number of items but not the dungarees and lounge jacket which Leen said he had been wearing.

The Gardaí carried out a cursory inspection of the house. Asked to explain why there were bloodstains in the fireplace of his bedroom, he rolled up his trousers and took a bandage off a sore on his leg and showed it to them as an explanation.

Downstairs, blood marks on the wall underneath a table on which there was a meat safe — used to store meat and keep flies away — were pointed out to him.

'Do you see those blood marks on the wall, how did they come there?' asked Supt Harte.

'That's the safe for meat. Would there be any meat in it?' asked Thady, and then, in the words of the Superintendent he 'rushed at' the safe and opened it, and the Superintendent had to hold him back 'to prevent him from interfering with it'.

Flynn said he couldn't explain why there were blood marks there, or why there were similar blood marks on the front of the safe and the table.

'What would have caused those stains on the floor under the table?' asked the Superintendent, offering him the opportunity to explain all the marks in the room.

'Only as I said before, that there was meat put into the safe the day it happened, and those stains may have been caused by the meat dropping onto the floor. I mean to say that the missus, my wife, was small and she would be taking out the meat from the safe and she would splash blood on the table.'

Fresh chips off the wall underneath the table, which had been described by Leen, were caused by pushing boxes up against the wall, said Thady Flynn.

Bloodstains on the back of the door were caused by dead fowl hanging from a hook there, he said.

Questioned about the clothes he produced, a bloodstained pair of boots and trousers, he replied, 'I really don't know how those stains came on them but I was helping to put the dead body on the table that night. They must have stained when I put the corpse up on the kitchen table when she was brought in that night.'

Thady Flynn went on to claim that his brother-in-law, Pat Joy, was jealous of him.

'I feel now I know what their game is. I will tell you all the story. There was another brother of my wife's, John Joy. He died here in this house eight or ten years ago and he left me £2,000. He left this money for my children, and the Joys are mad since then because I got all this money. Pat Joy now thinks when his sister is gone that I will reap all the reward and that's what's vexing him,' he said. He went on to allege that his wife's family had a history of insanity, with three close relatives committed to the asylum, where one uncle had died raving over twenty years previously.

'My wife also used to be a little nervy at times but I did not say anything about it for the sake of the children. She was a great little woman and even though she would go to Killarney she would have her work done before she would go,' he said. The statement was witnessed and signed at 6.15 p.m. that evening.

The cursory search of the house had also led the Gardaí to a wardrobe in nineteen-year-old Kathleen's bedroom. The wardrobe was locked, and when opened a bank deposit receipt for £1,100 in the name of the dead woman and her two daughters was found. A letter addressed to 'My dearest Tim, signed 'Always your fond pal, Ellie' and marked with a lot of kiss signs, was also discovered.

The following day, Flynn was to turn to his brother-in-law Pat Joy and tell him, 'The Guards are coming to clear up the situation for the children's sake.'

That same Thursday Flynn was again working with Leen in the fields, and he warned Leen: 'The Guards are suspicious of the overalls, and if they ask you anything about them tell them that you got them from me last July.' Flynn had in fact given Leen another pair of overalls, and the next morning he asked Leen where he had them. In his room, replied Leen. 'Well why did you not tell me that before, and I would have given them to the Guard?' said Flynn.

On Friday night, four days after the dead woman had been found, the Technical Bureau arrived in Killarney. A search of Thady Flynn's farm and house was carried out the following morning as Dr McGrath arrived, and the body was exhumed and the post mortem examination began.

By 11 a.m. a pair of bloodstained dungarees and a grey lounge jacket were found hidden in the barn under a pile of oats. In the pocket of the jacket were a pair of keys which opened the wardrobe which held the letter and deposit book and were in the possession of Mrs Flynn before her death.

Thady Flynn was questioned again that morning, by Superintendent Harte and Lawlor for almost three hours. He immediately admitted that the dungarees and jacket were his. But the bloodstains that marked both items of clothing were from rabbits, he said. Flynn said he had not seen either the dungarees or jacket for the past eight days. He had thrown them into the shed to dry after a day working in the rain, he explained.

He did not own the keys found in the pocket of the dungarees, and had never seen them before they were produced, he said. 'You see, as a farmer, I am not particular what I wear,' Thady Flynn told the two Superintendents. 'But I can dress as good as any man on Sunday, and I don't mind what I wear on weekdays and I did not mind wearing this old bloodstained dungaree when I was after handling the rabbits.

'I told you before on Thursday in the presence of my brother, John, that I wanted you to go to the bottom of all this. That I would help you. I want you to do so still for the month to come, or for the twelve months to come, and let them go to the end of a rope,' said Flynn, his ire rising.

Flynn claimed that Pat Joy and his wife's side of the family were trying to cause trouble for him — Joy even 'showed an angry face to the Beaufort Sergeant, didn't he?' asked Flynn. He went on to say that the National bank manager, Mr O'Heaney 'and the whole of County Kerry' would back up this allegation, and said that anyone could come to his house while he was away working in the fields and do anything they liked in his house.

Leen had been in the habit of going out every Sunday night to the local dance since he started on the farm the previous July. But on the night before Flynn's wife was found in the well he hadn't gone to the dance, wasn't that a strange one, asked Flynn?

He claimed a rumour was going around that he had been arguing with his wife on the night before she died, the Sunday, but he hadn't been in the house that evening he said.

'You can ask Leen who is in this house since 15 July 1942, had I ever an angry word with my wife? My little children can also tell and I will let you ask them alone. I will go away. My little wife was a good little woman even though she may take a half one of whiskey. She was a little nervous, there was insanity in her family. Leen can prove to you that myself and my wife were always on the best of terms and because of her little weakness I never said an angry word to her. She was the maker of my home. She was the best cook in the county of Kerry, and she always kept her home clean and neat,' said Thady Flynn.

Flynn said that he wasn't out of the potato field for more than five minutes the previous Monday. 'I will tell you that I left the potato pit and came out the gate onto the public road. I went back the road to Butlers for the shovel and I did not come near my own house at all. When I got the shovel from Butlers I came out onto the main road again and back up the road to the gate of my own potato field and went in that gate and down to the potato pits. I walked up and down to Butlers in the ordinary way and it took me about five or six minutes. I want to tell you that I met no one on the road and when I went for the shovel I did not come next or near my own house,' he said. 'I did not come near my own house. I did not put a foot across the road. I can give you that on oath,' he emphasised.

The only thing Leen would vouch for was that Hannah Flynn was 'a hard worker and kept a good house and table'.

However, since he had arrived at the Flynns' home, he had never heard either Hannah or Thady speak to each other. They conveyed messages to each other through the children, he said.

The Flynns' former housekeeper told the Gardaí that Hannah and herself would occasionally go to Killarney where they would go to Con McGillicuddy's or the Muckross bar in Killarney where they would have a maximum of two drinks, buying a round of port wine each.

Kathleen Flynn said that her father and mother slept apart for the past seven years. Her mother paid for all their education and clothing, and provided most of the food for the house. She had witnessed her father shouting at her mother, demanding money from her and calling her names. Both Donal Leen and herself said that there was no reason to suggest her mother ever drank.

Her father had become outwardly religious and was in the Third Order of St Francis religious society. But when he sat around the kitchen reading prayer books and Bible history, he was in fact watching his wife.

John Joe was to later say that after the Gardaí had interviewed his father, his father had approached him, saying 'You know I never opened my mouth to her in the past twelve months.' In a further effort to get his children not to speak out against him, he said 'Do

201

not be too hard on me.' He then gave him half a crown, an event so rare that John Joe easily remembered it.

The numbers of people who had witnessed Thady's deteriorating relationship with his wife increased as the investigators in the Technical Bureau spread their net. Mrs Ellen Doyle, Hannah's sister, who had been voluble at the wake, had stopped visiting the Flynn house six years previously. Thady had complained continually to her that Hannah was spending money on buying unnecessary things for the children, and was obnoxious in his behaviour. Her daughter, Theresa, said that she had heard Flynn say to his wife that he would 'kill her, burn her and bury her alive'.

Miss Aileen Rahilly, a teacher from Killarney who came to the house to teach the children music, had never heard Flynn and his wife speak to each other. Hannah told her that it would be a 'poor look out' for the children if they had to depend on their father and so she had to provide for them instead.

Tim Joy, a brother of Hannah, had often complained to Flynn that his wife was spending money in Killarney. He had not visited the house for six years until the funeral, because Thady had once produced a razor case and threatened to cut Hannah's throat.

Thady Flynn had formed a number of relationships with different women which his wife objected to loudly, and accused him of 'carrying on'.

In 1939 he began to correspond with a young married woman living in Killarney, and claimed that he would get her newly married husband a job in the Post Office by using his influence. The woman wrote to him four or five times, in ever more endearing terms, and they exchanged gifts. It was her letter, dated 24 December 1939 to Thady, that Hannah had discovered and kept locked in the upstairs wardrobe addressed to 'My dearest Tim'. She spoke coyly of the time they would 'spoil together', asking him, 'Don't you think so, but the right people never meet until it's too late, but that's destiny?' The letter was signed 'Always your fond pal, Ellie,' and followed by fifteen kiss marks and the words, 'Burn when read'. Hannah had shown this letter to the music teacher, Aileen Rahilly.

Hannah also accused Thady of having an affair with another woman, and said he was 'carrying on' with women. In May, Thady learned that his wife was about to consult a solicitor. He arrived at the office of Mr Henry Downing, a solicitor based in Killarney who had acted for his wife since 1936 and told him to tell Hannah to have sense and 'not be breaking up the home'. Hannah, however, called to Downing, and showed him a letter addressed to Thady from a woman. He subsequently wrote a letter to Thady at the behest of his wife, warning him not to associate with other women, otherwise proceedings would be issued against him. There was no reply to the letter. However, Thady subsequently told one of his workmen to intercept all post delivered to the house and bring it to him before his wife got to it.

When he was interviewed by Superintendents Lawlor and Harte, the point was put to him that there were rumours circulating about his unfaithfulness to his wife. 'There is no truth in that whatever, I am thankful to you for telling me that. The best pair in the world would have a word now and again. That's the way of life. For the twenty years I am married we lived like any farmers. We never had a word. It is awful for anyone to say that she ever went with any other man, or that I ever went with any other woman. I have always lived a strict life, and I never took a drink until 1919,' he said.

Reviewing the case, Supt Lawlor wrote: 'Donal Leen's statement to the Gardaí, which prompted the investigation, while of vital importance, was made by a person who had given evidence to the contrary at the Coroner's Court regarding Thady Flynn's absence from the potato field.

'For the Gardaí it was essential to obtain independent evidence corroborating Leen's statement that Thady Flynn had been absent from the potato field for half-an-hour to three quarters of an hour.

'Everyone who passed the main road on 16 November had to be traced and, as far as it was humanly possible, the time fixed at which each person passed the potato field in which Thady Flynn and Leen were working that day.'

'From the mass of information gleaned, it was established that a young lady had passed cycling on her way to Killarney at about 10.30 a.m. She had met Thady Flynn on the main road near Butler's cottage. At 10.45 a.m. two men passed along and had seen Mrs Flynn emerge from the back lane leading from her home to the main road and proceed by the main road up the front avenue towards the front lawn. A flock of turkeys were in the vicinity. These men did not see Thady Flynn in the field or on the road.

'Butler stated that Flynn called at 11.45 a.m. for the shovel and he was quite certain of the time, since he looked at his clock. Thus it was clear that Flynn did not obtain the shovel at the time stated, and that he must have left the main road soon after he had been met by the girl at 10.30 a.m. There is a lane leading from the main road at Butler's cottage to the back of Flynn's home, and he could have easily availed of this unfrequented route.

'Be that as it may, he was next seen by two men who were passing on the main road at 11 a.m. — at this time he was coming from his yard gate towards a field and in the direction of the main road. At about 11.30 a.m. when a rabbit buyer was going up the back lane to Flynn's house he met Thady. He was able to describe his dress and to notice he was not wearing dungarees. Thady exchanged a word with the rabbit buyer and continued on his way down the lane to the main road. Flynn must have gone to Butler's then, collected the shovel and returned to the potato field where he endeavoured to impress Leen that he had only been away a short time,' Supt George Lawlor wrote.

A two-hour reconstruction of Leen's account was undertaken by the Gardaí. Leen played himself, Supt Harte took on the role of Thady Flynn and Supt Lawlor acted as timekeeper for the reconstruction. They hitched up the horse and cart, and went to the potato pit which Supt Harte then opened and began to fill buckets with potatoes. They took four buckets from each of two pits, before Supt Harte left the field and later returned as Thady Flynn had done.

Flynn, however, was to escape being asked about the fifteen minutes which the reconstruction showed remained unaccounted for, as the recorded timings were never adduced as evidence in the subsequent courtroom drama.

On the following day, Saturday 28 November, Thady Flynn was arrested at his home and charged with the murder of his wife. 'He stared me right through, but never replied,' Supt Patrick Harte recalled.

Supt Lawlor and two other members of the Technical Bureau were injured and hospitalised after a collision with a truck in Co. Kildare on the way to the initial hearings in Tralee. The hearings had to adjourn a number of times over the next month because Supt Lawlor was still on sick leave and unable to attend.

On 29 April 1943 Thady Flynn's trial opened in Green Street Courthouse. The opening address by prosecution counsel Mr McCarthy, S.C., was one of the lengthiest ever delivered in an Irish murder trial. It outstripped addresses given in arguably more important trials in the previous 150 years, such as that of Robert Emmet who stood in the same dock in 1803 tried for treason, or Hurrish Sweep, the last man publicly whipped through the streets of Dublin in 1815, or John Mitchel and Charles Gavan Duffy in 1848, or the Invincibles and Fenians in subsequent years.

'The facts and circumstances of the case,' said Mr McCarthy, 'will establish that Mrs Flynn was literally hurled into eternity, and that, in addition, an attempt was made immediately following these tragic events to make what in fact was a murder appear to be really an accident, and to make it appear she had fallen into the well while attempting to rescue a turkey from it. It was a cruel and crafty scheme, designed to bluff and misguide those who might be making inquiries into her death — a scheme as skilful in its planning as it was wicked in its execution.'

Over 110 exhibits were to be brought into the court room, including scale models of the house and water well and detailed maps of the house and the surrounding farmland outhouses. The court heard that the murder had been carried out in the kitchen, and that Mrs Flynn had then been carried and dumped into the well. A turkey, a bucket and a hook at the end of a rope were then flung down the well after her.

'Apart from Leen's statement,' Supt Lawlor noted in his case-book, 'there were other matters which required explanation. How could Mrs Flynn have fallen down the well wherein lay the turkey, buckets, hooks and ropes and yet have all these articles remaining above her body? Undoubtedly strange things have happened and when a body is hurtling down twenty-two feet of space it is very difficult to visualise what position it will eventually take or what injuries it may receive. The bottom of the well was only two feet in diameter and to escape all these articles, including a live turkey, assuming of course it was an accident, was almost impossible.'

The court was told that the back kitchen, which was a lean-to building attached to the back of the house and leading to the garden and well, was minutely examined by members of the Technical Bureau. Over one thousand tiny flecks and smears of blood were found in that room which was no more than twelve feet by ten feet. A piece of human tissue was also found in the kitchen, and only a few of the blood marks were animal and not human. Many of the droplets could have been made by waving around a bloodstained instrument, said the State Pathologist, Dr McGrath. He also detailed the results of his post mortem examination and his inspection of clothing taken from Thady Flynn. A soaked bloodstain on the left leg of a pair of blue dungarees was human and not animal blood. The position of the staining also matched similar human bloodstains on a pair of underpants worn by Flynn at the same time as the dungarees. The chest portion, or bib, of the dungarees was also heavily stained with human blood.

Mr Casey in his opening address, for the defence, said that he charged Donal Leen with deliberate perjury. Far from admitting that the State case had been proved, he said that no jury would find Flynn guilty on the evidence of Leen.

But why had Leen not spoken out against Flynn before the Gardaí had contacted him a second time, asked Mr Casey?

'Because I was afraid,' said Leen under cross examination in the witness box. 'I was afraid because I was suspicious that he was after doing it, and I did not want to let him know that I knew anything about it,' he explained.

Flynn had pleaded 'Not Guilty' to the charge and his defence was a dual one, that he was not guilty, and secondly if guilty, that he was insane at the time he committed the murder.

Three doctors were called by the defence to prove his madness, but first, Rev. John Quinlan, a second cousin of the dead woman and a priest attached to the Liverpool archdiocese, said that he had noticed a change in Flynn since he had an accident some years earlier.

He had noticed something strange about his eyes, and he had begun to make incessant complaints concerning various matters in his home, including making allegations that his wife was drinking and that she was having an affair. Fr Quinlan, who had visited the Flynns' home, noticed that Hannah was 'always very much on her guard and did not wish to be left alone with her husband'.

The first doctor to give evidence was Dr John Dunne, Chief R.M.S., Grangegorman mental hospital, who had examined Flynn twice in Mountjoy jail as he awaited trial. He found that Flynn was suffering from 'delusional insanity'. 'This form of insanity,' he told the court, 'is known as systematic delusions which develops insidiously in men about Flynn's age and usually commenced with a sense of inferiority, depression and a suspicion that persons were talking about them or those that they loved. In every other way they might be normal but a person suffering from this disease is a grave threat.'

Dr Eamonn O'Sullivan R.M.S., Killarney mental hospital, also examined Flynn on a number of occasions in Mountjoy jail. Flynn told him he had been hearing 'voices' for the past eighteen months. On one occasion he thought he heard voices from heaven, and also thought that he was in heaven, the doctor said. Dr O'Sullivan asked him about his recent religious tendencies, and Flynn explained that he had 'heard voices from heaven telling me to mind my soul'. Flynn, was in his opinion, suffering from paranoia — a fixed systematic delusion centring on some object or person. A paranoiac imagined sinister motives for ordinary actions, and every paranoiac was regarded as a potential homicide.

A neurologist, Dr F. McMenamin, concurred, saying that Flynn had told him he heard voices, and recognised one of them as belonging to a man called Hanafin who had died some years previously.

The State in turn called witnesses to rebut the medical evidence given for the defence, commencing with Dr J. O'Sullivan who said that although Flynn had given 'grossly inaccurate' responses to questions put to him, he had not noticed anything peculiar about Flynn's behaviour.

Mr Sean Kavanagh, Governor of Mountjoy prison, said that he had not noticed anything abnormal about Flynn's behaviour. Equally Dr H. Roche Kelly of Limerick prison and Dr B.F. Honan, R.M.S., Cork mental hospital, had found no reason to believe Flynn suffered from paranoia.

The defence summed up their position by posing a number of questions. Why had Leen's statements to the inquest changed, why had no blood been discovered between the kitchen, which was where the attack allegedly took place, and the well?

'It had been suggested,' said defence counsel, 'that Flynn had been carrying on an intrigue with another woman. So far as an affair was concerned the evidence of motive did not assist them. As to the suggestion that his motive was to get control of the money his wife had got from her brother, what hope had Flynn of getting it when it was held in her name and the names of his daughters?'

Summing up on the 18th day of the trial, Mr Justice Overend said that if the jury came to the conclusion that Flynn knew his act was punishable by law he would not be insane in the sense that he would be exempt from the liability of the law. If, however, they found that he did not know of his liability, they would be justified in returning a special verdict of 'guilty but insane'. The case as defined by the facts would seem to show that Flynn was doing everything in his power to conceal the fact of what he had done, and that the turkey, the bucket, the ropes and the pothooks were put there to frame the occurrence as the result of an accident.

It took the jury over three hours of deliberations to return with a verdict of 'Guilty but Insane'. Flynn who had remained pale and seated as the verdict was read out, was sentenced to be detained in a criminal lunatic asylum at the pleasure of the Government.

'But what was the impelling motive for a husband to dispose of his wife in such a terrible manner?' Superintendent Lawlor asked. 'The letter found in Flynn's house by Supt Harte in a locked wardrobe in one of the girls' bedrooms spoke for itself.

'In some way his wife obtained possession of the letter, but her husband, Thady, came to know of it. He had made attempts to retrieve it, and, to prevent him from doing so she passed it to the eldest daughter who concealed it in her locked wardrobe and gave her the keys.

'Subsequent investigations brought to light the fact that there was another woman in the case. Mrs Flynn was cognisant of this affair and had approached her solicitor regarding it. In view of Mrs Flynn's sound financial position, she would probably have separated from her husband were it not for family considerations. Thady Flynn was aware that his wife had taken legal advice and this knowledge, added to his already embittered mind, possibly hastened her untimely death.'